THE NEW CAMBRIDGE HISTORY
OF INDIA

The Portuguese in India

THE NEW CAMBRIDGE HISTORY OF INDIA

General editor GORDON JOHNSON
Director, Centre of South Asian Studies, University of
Cambridge, and Fellow of Selwyn College

Associate editors C. A. BAYLY
Smuts Reader in Commonwealth Studies, University of
Cambridge, and Fellow of St Catharine's College

and JOHN F. RICHARDS
Professor of History, Duke University

Although the original *Cambridge History of India*, published between 1922 and 1937, did much to formulate a chronology for Indian history and describe the administrative structures of government in India, it has inevitably been overtaken by the mass of new research published over the last fifty years.

Designed to take full account of recent scholarship and changing conceptions of South Asia's historical development, *The New Cambridge History of India* will be published as a series of short, self-contained volumes, each dealing with a separate theme and written by a single person. Within an overall four-part structure, thirty complementary volumes in uniform format will be published during the next five years. As before, each will conclude with a substantial bibliographical essay designed to lead non-specialists further into the literature.

The four parts planned are as follows:

I The Mughals and their Contemporaries.

II Indian States and the Transition to Colonialism.

III The Indian Empire and the Beginnings of Modern Society.

IV The Evolution of Contemporary South Asia.

A list of individual titles in preparation will be found at the end of the volume.

THE NEW
CAMBRIDGE
HISTORY OF
INDIA

I · 1

The Portuguese in India

M. N. PEARSON

SCHOOL OF HISTORY,
UNIVERSITY OF NEW SOUTH WALES

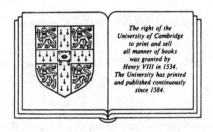

The right of the
University of Cambridge
to print and sell
all manner of books
was granted by
Henry VIII in 1534.
The University has printed
and published continuously
since 1584.

CAMBRIDGE UNIVERSITY PRESS
CAMBRIDGE
NEW YORK   PORT CHESTER
MELBOURNE   SYDNEY

CAMBRIDGE UNIVERSITY PRESS
Cambridge, New York, Melbourne, Madrid, Cape Town, Singapore, São Paulo

Cambridge University Press
The Edinburgh Building, Cambridge CB2 2RU, UK

Published in the United States of America by Cambridge University Press, New York

www.cambridge.org
Information on this title: www.cambridge.org/9780521257138

First published 1987
Reprinted 1990
This digitally printed first paperback version 2006

A catalogue record for this publication is available from the British Library

Library of Congress Cataloguing in Publication data
Pearson, M. N. (Michael Naylor, 1941–
The Portuguese in India.
(New Cambridge History of India)
Bibliography.
Includes index.
1. Portuguese – India – History.
2. Goa, Daman and Diu (India) – History.
I. Title. II. Series.
DS498.7.P36   1987   954'.004691   86–17100

ISBN-13 978-0-521-25713-8 hardback
ISBN-10 0-521-25713-1 hardback

ISBN-13 978-0-521-02850-9 paperback
ISBN-10 0-521-02850-7 paperback

Frontispiece: Mughal album painting of a European, about 1590.
London, Victoria and Albert Museum.

To
BEN *and* MATHEW

CONTENTS

General editor's preface	ix
Preface	xi
Rulers of Portugal 1385–1910	xii
Viceroys and governors of	
Portuguese India 1505–1961	xiii
Glossary	xvii
Maps	xix
Introduction	1
1 The Portuguese arrival in India	5
2 The system in operation	40
3 Evaluation of the official system	61
4 Indo-Portuguese society	81
5 Catholics and Hindus	116
6 Decline and stagnation	131
7 Toward reintegration	144
Bibliographical essay	163
Index	177

GENERAL EDITOR'S PREFACE

The New Cambridge History of India covers the period from the beginning of the sixteenth century. In some respects it marks a radical change in the style of Cambridge Histories, but in others the editors feel that they are working firmly within an established academic tradition.

During the summer of 1896, F. W. Maitland and Lord Acton between them evolved the idea for a comprehensive modern history. By the end of the year the Syndics of the University Press had committed themselves to the *Cambridge Modern History*, and Lord Acton had been put in charge of it. It was hoped that publication would begin in 1899 and be completed by 1904, but the first volume in fact came out in 1902 and the last in 1910, with additional volumes of tables and maps in 1911 and 1912.

The *History* was a great success, and it was followed by a whole series of distinctive Cambridge Histories covering English Literature, the Ancient World, India, British Foreign Policy, Economic History, Medieval History, the British Empire, Africa, China and Latin America; and even now other new series are being prepared. Indeed, the various Histories have given the Press notable strength in the publication of general reference books in the arts and social sciences.

What has made the Cambridge Histories so distinctive is that they have never been simply dictionaries or encyclopedias. The Histories have, in H. A. L. Fisher's words, always been 'written by an army of specialists concentrating the latest results of special study'. Yet as Acton agreed with the Syndics in 1896, they have not been mere compilations of existing material but original works. Undoubtedly many of the Histories are uneven in quality, some have become out of date very rapidly, but their virtue has been that they have consistently done more than simply record an existing state of knowledge: they have tended to focus interest on research and they have provided a massive stimulus to further work. This has made their publication doubly worthwhile and has distinguished them intellectually from other sorts of reference book. The editors of the *New Cambridge History of India* have acknowledged this in their work.

GENERAL EDITOR'S PREFACE

The original *Cambridge History of India* was published between 1922 and 1937. It was planned in six volumes, but of these, volume 2 dealing with the period between the first century A.D. and the Muslim invasion of India never appeared. Some of the material is still of value, but in many respects it is now out of date. The last fifty years have seen a great deal of new research on India, and a striking feature of recent work has been to cast doubt on the validity of the quite arbitrary chronological and categorical way in which Indian history has been conventionally divided.

The editors decided that it would not be academically desirable to prepare a new *History of India* using the traditional format. The selective nature of research on Indian history over the past half-century would doom such a project from the start and the whole of India history could not be covered in an even or comprehensive manner. They concluded that the best scheme would be to have a *History* divided into four overlapping chronological volumes, each containing about eight short books on individual themes or subjects. Although in extent the work will therefore be equivalent to a dozen massive tomes of the traditional sort, in form the *New Cambridge History of India* will appear as a shelf full of separate but complementary parts. Accordingly, the main divisions are between I. *The Mughals and their Contemporaries*, II. *Indian States and the Transition to Colonialism*, III. *The Indian Empire and the Beginnings of Modern Society*, and IV. *The Evolution of Contemporary South Asia*.

Just as the books within these volumes are complementary so too do they intersect with each other, both thematically and chronologically. As the books appear they are intended to give a view of the subject as it now stands and to act as a stimulus to further research. We do not expect the *New Cambridge History of India* to be the last word on the subject but an essential voice in the continuing discourse about it.

PREFACE

Indo-Portuguese history is still so small a speciality that people tend to co-operate. For useful discussions, and/or letting me read unpublished work, I want to thank: Rudolph Bauss; C. R. Boxer; Gervaise Clarence-Smith; Ashin Das Gupta; Teotonio R. de Souza; A. R. Disney; Jan Heesterman; Caroline Ifeka; Jan Kieniewicz; Stella Mascarenhas-Keyes; R. S. Newman; Geoffrey Parker; Dietmar Rothermund; Niels Steensgaard; Sanjay Subrahmanyam; John Villiers; George Winius.

I'm sure none of them will agree with everything which follows.

M. N. Pearson

RULERS OF PORTUGAL 1385–1910

HOUSE OF AVIZ

João I, 1385–1433
Duarte, 1433–8
Affonso V, 1438–81
João II, 1481–95
Manuel I, 1495–1521
João III, 1521–57
Sebastian, 1557–78
Henry, 1578–80

HOUSE OF SPANISH HABSBURGS

Philip II (I of Portugal), 1580–98
Philip III (II of Portugal), 1598–1621
Philip IV (III of Portugal), 1621–40

HOUSE OF BRAGANÇA

João IV, 1640–56
Affonso VI, 1656–67
Pedro II, 1667–1706
João V, 1706–50
José, 1750–77
Maria I, 1777–92
João VI, 1792–1826
Pedro IV, 1826–34
Miguel, 1828–34
Maria II, 1834–53
Pedro V, 1853–61
Luís I, 1861–89
Carlos I, 1889–1908
Manuel II, 1908–10

VICEROYS AND GOVERNORS OF
PORTUGUESE INDIA 1505–1961

All viceroys were also governors. Thus the serial number refers to governorships; those governors who were further honoured by being called viceroys have an asterisk. Gaps in the sequence, as between numbers 53 and 54, are because in these years there was a Council of Government. With a few exceptions, I have not included titles.

1* Francisco de Almeida, 1505–9
2 Afonso de Albuquerque, 1509–15
3 Lopo Soares de Albergaria, 1515–18
4 Diogo Lopes de Sequeira, 1518–22
5 Duarte de Meneses, 1522–4
6* Vasco da Gama, 1524
7 Henrique de Meneses, 1524–6
8 Lopo Vaz de Sampaio, 1526–9
9 Nuno da Cunha, 1529–38
10* Garcia de Noronha, 1538–40
11 Estêvão da Gama, 1540–2
12 Martim Afonso de Sousa, 1542–5
13* João de Castro, 1545–8
14 Garcia de Sá, 1548–9
15 Jorge Cabral, 1549–50
16* Afonso de Noronha, 1550–4
17* Pedro Mascarenhas, 1554–5
18 Francisco Barreto, 1555–8
19* Constantino de Bragança, 1558–61
20* Francisco Coutinho, 1561–4
21 João de Mendonça, 1564
22* Antão de Noronha, 1564–8
23* Luís de Ataíde, 1568–71
24* António de Noronha, 1571–3
25 António Moniz Barreto, 1573–6
26 Diogo de Meneses, 1576–8
27* Luís de Ataíde, 1578–81

28 Fernão Teles de Meneses, 1581
29* Francisco Mascarenhas, 1581–4
30* Duarte de Meneses, 1584–8
31 Manuel de Sousa Coutinho, 1588–91
32* Matias de Albuquerque, 1591–7
33* Francisco da Gama, 1597–1600
34* Aires de Saldanha, 1600–5
35* Martim Afonso de Castro, 1605–7
36 Frei Aleixo de Meneses, 1607–9
37 André Furtado de Mendonça, 1609
38* Rui Lourenço de Távora, 1609–12
39* Jerónimo de Azevedo, 1612–17
40* João Coutinho, 1617–19
41 Fernão de Albuquerque, 1619–22
42* Francisco da Gama, 1622–8
43 Frei Luís de Brito e Meneses, 1628–9
44* Miguel de Noronha, Conde de Linhares, 1629–35
45* Pêro da Silva, 1635–9
46 António Teles de Meneses, 1639–40
47* João da Silva Telo e Meneses, 1640–5
48* Filipe Mascarenhas, 1645–51
49* Vasco Mascarenhas, Conde de Óbidos, 1652–3
50* Rodrigo Lobo da Silveira, 1655–6
51 Manuel Mascarenhas Homem, 1656
52* António de Melo e Castro, 1662–6
53* João Nunes da Cunha, 1666–8
54* Luís de Mendonça Furtado e Albuquerque, 1671–7
55* Pedro de Almeida Portugal, 1677–8
56* Francisco de Távora, 1681–6
57 Rodrigo da Costa, 1686–90
58 Miguel de Almeida, 1690–1
59* Pedro António de Noronha de Albuquerque, 1692–8
60* António Luís Gonçalves da Câmara Coutinho, 1698–1701
61* Caetano de Melo e Castro, 1702–7
62* Rodrigo da Costa, 1701–12
63* Vasco Fernandes César de Meneses, 1712–17
64 Sebastião de Andrade Pessanha, 1717
65* Luís Carlos Inácio Xavier de Meneses, 1717–20
66* Francisco José de Sampaio e Castro, 1720–3

67 Cristovão de Melo, 1723
68* João de Saldanha da Gama, 1725–32
69* Pedro Mascarenhas, 1732–41
70* Luís Carlos Inácio Xavier de Meneses, 1741–2
71* Pedro Miguel de Almeida Portugal, 1744–50
72* Francisco de Assis de Távora, 1750–4
73* Luís Mascarenhas, 1754–6
74* Manuel de Saldanha e Albuquerque, 1758–65
75 João José de Melo, 1768–74
76 Filipe de Valadares Sotomaior, 1774
77 José Pedro da Câmara, 1774–9
78 Frederico de Guilherme de Sousa Holstein, 1779–86
79 Francisco da Cunha e Meneses, 1786–94
80 Francisco António da Veiga Cabral da Câmara Pimentel,
    1794–1807
81* Bernardo José Maria da Silveira e Lorena, 1807–16
82* Diogo de Sousa, 1816–21
83 Manuel da Câmara, 1822–5
84* Manuel Francisco de Portugal e Castro, 1826–35
    (Prefect) Bernardo Peres da Silva, 1835
85 Simão Infante de la Cerda de Sousa Tavares, 1837–8
86 José António Vieira da Fonseca, 1839
87 Manuel José Mendes, 1839–40
88 José Joaquim Lopes de Lima, 1840–2
89 Francisco Xavier da Silva Pereira, 1842–3
90 Joaquim Mourão Garcês Palha, 1843–4
91 José Ferreira Pestana, 1844–51
92 José Joaquim Januário Lapa, 1851–5
93 António César de Vasconcelos Correia, 1855–64
94 José Ferreira Pestana, 1864–70
95 Januário Correia de Almeida, 1870–1
96 Joaquim José de Macedo e Couto, 1871–5
97 João Tavares de Almeida, 1875–7
98 António Sérgio de Sousa, 1877–8
99 Caetano Alexandre de Almeida e Albuquerque, 1878–82
100 Carlos Eugénio Correia da Silva, 1882–5
101 Francisco Joaquim Ferreira do Amaral, 1886
102 Augusto César Cardoso de Carvalho, 1886–9
103 Vasco Guedes de Carvalho e Meneses, 1889–91

104 Francisco Maria da Cunha, 1891
105 Francisco Teixeira da Silva, 1892–3
106 Rafael Jácome Lopes de Andrade, 1893–4
107 Elesbão José de Bettencourt Lapa, 1894–5
108 Rafael Jácome Lopes de Andrade, 1895–6
109* Infante Dom Afonso Henriques, 1896
110 Joaquim José Machado, 1897–1900
111 Eduardo Augusto Rodrigues Galhardo, 1900–5
112 Arnaldo Nogueira Novais Guedes Rebelo, 1905–7
113 José Maria de Sousa Horta e Costa, 1907–10
114 Francisco Manuel Couceiro da Costa, 1910–17
115 José de Freitas Ribeiro, 1917–19
116 Augusto de Paiva Bobela da Mota, 1919
117 Jaime Alberto de Castro Morais, 1919–25
118 Mariano Martins, 1925–6
119 Acúrsio Mendes da Rocha Dinis, 1926
120 Pedro Francisco Massano de Amorim, 1926–9
121 Alfredo Pedro de Almeida, 1929
122 João Carlos Craveiro Lopes, 1929–36
123 Francisco Higino Craveiro Lopes, 1936–8
124 José Ricardo Pereira Cabral, 1938–45
125 José Silvestre Ferreira Bossa, 1945–8
126 Fernando Quintanilha e Mendonça Dias, 1948–52
127 Paulo Bénard Guedes, 1952–8
128 Manuel António Vassalo e Silva, 1958–61

GLOSSARY

This glossary is intended solely for the convenience of readers of this book. It makes no claim to being authoritative; nor does it cover all possible meanings of all the words; nor is it a work of linguistic reference.

aforamento	quit-rent
alvará	royal order or decree
araq	spirit distilled from palms
bhakti	Hindu devotionalism
cafila	convoy
Câmara	municipal council
carreira da India	Lisbon–Goa round trip
cartaz	passport; licence
Casa da India	India House, in Lisbon
casado	married man; householder
castiço	Portuguese born in India
chettyar	member of Coromandel Hindu merchant community
choli	Hindu blouse
Christão-Novo	New Christian; a convert from Judaism
colecta	tax on food
Conselho da Fazenda	financial council
cruzado	coin worth 400 *reis*, about 4 English shillings
descendente	mixed blood; *mestiço*
dhoti	Hindu male nether-garment
Estado da India	the Portuguese state in India
fidalgo	a noble or gentleman; 'son of somebody'
foro	land revenue
gaunkar	land controller
hajj	Muslim pilgrimage to Mecca
Indiatico	Portuguese born in India
jama masjid	congregational mosque
juiz	judge
keling	Tamil-speaking Hindu

mestiço	Eurasian; a person of Indo-Portuguese ancestry
náo	large ship
padroado	patronage
pan	betel leaf
pandit	Hindu teacher
paroe	light, oared boat
quintal	about 1 hundredweight (51 kgms)
reinol	Portuguese born in Portugal
rendas	tax-farming contracts
roteiro	rutter; navigational guide
ryotwari	Hindu system under which the state takes a proportion of the actual production of every cultivating family
satyagraha	'truth force'; Gandhian pacifist resistance
Senado da Câmara	municipal council
soldado	soldier; an unmarried man
sudra	bottom group in the Hindu caste hierarchy
taluka	district
tanador-mor	overseer
vania	member of Gujarat Hindu or Jain merchant community
vedor da fazenda	chief financial official
zamorin	title of the ruler of Calicut

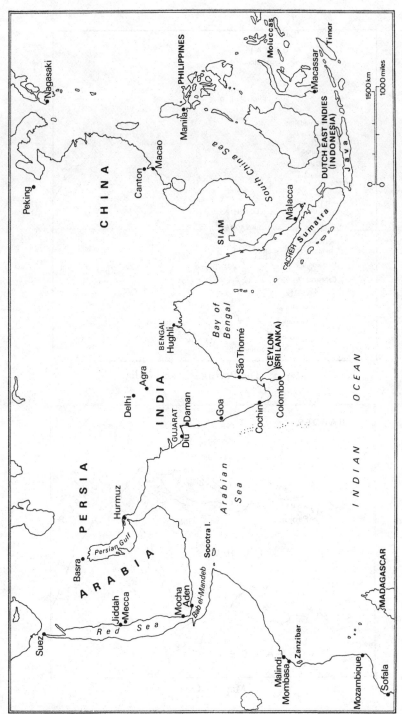

Map 1. The Portuguese and Asia

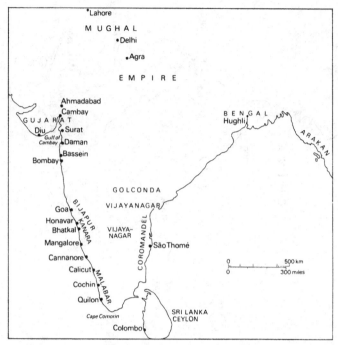

Map 2. The Portuguese and India

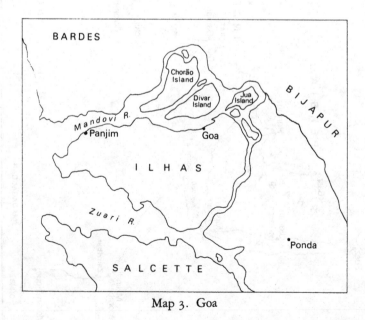

Map 3. Goa

INTRODUCTION

Portugal is the oldest territorial state in Europe; India is one of the world's newer nations. Yet ironically history is much more important, and controversial, for Portuguese than for Indians. It is true that historical writing played a role in the Indian national movement, for some of the writing of the first half of the twentieth century was designed to foster patriotism and pride. Today however Indians are commendably relaxed about their history, as can be seen in vigorous controversies over historical matters in which it seems that all possible points of view can be, and are, presented. These debates are intellectual; the validity of the Indian nation is not dependent on the outcome.

This has usually not been the case in Portugal; too often their history has had present political meanings. Robert Southey visited Portugal in 1796, and 1800–1, enjoyed himself, and spent years working on a huge, and never completed, history of Portugal. It was going to be a wonderful book:

I believe no history has ever yet been composed that presents such a continuous interest of one kind or another as this would do, if I should live to complete it. The chivalrous portion is of the very highest beauty; much of what succeeds has a deep tragic interest; and then comes the gradual destruction of a noble national character, brought on by the cancer of Romish superstition. (Quoted in Rose Maccaulay, *They Went to Portugal*, London, 1946, p. 164)

In Portugal history is indeed of interest, not only to historians but also to the general population and especially to the governing elite. A famous savant wrote in 1898 that 'Perhaps one could say that the memory of and pride in those past times of real although transitory greatness is still today one of the main bonds of our nationalism, one of the things which fortified, and still fortifies, us in those hard times which we later passed through' (Conde de Ficalho, *Viagens de Pedro da Covilham*, Lisbon, 1898, pp. vi–vii). All this was exacerbated during the Salazar–Caetano period. History joined religion as an opiate. It was blatantly used for present political purposes. Portugal tried to retain her colonies, disingenuously renamed overseas provinces. An important bolster was the claim that all were equal in Portugal, both metropolitan

I

and overseas. The criterion was not race but degree of 'civilization'. In a dictatorship where control over information was given a high priority, historians were enlisted to prove this claim for the past. In a country like Portugal, small, insignificant, thanks to Dr Salazar the poorest in Europe, history was used to foster pride and unity.

Since 1974 it has been possible for Portuguese to write what they like about their past and some have availed themselves of this opportunity. Yet among all classes and political tendencies, Portugal's past is still seen as 'important', and usually still as one in which the country can take pride.

The aim of my book is, naturally, to assess the influence or impact of the Portuguese on India. This is an ambitious and difficult task; in particular, sweeping generalizations must be avoided. Rather we need, as they say, to 'disaggregate the data'. When this is done, we find Portuguese influence varying very widely, ranging from massive to minuscule according to three criteria: time, place and category (for example, social, religious, economic, political). At a particular time, in a specified place, we may find a substantial Portuguese impact on a particular category of Indian life; change one or more of these criteria (say a different time or place) and the influence may well decrease to a considerable extent.

The conclusion, if I may anticipate the central finding of this book, is that in many areas the Portuguese impact was minor; in a few it was substantial. Overall there was much more co-operation and interaction than dominance. Let this not be misunderstood. This conclusion was reached on the basis of the evidence before me, and also, I believe, reflects an emerging consensus among specialists in the field. For those like myself who think in the most general way that it is 'wrong' for one group of people to impose their values, their political control, on others, the theme of this book will correctly be seen as one which is *positive* towards the Portuguese imperial effort. True, their leaders hoped to produce major change in India; most of the time they failed, and this, even if inadvertently, made their empire much less deleterious than the later more complete achievement of the British.

Needless to say, my conclusions are in no way influenced by anti-Portuguese or anti-Catholic feeling (whatever these two terms may mean). Several English authors in the late nineteenth century wrote books which criticized the Portuguese on invalid grounds, grounds which showed their own ethnocentrism (as indeed did Robert Southey).

There is a vast difference between racist attacks on the Portuguese, and a dispassionate investigation of their imperial career in India. This book attempts the latter.

C. R. Boxer said that his classic *Portuguese Seaborne Empire* (London, 1969) was 'the product of over forty years' reading, research, reflection and publication on and around its subject matter' (p. 392). I can only claim an interest going back twenty years. As I have tried to sum up what I have learnt in this time, I have become acutely aware of the huge gaps in our knowledge. This is the case for the whole period from the end of Spanish rule over Portugal in 1640 to the end of Portugal's Indian empire in 1961. Vast materials are available; so far they have hardly been sifted. In a book which attempts to reflect the existing state of scholarship, this will explain the brevity, and no doubt superficiality, of my coverage of this later period. Yet even for the comparatively well-researched sixteenth century there are still huge gaps. Consider only Vasco da Gama. We know almost nothing of his early career. On his fateful voyage in 1497–8, why did he (correctly) take an outward route which involved a huge loop far west into the Atlantic? Why was he so ill-informed about Indian conditions that he knew nothing of the status and power of the opulent zamorin of Calicut, and persistently mistook Hinduism for some sort of deviant Christianity? All this book can do is to attempt a synthesis of existing knowledge. Obviously I have drawn heavily on the work of others, and on my own past efforts. The gaps and errors in the book reflect in part the present feeble state of the field, in part my own ignorance.

Two guiding principles underlie this book. It is part of a series about Indian history, and by a person whose speciality is Indian history; I hope India is always to the fore in what I have written. Indeed, I have consciously tried to assess the Portuguese and their activities from an Indian angle, rather than from a European one. Thus in the central and crucial matter of evaluating the Portuguese impact on India, I have to some extent discounted large claims made then and now by Portuguese and other European authors, and been more influenced by the very silence of Indian records on the whole presence of the Portuguese. Yet I also found it necessary to include fairly detailed discussions of what may seem to be purely Portuguese matters. I did this because I strongly feel that the Portuguese in India cannot be seen in isolation: their actions, policies and prejudices were a result of a world view derived from their own European milieu. I had to make some attempt to describe this. If there is too much Portugal and not enough India – and I earnestly hope this is not the case – then I must fall back on blaming the sources. Portuguese sources are relatively full, and accessible; Indian sources for the topic and period are neither. There are obvious problems in using mostly sources from one side; I hope I have been able to transcend the limitations of Portuguese records for one interested in Indian history.

My second guiding principle was to be as comparative and analytical as possible. Here also I hope my book makes some contribution, for much existing writing on the Portuguese in India, and on the history of early European activities in India in general, is antiquarian in the extreme. Years of painstaking work in the archives produces only an elaboration on a political narrative, or more details about the life of some great man. I have tried to discuss such broad historical themes (related, of course, to the history of the Portuguese in India) as the nature of western 'impacts'; the peddling trade of Asia; European contact with Asia in what Jan Kieniewicz has called the 'pre-colonial' period, that is the period (which he extends through most of the eighteenth century) of European expansion, but not domination ('Contact and Transformation, the European pre-colonial expansion in the Indian Ocean world-system in the 16th–17th centuries', *Itinerario*, VIII, 2, 1984, pp. 45–58); and even what J. H. Plumb called society 'before the human-condition was radically changed by the growth of industry' ('The Underside of History', *Guardian Weekly*, July 1982, p. 18). Even when such themes are not overtly stated, they have been in my mind.

CHAPTER 1

THE PORTUGUESE ARRIVAL IN INDIA

Vasco da Gama's arrival near Calicut on 20 May 1498 was the culmination of a continuous, though spasmodic, Portuguese thrust into the Atlantic, south to the Cape of Good Hope, and on to India. This process began in 1415 when the Moroccan city of Ceuta was conquered. The Madeira and Azores islands were settled by Portuguese in the 1420s and 1430s, and in 1434 treacherous Cape Bojador was rounded. Great strides were made in the 1480s, culminating in the rounding of the Cape of Good Hope by Bartolomeu Dias in 1488. There followed a brief and rather mysterious hiatus, until de Gama's three small ships left Lisbon in July 1497. After spending May to October 1498 off the southwest Indian coast, he returned to Portugal in August 1499; not surprisingly, he was welcomed ecstatically.

The king, D. Manuel (1495–1521), immediately undertook extensive public works in Lisbon, designed to foster trade and future expeditions. Preparations for the second expedition, commanded by Cabral, were accelerated: he left in March 1500 with a huge fleet of thirteen ships and at least 1200 men. The sense of confidence and exultation of the time can be seen in the way work was started late in 1499 on the huge monastery of the Jeronimos in the suburb of Lisbon on the Tagus River from which the fleets left for India. Even more indicative was the renaming of the area where the monastery was to be erected (it took fifty years to complete): it was to be known henceforth as Belém (Bethlehem), the place where the Portuguese empire was born.

Historians have long debated the reasons for these voyages. Why was almost a century spent on thrusting down the West African coast, and why was it the Portuguese rather than some other European power who undertook these voyages? The much-quoted answer tells us that a member of da Gama's crew, when asked in Calicut 'What brought you here?' replied 'We seek Christians and Spices.' Such a reply was actually a cliché even in the fifteenth century; Portuguese kings in their letters explained not only the discoveries but almost everything else they did as being designed to 'serve God and make a profit for ourselves'. Some later Portuguese explanations, flying even further in the face of both facts and

5

probability, stress solely religious motives. Portugal's greatest poet Luis de Camoens in *The Lusiads*, Portugal's national epic, has a Portuguese reply to the question posed above: 'We have come across the mighty deep, where none has ever sailed before us, in search of the Indus. Our purpose is to spread the Christian faith' (William C. Atkinson, trans., *The Lusiads*, Penguin, 1952, p. 166). An official Portuguese publication issued in 1956, when their rule in Goa was gravely threatened, claimed that 'Commercial exploitation has never been the mainspring of Portuguese action overseas. Always religious in character, Portuguese expansion was yet not guided by a narrow proselytizing spirit, but by a spirit of gradual and tolerant assimilation.'[1]

History writing always reflects prevailing needs and moods. Consequently, in the period between 1955 and 1985 the Portuguese discoveries have often been explained in almost purely economic terms. Several things do seem to be clear. In the early fifteenth century Portuguese expansion was in large part a search for food, for Portugal was always a grain importer. Hence the settlement of the Azores and Madeira, and the rapid expansion of cereal and sugar production there. Hence also large-scale grain production in the Portuguese enclaves in North Africa. The search for new fishing grounds, when successful, especially in the north Atlantic, provided not only protein but also maritime training. But political imperatives also played a part. In Portugal, as elsewhere in Europe, seigneurial revenues were falling, and one escape from the 'crisis of feudalism' was to provide alternative outlets for bastards, younger sons, and other disadvantaged nobles. Such people received land on feudal terms in the Atlantic islands, and could gain glory, even knighthoods, fighting on the North African frontier.

Once started, the expansion fed on itself. As trade developed gold was needed; from the 1450s it came back in considerable quantities from West Africa. As sugar production expanded labour was needed; West Africa turned out to be a prime source of slaves and these flooded into the islands and metropolitan Portugal after 1443. But, ironically, one product not in short supply was spices, which of course became the *leit-motif* of the sixteenth-century empire. Until the 1470s there was no quest for Asian spices, for fifteenth-century Europe was well provided

---

[1] *Portuguese India Today*, 2nd ed. (Lisbon, 1956), pp. 31–2.

for by the traditional route through the Red Sea, to Alexandria and so to Venice.

The role of different social groups in Portugal in this expansion has been much debated. There is evidence, though this is a matter in dispute, that the rise of the Ottoman Turks in the eastern Mediterranean in the fifteenth century blocked some traditional Genoese investment areas. To compensate, great Genoese bankers turned to Portugal, and their investments provided some of the impetus and capital needed to finance the discoveries. The role of the peasantry is also controversial. Some historians have pointed to a population increase in the fifteenth century to compensate for the ravages of the Black Death; the expansion overseas was then necessary to provide a safety-valve. This however seems less convincing. Fifteenth-century Portugal was certainly a small and poor country, yet with a population of less than one million any surplus rural population was easily absorbed in the towns. It does seem clear that this urban migration weakened further the power of the nobles on their landed estates. The nobility in fact suffered not only from a labour shortage but also from a comparatively disadvantageous position vis-à-vis the monarchy, the House of Aviz which ruled Portugal from 1385 to 1580. This royal domination, which in part reflected changing economic and social forces in Portugal itself, was also a result of events in 1385. In this year the Portuguese king beat off a Castilian attack, so establishing his new dynasty. Most of his nobles had sided with the foreigners, and were either executed or exiled for their bad choice. The Portuguese nobility were thus facing crises both in their positions in the countryside and in their unusual subservience to the monarchy. The latter was forcefully brought home to them in 1484, when an over-mighty noble, in fact the top noble, the Duke of Bragança, was executed for treason. Expansion, new lands and new paths to glory had an obvious, even if atavistic, appeal.

The role of the crown is similarly a matter of debate and controversy. The image of Prince Henry the Navigator has long dominated. A younger son of D. João I (1385–1433), and knighted at Ceuta, he devoted his life, we are told, to the discoveries as a crusade to outflank the Muslims. In the fastnesses of Sagres, in the extreme southwest of the country, he established a school for mariners and navigators, and sent out expedition after expedition down the West African coast, following their progress with weary eyes until the Cross of Christ on their sails sank below the horizon. Recent research has modified this picture. The prince was not particularly learned, and the notion of his establishing a 'school' for navigators and scientists seems quite far-fetched. But he played a role nevertheless. Like other members of the royal family he had large estates and other economic interests in Portugal (among other things, he held a monopoly on soap making). While there may have been a religious or mystical element in his patronage of voyages of discovery, he also profited handsomely from the results, especially from imports of gold and slaves. Here also it seems economic man was dominant, even if not exclusively. Further, Prince Henry's activities, whatever their motives, do point to one central characteristic of the discoveries, namely the central role played by the crown. It is true that merchants, both Portuguese and foreign, often provided capital and even ships, yet the direction and much of the impetus came from the crown.

This direction was particularly important after the death of Prince Henry in 1460. It is possible to envisage the Portuguese standing pat around this time. The Atlantic islands were producing, a debased chivalry could perform its barbarous rituals in North Africa, and trade with West Africa was flourishing. The southern end of Africa seemed nowhere in sight. It was only a new royal push, this time from the future João II (1481–95), which led to further progress southwards. The way in which this was done encapsulated exactly the whole merchant–king nexus which produced the discoveries. In 1469 after some years of stalemate a merchant was given a wide-ranging concession. In return for a five-year monopoly on the trade in gold and slaves, he had to discover 100 leagues of West African coast a year. Thus were linked the merchant's search for profits, and the crown's desire, at least partly also with a view to profits, for further discoveries.

Historians have pointed to various other subsidiary elements to explain the progress and success of Portuguese discoveries. The country's location in the extreme southwest of Europe may have provided, by reason of greater contiguity, some small advantage. Portugal was at peace through nearly all the fifteenth century; energy could be channelled towards expansion. As in many other parts of Europe, the idea of discovery and foreign travel had some popular currency, fostered by Marco Polo's book and Sir John Mandeville's extremely popular, though bogus, *Travels*. Some Portuguese had behind them a tradition of seafaring, derived from the importance of fishing along the coast and indeed far out into the north Atlantic.

But this must not lead us to see the Portuguese as a race of hardy seafarers. Most Portuguese were peasants, in no way knowledgeable about the sea, nor economically dependent on it. The state of Portuguese navigational skills at the start of the discoveries is best exemplified by the way in which the fleet sailing to take Ceuta in 1415 had great difficulty getting across the Straits of Gibraltar. Yet soon this changed; the Portuguese experimented with and perfected both ships and navigational techniques to enable them to press on south into unknown seas.

Until the middle of the fifteenth century the Portuguese used small square-rigged vessels, similar to Mediterranean merchantmen. Such ships were adequate sailing before the wind, but had trouble returning to Portugal in the teeth of contrary winds. The crucial development was the perfection of the caravel around 1440. The lateen sails on these ships were copied from Arab practice. The advantage of course was that they could tack, and sail much closer to the wind. Indeed, sometimes both off West Africa in the fifteenth century and in the sixteenth century in western India, a ship would be square-rigged for sailing with a favourable wind, and then be re-rigged to lateen or a mixture of the two to sail into contrary winds.

In navigational skills also the Portuguese made progress which enabled them to sail far out of sight of land. From 1456 they were able to use a quadrant to measure star altitude and so determine latitude. In the 1480s solar observations and relatively sophisticated tables improved further their ability to work out their latitude. (The scientific determination of longitude of course remained a mystery for some three more centuries.) It would be incorrect to overemphasize these advances: Portuguese navigation in the sixteenth century could certainly be a hit or miss affair (literally), and many crusty old pilots scorned such new-fangled devices, preferring to rely on their experience of winds, tides and the run of the water to find their way.

A summary statement on motives is difficult to provide. The economic determinists have had things pretty much their own way recently. In part this is because one can measure gold and slave imports, and cultivation on the Canaries. But how to measure, or even demonstrate at all, Prince Henry's religious faith? Was it indeed that 'Religion provided the pretext, and gold the motive', or that 'Discovery was called into being by the search for wealth. Ostensibly it was a crusade for souls; if the Portuguese had built churches instead of baracoons, and sought conversions instead of slaves, they might be believed. Missionary work followed half a century behind man-stealing.'[2] Perhaps a better way to approach the matter is to remember that fifteenth-century people did not make the clear distinction between religion, economics and politics which we are used to making. To the Portuguese kings there may have been no contradiction or unconscious irony in their linking of service to God and profit for themselves. In 1565 the king, D. Sebastian, encouraged the viceroy in Goa to promote Christianity in the Indonesian island of Ambon, for this 'is an important means of making the country secure and would increase the profits to be made there' (Hubert Jacobs, ed., *Documenta Malucensia*, 2 vols., Rome, 1974–80, vol. 1, pp. 461–2). While giving primacy to economic motives, we should also try to see in the discoveries the same sort of complex intermingling of imperatives revealed in this letter: God, Caesar and Mammon altogether.

Apart from 'Christians and Spices', and Dr Johnson's later dismissive 'I do not much wish well to discoveries, for I am always afraid they will end in conquest and robbery' (John Wain, *Samuel Johnson*, London, 1974, p. 278), the other great cliché about the Portuguese discoveries is Adam Smith's famous statement that 'The discovery of America, and that of a passage to the East Indies by the Cape of Good Hope, are the two greatest and most important events recorded in the history of mankind' (D. K. Fieldhouse, *The Colonial Empires*, London, 1982, p. 3). We can pay unreserved tribute to the great navigational feats of 1487–1500. Da Gama on his voyage of 1497–9 was twice out of sight of land for ninety days continuously. Cabral in 1500 linked together four continents, for after leaving Europe he discovered Brazil, and then sailed to Africa and on to Asia. This tribute paid, what else can be said of the significance of the Portuguese voyages?

It is really incorrect to see these Portuguese voyages as completely new and unusual, for the Portuguese themselves and other Europeans had been trading, exploring and sailing long distances for centuries. When Rome was at its height its merchants traded extensively in the Arabian Sea. Later Europeans like Marco Polo travelled vast distances overland and by sea. Norsemen and Vikings settled Greenland, Iceland and even North America. Thus a case can be made that the Portuguese,

---

[2] Respectively Carlo M. Cipolla, *European Culture and Overseas Expansion* (Harmondsworth, 1970), p. 101, and Peter Padfield, *Tide of Empires*, vol. 1, '1481–1654' (London, 1979), p. 32.

far from being *sui generis*, were in fact building on a long tradition of discovery. The difference with these earlier efforts then lies not in the discoveries as such, but in the use the Portuguese made of them; unlike their predecessors in other areas, they built on their voyages and tried to produce a major politico-military impact on India. But it is worthwhile to investigate the word 'discovery' a little more closely. Is it too pedantic to point out that there were already people living in Brazil, and in West Africa; indeed West Africa was linked by trade routes, albeit rather rudimentary, with other areas of Africa and so with a wider world. In these areas it is more correct to describe the Portuguese as the first Europeans to arrive.

This point can be made much more strongly in the case of the Indian Ocean, and western India. When da Gama sailed up the East African coast in 1498 he sailed into a familiar world, and one already linked to the Mediterranean and Europe. Arab traders had penetrated, converted, settled and intermarried as far south as Sofala, and linked all littoral East Africa north of here with other parts of the Indian Ocean as well as the Red Sea and Europe. That this was not a new and isolated world was soon made depressingly clear. When da Gama's ships arrived at Mozambique island the Muslim ruler thought the Portuguese were Muslim also, and welcomed them. When he discovered they were Christian, age-old prejudice from North Africa, the Mediterranean and the Crusades surfaced – his demeanour changed to one of hostility. On their side, the brutal anti-Muslim campaign on which the Portuguese soon embarked was in many respects simply a continuation of their reconquest of Portugal and their crusade in North Africa.

A dismally familiar world then, and also one in which the Portuguese were not the first Europeans. For centuries scattered European traders and travellers had adventured through the Middle East to the Indian Ocean. In 1338 six Venetians travelled overland to India to trade; in this same century other Italians, successors of Marco Polo, traded in China. These contacts became more rare once the 'Pax Mongolica' collapsed in the middle of the fourteenth century, but we know of several other European visitors to India in the fifteenth century. One of them was Pero de Covilham, sent out by the Portuguese king D. João II in 1487 to investigate conditions in the Indian Ocean. He visited Cannanore, Calicut, Goa, Hurmuz, and also East African ports as far south as Sofala. It is likely that he met other Europeans in Calicut at least.

The contact went both ways; some Muslim merchants in India and Asia around 1500 knew something of Europe, and spoke European languages. These people usually had spent time in North Africa and traded in the Mediterranean, where they had contact with Venetians and other Italians. When da Gama got to Calicut he was met by two Tunisian Muslims who spoke Castilian and Genoese. In September 1498 he came across a Polish Jew who spoke, reputedly, Hebrew, Venetian, Arabic, German and a little Spanish. The movement of trade goods was also well established between Asia and Europe. From Roman times, with occasional fits and starts, Asian products had moved through the Red Sea to the Mediterranean, being paid for usually by bullion. Nor should we see the world of the Indian Ocean as discrete and parochial: trade and travel within Asia was well developed. We should remember here the famous voyages all over the Indian Ocean, from 1405 to 1433, of the Chinese Muslim eunuch Cheng Ho. His expeditions provide an interesting counterpart to the beginnings of Portuguese expansion at the same time. The most obvious difference is that Cheng Ho got much further, and mounted far larger expeditions. Is it totally unprofitable to speculate that had imperial policy not changed after his death in 1434, Chinese expansion *might* have continued around the Cape of Good Hope and even up to Europe? Certainly Braudel and Needham and Wallerstein have toyed with the idea.[3] In any case, Cheng Ho was by no means the only long-distance Asian traveller in the fifteenth century.

There was, then, some travel and much trade between Asia and Europe before da Gama. Perhaps however our terminology is confusing the issue. It may be more correct to think of a Eurasian area in which trade and travel occurred, rather than of two discrete areas called 'Asia' and 'Europe'. Within Eurasia trade took place, with different routes and different products being moved by different people at different times. In the fifteenth century the two most important long-distance luxury trades were in gold and spices. These and many other products moved on many different routes to various destinations within Eurasia. *One* of these destinations was the Mediterranean, and on this route the main traders were Muslims and Venetians. In the early sixteenth century the Portuguese took over part of this trade, and used a different route, that

[3] Fernand Braudel, *Civilization and Capitalism, 15th–18th Century*, vol. II (London, 1982), p. 581; Joseph Needham, *Science and Civilisation in China*, vol. IV, part 3 (Cambridge, 1971), pp. 501–2; Immanuel Wallerstein, *The Modern World-System*, 2 vols (London, 1974–80), vol. I, pp. 52–63.

around the Cape, which was external to Eurasia. Yet the end result was the same: spices and bullion still reached various destinations within Eurasia, among them the Mediterranean.

Yet even if this be a correct way to conceptualize the Portuguese presence, some cautions must be provided. A few European traders and adventurers in the Indian Ocean in the fifteenth century are not in the same category as the massive Portuguese irruption in the early sixteenth century: it will be remembered Cabral left Lisbon with at least 1200 men. Nor indeed can the degree of European knowledge of Asian matters in the fifteenth century have been really detailed. It is possible that the Venetians, the main Mediterranean contact with Egypt, knew much more than they told the Portuguese, but certainly da Gama made such obvious mistakes as to call into question any claim that the Portuguese knew much about the Indian Ocean before 1498. He apparently knew nothing of the status and prestige of the zamorin of Calicut, the opulent ruler of a great port city, and dominant on all the Malabar coast, because his presents for the zamorin were trifling in the extreme. Nor apparently did he know anything of Hinduism, for he and his companions mistook a Hindu temple for a (presumably rather strange, even schismatic) Christian church. Indeed he returned to Portugal still thinking the Hindus of Malabar were Christians of some sort. And the Asian lack of knowledge was rather comparable, as is seen in a charming contemporary account of the arrival of the Portuguese in Sri Lanka. The king was told that they were 'a race of very white and beautiful people, who wear boots and hats of iron and never stop in any place. They eat a sort of white stone and drink blood' (quoted in C. M. Cipolla, *European Culture and Overseas Expansion*, Harmondsworth, 1970, p. 84).

What then can we conclude about the general significance of the Portuguese voyages in the fifteenth century? One point seems now to be uncontested: that their importance was much greater for Europe than for Asia. As a recent historian of western colonialism puts it, they 'liberated Europe from a geographic and mental cell'.[4] As to trade, we have already noted that the Cape route merely provided an alternative route for Eurasian trade; any significant European impact on Asian trade came only in the later eighteenth century. But if we follow the received wisdom of today and see a decisive European impact on Asia, consequent mostly on the industrial revolution, only in the eighteenth

[4] D. K. Fieldhouse, *The Colonial Empires*, 2nd ed. (London, 1982), p. 4.

13

century, can we then claim that the Portuguese are the necessary precursors, the ones who showed the way to later more successful Europeans in Asia, who moved beyond expansion to domination? The answer seems to be negative. Developments in technology made possible the Cape route, and knowledge of these developments was not restricted to the Portuguese. Someone from Europe was 'inevitably' going to make this voyage sooner or later. We have tried to explain why the Portuguese were first, yet had they not succeeded someone else, probably the Spanish, would have done it. It may be remembered that a ship of Magellan, a Portuguese in Spanish service, in 1522 rounded the Cape from east to west.

A second point is more basic. One cannot see the Portuguese as the necessary precursors to the European expansion which in the eighteenth century became world dominance, thanks to the industrial revolution and related scientific and technological developments. The point surely is again that these developments must have produced western European dominance, at least for a time. The fact that the Portuguese rounded the Cape of Good Hope some two and a half centuries previous to this then had no bearing on the outcome. Portuguese navigational triumphs in the fifteenth century must be seen as strictly a *tour de force*.

Finally, and before the focus swings to India, we must try to describe these Portuguese stepping ashore in Calicut in 1498 after ten months at sea. The stereotype is of people belonging to a *different category*, a new *genus*, arriving: different religion, culture, skin colour, even degree of civilization, for we are often told that the Portuguese were the standard-bearers of a new, more advanced, Christian impact on Asia. What sort of society did they spring from?

Portugal in 1500 had a population of 1 million at most, giving a low density of about twelve per square kilometre. By 1640 the total was close to 2 million. Perhaps 15 percent of these people were urban dwellers, a high percentage for Europe at the time. Lisbon was by far the largest city, with about 70,000 inhabitants in 1527, and as many as 110,000 by 1629. The composition of this population was far from stable. The broad equation is that Portuguese left for overseas – between 3000 and 4000 a year in the sixteenth century – and were replaced by slaves, of whom some 2000 entered every year. The slave trade had started in the 1440s, and even by the next decade 1000 were coming in each year. Their labour developed agriculture on the Atlantic islands and in southern Portugal, and most Portuguese households of any wealth had household slaves. Portugal had a much higher percentage of slaves than any other European country, something which both foreigners and Portuguese commented on. In the ports, and trade areas like the Algarve, slaves could make up 10 percent of the population; in the early seventeenth century in Lisbon the proportion was even higher.

A second distinctive element in the population, one deliberately made to be external during the sixteenth century, was Jews. Just as slavery was not very extensive in fifteenth-century Portugal, so also Jews were not particularly singled out. Portuguese clothes, food, medicine and entertainment owed much to Jewish (and Muslim) influences in this more tolerant, or indifferent, era. Indeed, the first eleven Portuguese incunabula were all in Hebrew. Many Jews expelled from Spain in 1492 moved to Portugal. The formal break came in the 1490s when two Portuguese princes married Spanish princesses, and as part of the marriage contracts agreed to adopt Spanish practices of intolerance and bigotry towards Jews. In 1496 D. Manuel decreed that all Jews and Muslims who refused baptism were to be expelled; one author claims that the seizure of the goods of those expelled helped to finance da Gama's voyage. Yet to his credit Manuel refused a total pogrom. Conversion was made to be a very *pro forma* matter, and the converts, called New Christians, were given twenty years (later extended) to instruct themselves in the Christian faith. In part this relative tolerance was forced on Manuel by the prominent role of Jews in Portuguese trade, commerce and finance, a role which the same families, now formally New Christians, continued to play. Nevertheless, during the sixteenth century this community was often threatened by the increasing drive for Catholic purity fostered by the Counter Reformation and symbolized by the Inquisition, which was established in Lisbon in 1536 and became fully operational in 1547. Here as elsewhere one sees a tension between deference to God and to Mammon. An incident in 1627 illustrates this clearly. The New Christians had been under increasing pressure from the Inquisition. Finally this was eased a little in return for a huge loan of 1,500,000 cruzados to the Portuguese crown. Yet although crypto-Jewish wealth could buy this sort of official semi-tolerance, it could not ease the general contempt which most sixteenth-century Portuguese showed to New Christians: the records are rife with casually racist remarks against them.

One other demographic feature may be noted: low life expectancy. Plague was the worst killer, especially in 1569–70. In this great outbreak (only one of several during the century), mortality in Lisbon in June 1569 was 50 or 60 a day, in July 300 to 400, and later up to 700. A modern estimate finds 50,000 deaths in Lisbon, a city of about 100,000, during this epidemic. The 'big people,' including the king, left precipitously and returned only when the outbreak was ended. Similarly, when the elite in April 1581 were called on to elect Philip II of Spain as King of Portugal, plague in Lisbon forced them to meet outside the city, at Tomar. Yet even the elite was far from immune to high mortality, as is dramatically illustrated by the longevity of the royal family in the sixteenth century. D. Manuel, who lived from 1469 to 1521, had thirteen children by three wives. Four predeceased him, and nine died before the age of forty. His successor, D. João III (1521–57), had ten children, whose average life span was some 7.6 years: the most long-lived died at twenty-two.

Such fearsome mortality bred religiosity. At the elite level this found partial expression in an increasingly intolerant Catholicism, symbolised by the Inquisition or by the way in which Portugal was the only European Catholic country which accepted all the decisions of the Council of Trent (1545–63) and applied them rigorously. In the early seventeenth century Portugal boasted some 400 convents; one person in 36 was a priest or member of a religious order. An account of a shipwreck in the Arabian Sea in 1585 illustrates well the hold of formal religion in moments of crisis. Those on board 'all wished to confess at the same time, and so loudly that they could all hear each other . . . one man, who could not wait . . . without further delay told his sins out aloud, sins which were so grave and so great that the priest had to put his hand in front of his mouth, shouting at him to be silent.'[5]

Yet at least partially among the elite, and almost absolutely among the bulk of the population, folk religion retained its sway, and indeed continued to do so into the twentieth century. This dominant religious strain was characterized by belief in magic, the evil eye, witches, miracles, love potions, all thinly overlaid with a veneer of Catholicism. Folk practice influenced all aspects of life, and all classes. In 1501 D. Manuel told Ferdinand and Isabella there were men with four eyes at Sofala. Seven years later a respected author reported snakes a quarter of a league long in Senegal. In 1544 men with no heads were reported to live in the interior of Angola. This belief in the fabulous spread over into illness. Diarrhoea, prevalent in Portugal for centuries because of lack of

[5] Charles David Ley, ed., *Portuguese Voyages, 1498–1663* (London, 1947), pp. 268–9.

hygiene, could be cured by annointing the body with a powder of goat dung and egg whites. As late as 1933, forty miles (64 kilometres) from Oporto, an epileptic woman was thrashed until unconscious and then burnt to death in order to exorcise her of an evil spirit. Her peasant tormentors thought she would rise from the flames free of the spirit. That this occurred in the north is in fact a little atypical, for generally religious observance, and rigidity, decreased in Portugal from north to south. In the twentieth century the southern areas of Alentejo and the Algarve were classified as mission fields, such was the laxity in these areas.

Messianism is another example of folk religion lightly overlaid with Christian belief; it has important political implications. The prevailing belief, based on Celtic and Jewish legends, was that a Hidden One would return and establish a universal monarchy under Portuguese rule. After 1578 this belief became the phenomenon of Sebastianism. D. João III had died in 1557 leaving as his heir a three years old grandson, Sebastian. He grew up a little deformed both physically and mentally. In 1578 he led on crusade the flower of the Portuguese nobility to their, and his, death at the battle of El-Ksar el-Kebir in Morocco. He was succeeded by his great uncle, D. Henry, a cardinal. His death in 1580 ended the Aviz dynasty and led to sixty years of Spanish rule in Portugal. Not surprisingly, tales soon spread that the Hidden One was in fact D. Sebastian, who would return to free his people. False Sebastians continued to appear, usually acquiring large peasant followings, and even some elite support. Like other folk beliefs, this also continued into the twentieth century as an influential strain in Portuguese popular culture.

One other religio-political strain in sixteenth-century Portuguese thought needs to be noted. We have described anti-Jewish sentiment; anti-Muslim feeling was much more virulent, based as it was not only on religious antipathy but also on political and military conflict. It will be remembered that the reconquest was completed only in 1249. This did not lead to any abatement of hostility to Muslims. The example of Spain was influential here, with her wars against Muslim Grenada: indeed the final Morisco revolt in southern Spain occurred as late as 1568. More important was the taking of Ceuta, and involvement throughout the fifteenth and sixteenth centuries in North African affairs. D. Sebastian's death was thus only one instance of a tradition of Portuguese–Muslim hostility, a tradition which influenced all elements of Portuguese society, and which contributed powerfully to Portuguese actions in the Indian Ocean in the sixteenth century.

Among the elite in the sixteenth century there were other influences at work, though disentangling them is difficult. Co-existing with religious bigotry and supersitition was a feeble Portuguese version of the Renaissance, including humanist influences from other parts of Europe. Confusingly, the tendency of both these was strictly speaking reactionary, for they promoted a return to an ancient intellectual tradition. Yet the second dominant intellectual strain was the excitement, the vast new knowledge, produced by the explorations and discoveries of the fifteenth and sixteenth centuries. As Godinho stresses, concepts of space, time and number were all radically changed as a result: as a telling example, quantification was done much more now.[6] It seems however that some of this spirit of inquiry, or rebirth, was stifled later in the sixteenth century as the Counter Reformation imposed its shackles. Portugal lay under a strict censorship of books; Garcia d'Orta's classic inquiry into Asian botany and medicine was neglected by his fellow Portuguese, but not by other Europeans. Portuguese painting concentrated on religious subjects, education was minimal, and dominated again by the church. In many ways D. João de Castro, governor of Portuguese India from 1545 to 1548, summed up in himself these conflicting trends. On the one hand he was a Renaissance man. In his *roteiros* (rutters, navigational guides), he was especially concerned to test and correct Ptolemy's information on East Africa and the Red Sea. Yet these rutters also show Castro the scientist and discoverer at work, so that, as Elaine Sanceau well says, he was a 'true son of that strange century that looked forward and back'.[7] But his military actions in India show a fanatical anti-Muslim at work, a man responsible for slaughter on a vast scale. Add to this his personal religiosity, complete with draconian fasts and scourgings, and a notorious failure to comprehend financial matters, and one has a person who, in his complexity, sums up much of the intellectual life of the sixteenth-century Portuguese elite.

Such varying and contradictory influences make clear that the Portuguese elite was not static in the sixteenth century. This was indeed a century of turmoil and change, the religious and intellectual aspects of

<hr/>

[6] V. M. Godinho, *Os Descobrimentos e a Economia Mundial*, 2nd ed. (Lisbon, 1981–3), vol. I, pp. 15–45.
[7] Elaine Sanceau, *Knight of the Renaissance: D. João de Castro* (London, n.d.), p. 221.

which we have already noted. In military matters, it has been claimed that the period 1450–1530 saw in Europe a series of fundamental changes – improved fortifications, the use of artillery in naval warfare, the use of infantry, the development of hand-held guns – which added up to a revolution. From then until the late eighteenth century there were only changes of scale. The nature of the Portuguese state also changed fundamentally, for under D. Manuel (1495–1521) we see the founding of a bureaucratic and mercantilist state, one which reduced further the power of the nobility, and began to regulate crafts, and to provide a minimum at least of social service. One aspect of these changes (which were not found only in Portugal) was the way in which Portuguese kings increasingly ignored the people as embodied in the Cortes, and instead ruled through their dependent and subservient advisors. Yet whatever the degree of royal domination, and the growth of impersonal bureaucratization, this was still a very small elite, in which most people knew each other, and indeed were related to some degree. The still-casual atmosphere, the pre-modernity of the system perhaps, is well illustrated in an account of how da Gama was chosen, fatefully, to command the first fleet to India. D. Manuel was sitting in the council chamber reading documents (a 'modern' activity) when da Gama wandered through the room ('pre-modern' casualness). The king invited him to command the expedition. Long discussion ensued, during which the king ate a meal and later, with da Gama still tagging along, retired to a robing room.

Such courtiers, together with other members of the nobility clustered in servile fashion around the king, or sent off to prove themselves overseas, made up one group in sixteenth-century Portuguese society. The nobility in the broadest sense included perhaps 20,000 people, and was rather diverse internally. It included not only people with titles, but also successful lawyers and bureaucrats, and a host of people called *fidalgos*, 'sons of somebody'. In the sixteenth century the gentry generally became less rustic, more attracted to the benefits of patronage at court and commercial activities. Here they merged into a second social group, that of merchants, among them New Christians. This group however failed to improve its position along the lines laid down in say England or Holland. Those of them who were New Christians were subject to arbitrary persecution and confiscation. Foreign capitalists could frequently compete successfully, notably Genoese and Fugger representatives. Portugal's still-born bourgeoisie also suffered from a lack of capital, and unequal competition from a mercantile-minded king and nobility. Portugal's failure to profit from and build on her sixteenth-century successes stemmed in large part from the inability of her merchants to evolve into mercantile capitalists.

The vast bulk of Portugal's population, perhaps 80 percent of the total, were peasants caught in a situation which remained stagnant into at least the eighteenth century, and which was largely unmonetized and unaffected by the market. Here was the stratum of the population, a huge one, in which folk religion remained dominant. Here were the people who laboured on noble or clerical estates, or leased land from them, paying in return at least one-third, and sometimes seven-tenths, of their production in rent and other taxes. These were the people who ate, when they ate at all, the Mediterranean staples of bread, olive oil and wine: meat and fish were luxuries. And these were the people who escaped, when they could, to the towns, and from there overseas. Yet this emigration from rural Portugal constitutes an indictment of Portuguese agricultural management and of her productivity. About 65 percent of Portugal is cultivable; in the sixteenth century about 25 percent was used (a proportion which had hardly increased in the second half of the nineteenth century). An acerbic French visitor in the 1530s expatiated on what seemed to him to be Portuguese backwardness. Much of the country was uncultivated, and even unpopulated. The results of this agricultural inefficiency, coupled with natural disadvantages, were significant. In the sixteenth century Portugal imported about one-fifth of its grain requirements, while an important motivation for the early fifteenth-century expansion was grain imperialism: to find better land, in North Africa and the islands, on which food could be grown. It cannot be stressed too strongly that sixteenth-century Portugal was a poor country, with the bulk of the population suffering from disease and mortality rates high. As Braudel noted, 'It was a country rotten at the core, an enormous deadweight of which Philip was to find himself master in 1580.'[8] Indeed, anyone who travels today on the western Indian coast and in Portugal will be impressed by the appearance of fecundity, of lush vegetation, in the former compared with the rocky, infertile and barren appearance of much of Portugal. At least visually and initially, Goa must have looked like paradise to a sixteenth-century Portuguese peasant.

[8] Fernand Braudel, *The Mediterranean and the Mediterranean World in the Age of Philip II* (London, 1972–3), vol. I, pp. 585–91.

Several other matters must be touched on briefly to conclude this sketch of sixteenth-century Portugal. In the home the main item of furniture was a bed; chairs were unusual, and reserved for the head of the family. Most people, probably following Muslim practice, sat on the floor. Spoons also were rare, and forks unknown. The only usual utensil was a knife, which in the fifteenth century was brought along to a meal. In the next century the host began to provide these. In the cities people lived and worked grouped in streets and quarters based on professions. Until the later sixteenth century the government attitude to city hygiene and other conveniences was strictly *laissez-faire*. Only under the Spanish kings was a start made to provide pavements or drainage.

Attitudes to legitimacy and sex seem to have become stricter during the sixteenth century, another result no doubt of the Counter Reformation. Before this time adultery and partnerships without benefit of sacraments were rife, and illegitimate children were produced in gay abandon, even by male and female clerics. Prostitution and homosexuality were common. When public morality tightened up in the sixteenth century, this still applied mostly to the elite, the only ones who usually indulged in 'legal' weddings performed by a priest. The partners were comparatively young – the male typically fourteen to sixteen, the female twelve to fourteen. Differing notions of modesty were revealed (literally) by fifteenth-century clothing: a man in his codpiece (sometimes made of flamboyant brocade) could reveal almost all while women wore much less revealing clothes, and indeed often were veiled. Two sixteenth-century accounts make clear these divergent mores. A member of Cabral's voyage to Brazil in 1500, a male scribe from a good family, rhapsodized over the forms of the naked Tupi Indian girls they found there. 'These were very young and pretty, and had abundant long black hair down their backs. Their private parts were tightly knit, well raised, and half free from hairs; thus we were not at all ashamed to look at them.' There are strong overtones of an early version of the noble savage myth: another girl 'was so well made and so rounded, and her private parts (of which she made no privacy) so comely that many women in our country would be ashamed, if they saw such perfection, that theirs were not equally perfect.'[9] Portuguese women, on the other hand, were socialized very differently. A noblewoman captured by East African Kaffirs in 1552 at first resisted being stripped by them, 'for she was of a nature to prefer being killed by the Kaffirs to being left naked

[9] C. D. Ley, *Portuguese Voyages*, pp. 46–7.

21

before all people'. Finally succumbing, 'she flung herself on the ground immediately, and covered herself completely with her hair, which was very long. She made a hole in the sand in which she buried herself up to her waist, and never arose from it again.'[10]

The last question we must ask is whether Portugal was a nation in the sixteenth century. Most historians of Europe would put the rise of nationalism, as opposed to patriotism or chauvinism, much later than this. Yet at the least patriotism was well developed in Portugal, in part no doubt because as early as the mid thirteenth century Portugal was reconquered from the Muslims, and her boundary with Spain fixed. In terms of fixed boundaries she is thus the oldest state in Europe. Yet even before the period of Spanish rule from 1580 to 1640 there were occasional skirmishes, even wars, with Portugal's only neighbour. Anti-Spanish feeling ran deep in Portugal; this led to the reassertion of independence in 1640, and more generally to the creation of closer Portuguese identification in the face of this common enemy. Only the nobility was largely immune from this, hence their pusillanimous, if not disloyal, stance in 1580 and on several other occasions. The Cortes of 1562 reflected more clearly Portuguese feeling. It was worried that the young D. Sebastian, then aged eight, was being turned into a little Spanish dandy. They advised: 'Let him dress Portuguese . . . , eat Portuguese, ride Portuguese, speak Portuguese, all his acts be Portuguese' (quoted in H. V. Livermore, *A New History of Portugal*, Cambridge, 1966, p. 152). Yet even patriotism, let alone nationalism, should not be stressed too much. It surfaced at times of crisis in Portugal and in Asia, but we must again, and finally, remember that the bulk of the population knew nothing of the world beyond their village. King, Cortes, Spanish, even church were unknown and unregarded.

This rather lengthy background may have taken us too far. Yet it seemed vital to provide this foundation, for only thus is it possible to assess accurately the nature and degree of the Portuguese impact on India, and the Indian impact on the Portuguese. We can now begin our analysis of this matter.

The state of our knowledge of sixteenth-century India does not allow us to attempt the sort of sketch which we have just provided for Portuguese society. In any case this is hardly necessary, for few people in India were affected by the arrival and activities of the Portuguese in this

[10] *Ibid.*, p. 257.

century or later. The total population of India at 1600 is estimated at 140 or 150 million, with around 110 million of these living within the Mughal empire. (At this same time Portugal's population, it will be remembered, was about 1,500,000.) The great bulk of this comparatively teeming mass of people never knew of, saw, or were concerned with the Portuguese. One of our main aims is to delineate clearly just who were affected, and how they responded; to do this we must first describe the political–economic situation in the Indian Ocean and especially in littoral western India at the time of the arrival of the Portuguese. We can then consider the Portuguese attempt to change this situation to their own advantage.

There are two important areas of debate concerning the situation in the Indian Ocean around 1500: what community did seafarers belong to, and what economic position did the merchant passengers have? It has been generally assumed that the ships of the ocean at that time were nearly all Muslim-owned and manned. Indeed, at one time scholars talked of a period of Arab dominance. This, however, if it ever existed had certainly ended by the sixteenth century. The situation was in fact quite complicated at 1500. Muslims no doubt did control the bulk of the trade, and manned most of the ships, but this does not mean they owned all the cargo on board these ships, and in any case these Muslims were very diverse indeed. Some big merchants, and famous pilots, came from the Middle East, especially the Red Sea and Hadramaut areas. However, the majority of Muslim ships were owned by more recently converted Muslims from Gujarat, Malabar and Bengal. The activities of these traders were often geographically divided: thus trade to the Red Sea from Malabar was controlled by Middle East Muslims, but the eastward traffic to Malacca was handled by various Indian Muslims.

We must not overemphasize the degree of Muslim dominance. Even when Hindus stayed ashore, they still could own large parts of the cargo of a ship owned and crewed by Muslims. There is also good evidence of Hindus of various castes trading overseas, for example from Gujarat to East Africa, and down the western Indian coast. *Vanias* traded to, and were resident in, Red Sea and Hadramaut ports from pre-Portuguese times to the end of the eighteenth century and indeed until today. From within Hindu India as a whole the main seafaring group at 1500 was apparently the *chettyars* of Coromandel, who had a very important role in trade in the whole Bay of Bengal area, and especially from Coromandel to Malacca. They were joined in this trade by another southeast Indian trading community, the Chulia Muslims. We have much less evidence about who travelled on coastal craft, but one would expect more of a communal mix here, with both Hindus and Muslims participating. Finally, it does seem clear that the crews of all these ships were overwhelmingly Muslims, hailing from a wide range of Muslim littoral communities. Yet here again Muslim dominance was not complete. Various lower-caste Hindus in both Malabar and Gujarat sailed ships on coastal routes, and also engaged in fishing.

The communal allegiance of people on board ships was thus rather various. The same comment applies when we look at the motives which made people take ship. Some passengers on the Red Sea route were Muslim pilgrims, but these people (and indeed everyone else on board ship including the crew as well as passengers) also traded. It is here that we enter the second, and more important, debate over activities in the Indian Ocean at 1500: who were the maritime traders?

The problems arise when we consider the claims of the important Dutch historian J. C. Van Leur.[11] He found pre-nineteenth-century Asian trade to be virtually changeless, done mostly by petty pedlars, characterized by the exchange of luxury goods small in bulk but high in value, and dominated by politically powerful coastal lords. As several scholars have pointed out, there are problems with all four of these claims. First, Asian trade was not completely changeless, as we have had, and will have, occasion to notice. There were positional changes at least, even if one can find common underlying themes and trends.

Van Leur's depiction of the pedlar, a petty merchant travelling from port to port with a few bales of goods, and little financial backing, is also questionable. No doubt many such did exist, but other people who traded had huge capital resources. Indeed, the Portuguese accounts frequently expatiate on the, to them, colossal wealth of the Hindu and Muslim merchants of Gujarat. Similarly, the Red Sea Muslims were far from being pedlars, and nor apparently were some of the *chettyars*. It is true that the richest merchants would usually not travel by sea themselves, yet their agents also cannot be considered to be pedlars in Van Leur's sense.

Nor can we follow him in his characterization of the goods traded. Luxuries were of course exchanged – indeed India's prime import was bullion – but many more mundane goods were also carried by sea. The best example is cotton cloths from Gujarat, Coromandel and Bengal,

[11] J. C. Van Leur, *Indonesian Trade and Society* (The Hague, 1955).

some of it costly fine stuff but the majority coarse cloth, especially from Gujarat, designed for everyday wear and exported all over seaborne Asia. It was these cloths which paid for many of the spices of southeast Asia. Indeed, in the sixteenth century in some agreements between the Portuguese and the suppliers, the price of the spices was fixed in cloths, not money. Food, especially rice, was also traded by sea within the Bay of Bengal, in Indonesia, and up and down the west coast of India: Indian rice even went to Aden, Hurmuz, and Malacca.

The fourth claim, of domination by coastal lords over the trade of the pedlars, is more difficult to assess, partly because it strikes a sympathetic chord for recent Marxist historians. To explain India's lack of economic development in the seventeenth century they claim either that the Europeans nipped nascent Indian capitalism in the bud, or that oppression from the political elite created such insecurity that economic development was hindered. But both Van Leur and the Marxists fly in the face of the available evidence. Most port controllers saw correctly that it was in their interests to increase the trade of their port. Merchants could and did respond effectively to the few who were extortionate, whether by moving, by shutting up shop, or by appealing to higher authority. Medieval Asian cities were not as autonomous, nor as dominated by merchant elites, as were comparable European (but not, it will be remembered, Portuguese) cities, but the merchants were far from being powerless. Van Leur, however, ignored the existence of these powerful merchants who were not connected to the political elite.

We have now to consider which were the major sea-trade routes in the Indian Ocean at 1500, and list the most important products traded. The routes sailed were all governed as to timing, and to some extent also as to direction, by the monsoon winds, if we exclude very minor coastal trade done in oared boats. The glamour routes, on which historians have focussed too much attention, can be listed first. At 1500 the longest route was from Aden to Malacca, via either Gujarat or Malabar. The goods entering the Red Sea included cottons, indigo, spices, and drugs, while from this area came European woollens, silks, and bullion. Gujarat provided most of these cloths and indigo, and took much of the bullion. From Malabar, especially through Calicut, came some of the pepper, and cinnamon transhipped from Sri Lanka. Malacca, the great entrepot, received cloths from India and bullion from the Red Sea, and provided in return pepper, mace, nutmeg and cloves from eastern Indonesia and Chinese goods, especially silks and porcelain. A second major route, dominated by Gujaratis, brought ebony, slaves, ivory and gold from East Africa to India. Cloths, beads and foodstuffs were provided in return.

From the Hadramaut, and the Persian Gulf via Hurmuz, came horses, pearls from the gulf, Persian silks and carpets, and dyes. In the Bay of Bengal area, Bengal exported cloths and foodstuffs, while Coromandel provided cloths and yarns. In the south Sri Lanka produced precious stones and cinnamon, and to the east Pegu took cloths and exported precious stones and metals. Mme Bouchon has described for us a typical Gujarati voyage.[12] The ship would leave Gujarat with textiles, opium and copper in May for Malacca, arriving at the end of June. Part of the cargo would be exchanged for silks and porcelain from China, and spices, and the ship would then proceed to Sumatra for pepper. From September to March the ship traded in Pegu, Tennassarim and other Bay of Bengal ports for rice, lac, and rubies. It would also call at Pedir and Pasai for pepper. Leaving southeast Asia, the ship then sailed to the Maldive islands, where it remained during the monsoon taking on supplies. Then the ship would either return to Gujarat, or go on to Aden to pick up Red Sea products and bullion, which would be taken back home to vanish in Gujarat or again be re-exported.

These are long-distance routes, involving voyages of some weeks at least, and perhaps dominated by big merchants rather than pedlars. We know much less about coastal trade in the fifteenth century, but clearly at 1500 it was extensive, with numerous small ships engaged in transporting local products to the great entrepots for re-export. Cinnamon usually came up from Sri Lanka to Calicut. Malabar pepper came overland or by sea to the same entrepot. Sumatran pepper came by sea to Malacca, as did other Indonesian and Chinese products. Other coastal trade was simple exchange of goods not destined for re-export: thus Gujarati and Coromandel cloths were carried to ports in their immediate vicinities on the west and east coasts, and around to Pegu. The trade in food, especially rice, was very extensive. Kanara supplied other areas on the west coast of India, Malacca got its rice from Java, Siam and Pegu.

At 1500 none of the major states of India played any important role in maritime affairs. In the north, the declining Lodi sultanate, and then the new and expanding Mughal empire, were entirely land based in

[12] G. Bouchon, 'Le Première Voyage de Lopo Soares en Inde (1504–1505)', *Mare Luso-Indicum*, III (1976), 196–8.

terms of both resources and ethos. The vast bulk of the revenue of the Mughal state came from land revenue. A small part was derived from other land-based sources – for example, various tolls and transit fees. Only perhaps 5 percent came from customs revenue. It is true that some of the land-based revenues related to trade: thus crops grown for export paid land revenue, while some transit taxes were paid on goods destined for export. Nevertheless, the revenue resources of the Mughal empire were overwhelmingly from the land.

This fact interlocked with, and no doubt helped to create, a North Indian Muslim ethos which was again oriented to the land. The Mughals came from interior Asia. Babur (1526–30), the first of the dynasty, never saw the sea. Akbar (1556–1605), his greatest successor, responded with puzzlement and delight when he first saw it, in the Gulf of Cambay at the age of thirty. For this militarily-oriented elite culturally sanctioned activities were land activities, especially heroic cavalry charges and more prosaically the struggle to control more land and so more resources. To quote only one of several contemporary Muslim aphorisms: 'People who travel by sea are like silly worms clinging to logs.'

All this applies equally well to the southern states. In the Deccan the Muslim political elite was preoccupied during the sixteenth century with establishing independent states after the Bahmani disintegration late in the previous century, then with struggles between themselves and with Hindu Vijayanagar further south, and after 1565 and the end of Vijayanagar with expanding over its ruins. In none of these elite preoccupations did maritime matters play any role at all.

At first sight the *hajj* appears to be different. Muslim rulers, especially newly established ones were concerned, either for reasons of personal piety or in order to impress the orthodox, with making it possible for the faithful to travel to Mecca and Medina. For our present purposes, the point is that while the Mughals at least, and presumably other rulers also, patronized this activity, this did not mean that they became actively involved in maritime matters. The clearest proof of this is that Akbar was prepared to take passes from the Portuguese in order to be allowed to send off his pilgrim ships. The object of the exercise was to send people to the Holy Cities; the means were subordinated to this end, and the traffic did not involve state political concern with the sea.

The same applies to the private trading activities of the Indian political elite. Particular nobles and ladies of the royal harem (usually using agents) did send off goods on their own accounts and did sometimes lend money to other sea traders. At least in the sixteenth century this was a minor activity in terms of the incomes of most of this elite, and usually did not lead to any involvement on their part in political action directed to the sea.

The only exception to this general rule concerns the relatively small number of state officials or quasi-officials who derived major parts of their incomes from taxes on maritime matters, or from their own sea trade. There is a continuum here, ranging from say the police chief of Agra, who derived no revenue, even tangentially, from maritime matters, to the collector of customs at Surat, whose entire income might come from taxing sea trade. We must remember, however, that a port official, or governor, could also receive part or all of his income from land revenue. Thus the vast majority of officials in any of the major states were at the first end of our continuum. In the middle were primarily land-based people, part of whose income came from taxes on goods destined to be exported by sea: for example, nobles whose revenue came from cotton producing areas, or local chiefs who collected dubiously sanctioned tolls on the bullock carts going from Agra to Surat. At the other, and very atypical, extreme are a small number of people like customs collectors and governors of port cities. These people were sea-oriented, at least in part. They themselves were landlubbers, but a crucial part of their revenue came from taxes on sea trade, and from their own trading activities. They were concerned to see this trade continue.

Apart from these servants of large, land-oriented states a few other political leaders have to be included in this end of our continuum. These were the rulers of seaboard states which were focussed on particular port cities. The best examples of these are the rulers of Malabar: the zamorin of Calicut, and the rajas of Cochin, Cannanore, Quilon and various other minor ports. Comparatively little of the revenue of such rulers came from the land; rather, an important part of state income was based on direct and indirect profits from sea trade. Customs duties and port charges are most obvious here, but we must also include land revenue on areas producing pepper, various taxes and charges to do with its transport and weighing, and the market cesses and charges deriving from the role of their ports as entrepots.

It was this small number of political elite, some fully independent, others in tribute relationship, and others more formally officials of a larger state, who were crucially oriented to sea matters in India at 1500. Even so, most of these people took a rather passive role when they could. They tried to increase the trade of their particular port or city, and to ward off threats to it, but none of them pursued more active policies, such as trying to force traders to call. Similarly, while most of them traded rather extensively on their own account, and no doubt their use of their political power helped such private trade, they did not go beyond this to try, for example, to engross large areas of trade for the state or themselves. Nor, during the whole century, did any of these people have navies in any way comparable to the contemporary Ottoman Turks or Portuguese.

The Portuguese have the dubious distinction of being the people who introduced politics into the ocean. We can briefly recapitulate the situation at the time of their arrival. On particular routes particular merchant groups were dominant. Thus *chettyars* and Chulia Muslims dominated trade between Coromandel and Malacca, Gujaratis were important in western Indian coastal trade, and participated on other routes also. Middle East Muslims dominated the Calicut–Red Sea route. In every case, however, this position was achieved by superiority in peaceful commercial competition. We have no evidence of any use of force at all. Similarly, the rulers of the great trade centres of the ocean, Malacca, Calicut, Hurmuz, Aden and the several ports of the Gulf of Cambay (in 1500 principally Diu, Cambay, Broach, Rander and Surat) owed the success of their ports to location, good facilities for visiting merchants and in some cases productive hinterlands, but not coercion. No warships patrolled forcing ships to call at any of these ports. Those who traded there did so because they wanted to.

Not that this was some sort of pre-European Golden Age. Among the merchants competition was fierce, even cut-throat; a lone outsider would find it almost completely impossible to break in on one of the established quasi-monopolistic routes. There is evidence of some extortion at customs houses, and of arbitrary actions by local officials. As a further blemish, piracy was widespread in the Indian Ocean at the start of the century, and land powers took few steps, and these mostly ineffective, to control it. The fact remains that the ocean at 1500 was genuinely a *mare liberum* where no state tried to control maritime matters.

Arriving then to this situation, what were the politico-military aims of the Portuguese? First, one cautionary note must be sounded. The previous discussion of Portuguese society has noted that religion, politics and economics were not clearly distinguished in the sixteenth century; frequently all three combined in a confusingly intermingled way. The great chronicler Diogo do Couto claimed that 'The Kings of Portugal always aimed in their conquest of the East, at so uniting the two powers, spiritual and temporal, that the one should never be exercised without the other' (*Da Asia*, 15 vols., Lisbon, 1778–88, VI, iv, 7). Yet heuristically religion and politics need to be separated, albeit artificially, simply in order to give this exposition some coherence.

Politics and economics cannot be so separated, for the basic Portuguese aim in India in the sixteenth century was, by the use of military force, to enrich their state and themselves. The general object was two-fold: to try and monopolize the supply of spices to Europe, and to control and tax other Asian trade. Right from the start the method was to be force. Manuel in 1499 precipitously took the title of 'Lord of the conquest, navigation and commerce of Ethiopia, Arabia, Persia and India'. The second expedition, led by Cabral, indulged in various atrocities in Calicut and at sea in 1500. A fundamental debate at court in 1501 centred on the question of whether the Portuguese in the Indian Ocean should try to be peaceful traders, or should attempt a monopoly. The decision (and we will analyse this basic matter later) was to use force. In 1502 da Gama was sent back to India. He was told to build forts, and to leave a fleet permanently in the Indian Ocean.

Factories thus rapidly gave way to forts. The first factory, at Calicut in 1500, was soon destroyed. In that same year Cochin was substituted, and Cannanore added a year later. In 1503 a small fort, the first for the Portuguese in India, was built at Cochin, and a fort at Cannanore followed two years later. In this same year, 1505, the first viceroy, Francisco d'Almeida, was despatched to India to establish formally the State of India. He took with him very wide-ranging instructions. Forts were to be established, and not for defensive purposes but in order to enable the Portuguese to control the trade of the Indian Ocean. Almeida, however, demurred, and it was his successor, Afonso de Albuquerque (1509–15), along with da Gama the great hero of Portuguese India, who laid the foundations of the empire.

Albuquerque is often hailed as a great strategist. His son said he

... often used to say that for the preservation of India, and for the prevention of troubles arising from that territory to the Kings of Portugal, there were four main things, of which their possession by the Portuguese must be made very strong and very sure. These were: Aden, in order to have dominion over the Straits of Meca, before the Grand Sultan [of Turkey] could forestall them in their seizing it; Ormuz, so as to have supreme rule over the Straits of Bacora; and Diu and Goa, for the sovereignty of all the other districts of India. And with these four places assured to Portugal, and fortified with very strong fortresses, she could avoid many other unnecessary expenses to which she was now subject. (*Commentaries of Afonso Albuquerque*, 4 vols., London, 1875–84, vol. IV, p. 24)

It is, however, unclear how much of this geopolitical design was his, and how much was laid down in Lisbon. In any case, he rapidly achieved control of several port cities in India and the Indian Ocean. Goa was taken in 1510, and next year the great Southeast Asian entrepot of Malacca. Hurmuz, at the mouth of the Persian Gulf, followed in 1515. The area of land acquired was in each case tiny, but the strategic value of these three cities was immense. As Albuquerque told the king (with some exaggeration) in a valedictory: 'I leave the chief places of India in your Majesty's power, the only thing left to be done being the closing of the gates of the Straits' (*Cartas de Afonso de Albuquerque*, 7 vols., Lisbon, 1884–1935, vol. I, p. 380). The reference is to his repulse before Aden in 1513; later Portuguese attacks here also failed, and this was correctly seen at the time as a crucial gap in the system. The king was informed in 1538 that if Aden were taken 'India would be sealed off, with the key in your hands' (Luciano Ribeiro, 'Ainda em torno do primeiro cerco de Diu', *Studia*, no. 18, 1966, p. 280).

Further conquests followed spasmodically throughout the sixteenth century. A fort was established at Colombo in 1518, and Portuguese involvement in Sri Lanka increased through the century; by its end they controlled most coastal areas. Around 1530 a move to the north of Malabar occurred, symbolized by Goa becoming formally the capital of Portuguese India in 1530. Another great port city, Diu, was conquered in 1535. A year earlier Bassein had been acquired. The aim was to control the huge sea trade of Gujarat; to increase the effectiveness of patrols across the mouth of the Gulf of Cambay, Daman was taken in 1559. Other forts were erected all around the Indian Ocean littoral: several in East Africa, in the Moluccas, and on the Konkan and Malabar coasts in India. Portugal finished up with a string of some fifty forts and fortified areas, and a total fleet of up to 100 ships of various sizes in different areas.

These forts were acquired in several ways. Sometimes a local ruler, acting either under duress or with an eye to his own advantage, would give the Portuguese permission. More often conquest was the method. In India, the raja of Cochin saw a chance to increase his power in relation to his nominal overlord, the zamorin of Calicut, and happily became a puppet of the Portuguese, and a wealthy one at that. Diu, Bassein and Daman were acquired by treaty, but with a strong element of duress also. Goa and Malacca were conquered.

We will discuss in detail later the role of Indians in the Portuguese Indian economy and society, but we should note here that even Portuguese conquests sometimes were aided by local people. In sixteenth-century Indian terms this was not treachery, for the voracious demands of the modern nation state were of course not yet present. As is well known, da Gama's pilot from Malindi to Calicut was the distinguished Muslim navigator Ibn Majid. Cabral used two Gujarati pilots for the same voyage. In the early years several Jews, both Ashkenazi (like Gaspar da India) and Sephardim, these often being refugees from Spanish persecution, provided detailed and invaluable advice, and interpreter services, for the Portuguese. A Hindu adventurer, Timmayya (Timoja), provided Albuquerque with crucial advice and encouragement prior to the taking of Goa. Throughout the century on Portuguese ships, both naval and trade, the crews and even the soldiers were more often local people than metropolitan Portuguese. Even on the huge carracks bound for Portugal there would be only a handful of Portuguese or *mestiço* (Eurasian) officers. On big expeditions there would be at least as many local Indian troops as Portuguese. The first Portuguese expedition east of Malacca is perhaps symptomatic of the whole: after the town was taken Albuquerque sent off a small fleet to 'discover' the Moluccas. The fleet had Javanese pilots, and a local merchant ship with a rich Muslim Malaccan merchant on board preceded the Portuguese to prepare the way for them. In India later in the sixteenth century and after, the Portuguese employed Indians as ambassadors-cum-spies in neighbouring courts; the information collected by these people was often invaluable in preventing an attack, or exposing weakness in a hostile Indian court.

The Portuguese in the sixteenth century were not operating in a isolated Indian Ocean world. Their activities threatened established interests in Venice, Egypt and the Ottoman empire especially, for they for a time came close to blocking the lucrative spice trade via the Red Sea and the Persian Gulf to the Mediterranean. In the first decade it was

Mamluk Egypt which was most affected by these Portuguese successes, because of their huge revenues from taxing the spice trade. When the Portuguese blocked the Red Sea trade in 1502 the Mamluk sultan asked the Pope to force the Portuguese to stop doing this, on pain of Egyptian harassment of Christians and destruction of the Holy Places in Palestine. It is characteristic of the brio of the Portuguese in this first flush of conquest that Manuel replied defiantly that his forces could occupy Mecca and Medina, and destroy the Prophet's tomb. Abandoning diplomacy, the Mamluks in 1507 sent off Amir Husain with a large fleet to the Indian Ocean. With local help he defeated a Portuguese fleet at Chaul in 1508, but was himself decisively defeated off Diu in 1509. This defeat caused consternation not only in Cairo but also in Venice. The oligarchy in this Mediterranean port city had consulted with Cairo over the Portuguese threat to their mutual interests, and even, in a triumph of economic interest over Christian solidarity, covertly provided military supplies to the Egyptians.

Nor indeed were the Venetians the only Christian opposition. Portugal and Spain had been allocated shares of the undiscovered world by the Pope in the well-known treaty of Tordesillas in 1494. It was, however, not clear where the line of demarcation went in the Pacific; nor was the huge width of the Pacific appreciated until Magellan. There ensued in the 1510s something of a race, as the Portuguese, aroused by rumours of Castilian fleets bound for Sumatra, Malacca, and even Sri Lanka, pushed east as quickly as possible. These fears were exacerbated after Magellan's crossing of the Pacific in 1522. It was from this time that the Portuguese tried to establish a military presence east of Malacca, in the Moluccas. Their attention even extended to China, where attempts in the early 1520s to control Chinese trade were repulsed by the coastguard fleet. The Portuguese returned here, and then only on sufferance, in 1557 when Macao was founded.

The main opposition, however, continued to come from Muslim powers in the Middle East. Falling revenue from the spice trade was the last straw for the already moribund Mamluk empire. It was easily conquered in 1516–17 by a formidably efficient and expansionist Ottoman empire. From their Mediterranean experience the Portuguese were already well aware of the military prowess of the 'Rumes', or Turks. A major reason for Albuquerque's decision to take Goa in 1510 was the presence there of large numbers of Turks, many of them survivors of the defeat of the Egyptian fleet off Diu by Almeida the previous year. Albuquerque thought this threat had to be nipped in the bud. The conquest of Egypt, and Ottoman probes down the Red Sea before and after this, simply increased Portuguese fears. After many rumours, the worst happened at last in 1538. A large Turkish fleet despatched by Sulaiman the Magnificent sailed down the Red Sea, took Aden, and with local help laid siege to the new Portuguese fort in Diu. Its epic, and successful, defence by the Portuguese was one of their greatest triumphs in Asia. Yet this did not end the threat from Turkey. In 1546 they took the important port of Basra, at the head of the Persian Gulf. In 1551–2, Piri Reis with 23 galleys sacked Mascat and unsuccessfully besieged Hurmuz. Hostilities continued intermittently thereafter; in the 1580s a freebooting Turkish fleet achieved some success against the Portuguese off the East African coast. Around this same time Turkish support contributed to the rise of Acheh in Sumatra, the focus of a very successful, though in Portuguese eyes illegal, spice trade to the Red Sea.

Many historians have seen any threat to the Portuguese in the Indian Ocean ended by Almeida's victory at Diu in 1509. A more correct depiction would show, through most of the sixteenth century, competition between the Portuguese and the Ottomans as both tried to expand in the Indian Ocean. This point indeed was stressed by my predecessor in a Cambridge series. Ross claimed 'it is quite conceivable that if one of their fleets had succeeded in driving the Portuguese out of their fortresses on the Indian coast, the establishment of the Christian power in India might have been indefinitely postponed' (E. Denison Ross, 'The Portuguese in India, 1498–1598', in *The Cambridge History of India*, vol. v, Delhi, 1968, p. 27). This was relatively equal competition; the Portuguese 'won' mostly because they reached the area a few years before the Turks, and also because Turkey had many other interests. For her the Indian Ocean was a sideshow compared with campaigns in the Mediterranean and Balkans, and the endemic war with Safavid Iran.

What sort of government structure did the Portuguese set up to rule their far-flung empire? At first sight the system seems to be marvellously articulated and centralized. At the top was the king in Portugal (after 1580 in Madrid), assisted by his officials. However, as a letter written in Goa received a reply at the earliest only after ten months had elapsed, the kings and their officials in Europe could lay down policy only in the most general terms. It was the authorities in Goa, and their subordinates, who made the running.

The head of the Portuguese *Estado da India* (state of India) was the viceroy or governor, resident first in Cochin and after 1515 usually in Goa. A viceroy enjoyed a slightly higher status than did a governor, but their functions and powers were really identical. They were heads of the civil and military government of the whole state from East Africa to the Moluccas and Macao, in theory responsible only to the king, and to God.

To assist him in Goa the governor had at first a loosely organized council. These early councils were not institutionalized; they were called into session more or less at the whim of the governor, to give advice only on specific, usually military, matters. There was no fixed membership or procedure, though the members were always *fidalgos*. Thus in 1510 after Albuquerque had taken Goa, he had to call a council to get approval before he could build a fort. Similarly, councils of important people were often called on board ship, to ratify decisions already taken, to seek advice or to share blame. In these councils the governor was often only first among equals. If he ignored the advice of the council, and for example proceeded with an attack, those disapproving of the action would usually not help him. In most cases however a consensus was reached and adhered to by those present.

By 1563 the council had evolved and become more institutionalized as the Council of State. Its members, as of 1604, were the governor as president, the archbishop of Goa, the chief inquisitor, two or three of the older *fidalgos* resident in Goa, the head of the High Court, the captain of the city of Goa, and the *vedor da fazenda*, or chief financial official.

Religious affairs were usually handled independently of the civil authority by the archbishop or by the heads of the several orders, though there were some famous cases of God in his Goan incarnation trying to influence Mammon and vice versa. There was also the municipal council, elected by the Portuguese and Eurasian population and at times an influential force on the government. Four areas of authority can thus be distinguished: in financial matters the *vedor*, and later the *conselho da fazenda*; in religious affairs the clerics; in legal matters the High Court; and in local government the municipal council. Only over the first did the governor exercise appreciable control. However the governor, assisted by the Council of State, did control military matters and external relations, in a manner befitting the head of what was and in most respects remained a society dominated by the ethos of the *conquistador*.

The state government in Goa was a macrocosm of that of the other areas and forts. Each had a captain, usually assisted by a *vedor da fazenda*, other minor officials such as clerks, and more important the factor, who supervised the royal trade in the area. There were also various clerics, a judge, and in the larger areas a municipal council.

The object of all these forts and captains was to enable the Portuguese to achieve several economic aims. These may be listed as: a monopoly of the spice trade to Europe; a monopoly on the trade between various specified ports within Asia; the control, direction and taxation of all other trade in the Indian Ocean; private trade, done on their own behalf by most Portuguese living in Asia.

In many ways the rationale, and the necessity, underlying all of these economic aims was the fact that a small, poor and distant country like Portugal could not hope to have a large impact on Asian land areas. Nor could it maintain its empire solely for reasons of prestige. The empire had to sustain itself, and the only way this could be done was from controlling and taxing sea trade, for only here were the Portuguese at a decisive advantage in Asia. Concretely, this can be seen if one studies Portuguese revenues. In Goa itself the revenue derived from customs duties as a percentage of the total from all sources in the sixteenth century was around 60 percent, while in the whole empire the percentage was closer to 65. And indeed some other items of revenue were also derived from sea trade and control, such as booty from captured Asian ships engaged in 'illegal' trade.

We will conclude this chapter by sketching the official policy concerning the first three of these Portuguese aims. Chapter 2 will describe in some detail local reactions to their system. Chapter 3 will discuss internal Portuguese factors which affected their success, and will conclude with a general analysis of three broad characteristics of the Portuguese empire in India.

As soon as they got to India the Portuguese tried to monopolize all trade in spices. Throughout the century and later a stream of decrees and instructions from Portugal and Goa insisted that all trade in spices was reserved entirely for the Portuguese crown and its agents. If this monopoly could be enforced the Muslim powers in India, the Red Sea and Egypt would lose their most profitable trade, while the Portuguese could buy cheap in Asia and sell dear in Europe.

Offenders against this policy were harshly treated. Official decrees laid down that any Portuguese transgressing was to lose all his property and his salaries; a Muslim was to be imprisoned after forfeiting all his goods and the ship in which the forbidden article was found. In practice Muslim offenders were often killed at once. Occasionally a closely regulated trade within Asia was permitted, and puppet rulers sometimes were conciliated by being allowed to trade in pepper in limited quantities. Further, the crews of ships returning to Portugal were paid partly by being allowed to take small quantities of spices with them. Nevertheless, the broad generalization is still true: Portugal did try to reserve all spice trade within Asia to agents of the king, and to restrict the transport of spices to Europe to Portuguese ships sailing via the Cape of Good Hope.

The second area of involvement consisted of voyages to specified places within Asia on a monopolistic basis; only the designated ship could make a given voyage in a particular year. Cargo space on such ships thus sold at a premium. In the earlier sixteenth century voyages of this kind were done in royal ships, though a large part of the goods carried belonged to private merchants. Later it was decided that such a method meant that the king had too much of his own capital tied up in ships and incidental expenses, so from the 1540s at least individuals were licensed to undertake these voyages. Such licences, like appointments to official positions, were given out on several grounds. Sometimes they were given as rewards for meritorious military service. Others were given as dowries to the daughters of prominent but impoverished *fidalgos*, while some formed part of the perquisites of a particular post. Most of the voyages however were sold to the highest bidder, either directly by the crown or by the person who had been granted the voyage for one of the above reasons. They could be extremely lucrative for the holder. Among the seventeen voyages 'owned' by the holder of the post of captain of Malacca was that to Macao. He could make up to 10,000 cruzados from it, or could sell his rights to it for 5–6000 cruzados. The best of all was that from Goa to Japan via Macao, which even in the 1560s produced a clear profit of about 40,000 cruzados, and later much more.

The third area of Portuguese involvement constituted an attempt to control and tax trade carried on by everyone else in the Indian Ocean. It was here, in their *cartaz–armada–cafila* system that they produced their greatest impact on Asian trade. The main instrument used was the *cartaz* or passport backed up by armadas. Passports were something new for Asian merchants, but the Portuguese justified them, at least to themselves, with a legal underpinning.

In the fifteenth century, as we saw, there was no attempt to control sea trade; those states which profited from the presence of foreign and local merchants did so because they provided attractive conditions for these merchants. In juristic terminology the Indian Ocean was a *mare liberum*, there being no concept of sovereignty over it except in some coastal areas and rivers. The Portuguese justification for their attempt to control sea trade in Asia completely was based on their claim to be lords of the sea in Asia. In Europe the seas were open to all, but this did not apply in Asia to non-Christians. Nor did they have any right of passage, because before the arrival of the Portuguese no one had claimed the sea as his property. There being then no preceding title, there was no present or future right of passage, except for that licensed by the Portuguese.

All ships trading within Asia were thus required to take a pass, or *cartaz*. These were issued by the competent Portuguese authority. The pass stated who was the captain of the ship concerned, how big the ship was, and what crew it carried. The quantity of arms and munitions allowed was strictly limited. The ship had to call at a Portuguese fort to pay customs duties before it proceeded on its voyage. A cash security left at this fort served as a guarantee that the ship would call there on its return voyage also, to pay more duties. Enemies of the Portuguese and forbidden goods such as spices were not to be carried.

Any ship without a *cartaz* was automatically' confiscated as a fair prize, and its crew either killed at once or sent to the galleys. Even a ship with a *cartaz* was subject to confiscation if its conditions had not been fully met. In 1540 a Gujarati ship was confiscated merely because its *cartaz* said it was bound for Kishm, but, judging by its position when the Portuguese checked it, it could not have been going there.

The ultimate implications of these Portuguese claims to control the sea can best be seen in an incident in 1540. The governor of Surat, Khwaja Safar, had built a new fort to protect his port. The Portuguese viceroy wrote to his overlord, the sultan of Gujarat, asking him to make Khwaja Safar demolish his fort, 'because it was bad to build a fort there when there was no need for it at all; because if he was a true friend of the king of Portugal he would not build forts on the edge of the sea, which belonged to the Portuguese, and because no one was ever going to attack him from the sea except the king of Portugal, who would only do so if he did not keep the peace which had been established between them' (Gaspar Correa, *Lendas da India*, 4 vols., Lisbon, 1858–64, vol. IV, p. 143).

The fee charged for issuing the *cartaz* was negligible; the profit for the Portuguese came from the obligation imposed on the ship concerned to call and pay customs duties to the Portuguese at a Portuguese fort. This was the essence of the arrangement, for we saw earlier how crucial were customs duties to total Portuguese revenues.

Later in the sixteenth century the Portuguese were forced to put into effect their third strand of trade control, the *cafila*. This consisted of a convoy of small local merchant ships guarded by a Portuguese fleet. This system was introduced to increase the security of ships sailing under Portuguese auspices; if they were sunk by pirates Portuguese revenues would suffer. From Goa 2 or 3 *cafilas* set sail north each year, bound for the ports of Gujarat. Two hundred or more ships could be included. The *cafilas* south to the Kanara area were equally vital, for from there came food. Goa, like Portugal, had a heavy rice deficit in the sixteenth century, so that each year a fleet of at least 100 small boats made 2, 3 or 4 voyages to the Kanara ports and brought back rice for Goa. The third regular route was further south to Cape Comorin. Ships from Malacca, Coromandel and even Macao would be collected and escorted up to Goa, picking up on the way other ships from the Malabar ports.

As with the *cartazes*, these *cafilas* in theory embodied two principles; profit for the Portuguese customs houses and protection for the native traders. In fact, pirates sometimes did attack *cafilas* and loot ships in them, but it can be conceded that ships in *cafilas* were safer than those sailing alone. Nevertheless, it is clear that many native traders would just as soon have taken their chances outside the *cafila* system, and certainly would have preferred not to have to call at Goa to pay duties and engage in virtually forced trade. Thus the escort fleet had two functions; to guard the merchant ships from pirates, and to make sure none of these same merchant ships slipped away to trade outside the Portuguese system.

CHAPTER 2

THE SYSTEM IN OPERATION

A brief analysis of the Portuguese success in monopolizing the trade in spices will begin our discussion of this system, and of Indian responses to it. It will be followed by discussions of Portuguese policies and Indian reactions concerning the horse trade, general trade control, and technology. These case studies will reveal several problems for the Portuguese: their need to take into account local pressures; problems with their own system in practice; regional variations; and changes over time during the sixteenth century. This whole discussion of 'reactions' to the Portuguese 'impact' should indeed call into question the very validity of these terms, for the implications, of a dynamic west impacting on a static east, are clearly incorrect.

There is now a considerable body of writing on the spice trade of the sixteenth century, focussing on the trade to Europe. The first point to make clear is that this was in fact a rather minor part of the total Asian trade in spices. In 1500 Europe took, at the most, one quarter of total Asian production of spices. The greatest consumer of pepper was China, which took perhaps three quarters of total Southeast Asian production. Over the sixteenth century Europe's share rose considerably, as her consumption increased thanks to comparatively lower prices. The result was that Asian production of spices during the sixteenth century may have doubled to meet this increasing demand not only in Europe but in Asia also.

We can quickly sum up the basic trends in this trade to Europe. The Portuguese arrival in the Indian Ocean meant that for perhaps fifty years the trade through the Red Sea to the Mediterranean and so to Venice suffered greatly, though not consistently. But in the second half of the century the Mediterranean trade revived to equal Portuguese trade via the Cape. Thus from 1550 the Portuguese share, and also total amounts brought to Lisbon, fell. Venice's trade, and what was left of Portuguese trade, was finally destroyed when the Dutch took over the production areas for most spices during the seventeenth century, and were thus able to impose a much more efficient monopoly than the Portuguese had ever done.

During the fifteenth century in Europe it seems that demand for spices, for flavouring and preserving meat, rose, while the European price was stable or fell. The route via the Red Sea was a difficult one, not only because of the danger of shipwreck but also because of the high charges levied on the trade, especially in Mamluk Egypt. For this reason, although the increase in price of a kilo of pepper as it changed hands was enormous – costing 1 or 2 grammes of silver at the production point, it was 10 to 14 in Alexandria, 14 to 18 in Venice, and 20 to 30 in the consumer countries of Europe – the net profits made by Venetian merchants were a comparatively modest average of 40 percent. (I use several measures of weight and currency in this section. The figures are meant only to show comparative trends.)

The opening of the Cape route should have produced huge long-term profits for the Portuguese, for they could avoid all the difficulties and taxes of the Red Sea route. In theory they could buy for 1 or 2 grammes of silver, and sell for at least 20 in Europe, with only transport costs to be met. A recent estimate finds the Portuguese paying at the most just over 6 cruzados per quintal for pepper and freight in Malabar, and getting a minimum price of 22 cruzados in Lisbon. The profit was thus 260 percent and, assuming a minimum annual export from Malabar of 25,000 quintals, annual profits came to 410,000 cruzados.[1] An alternative costing from later in the century finds, after accounting for shrinkage, wastage, shipwrecks and freight, profits of 152 percent. Even if the costs of the forts in the Malabar towns from whence the Portuguese got the pepper are included, the profits in Lisbon still reached nearly 90 percent.[2]

Other estimates point to even higher profits on pepper, this being always the main product brought back to Lisbon. A typical voyage of 1520–1 on the Lisbon–India route has been described as follows: three Portuguese ships arrived in Cochin carrying 20,000 cruzados in specie, and 64,000 cruzados worth of goods. The ships had also picked up in Mozambique some ivory, so the total capital available was 96,000 cruzados. This was spent on 30,000 quintals of pepper, at $2\frac{1}{2}$ cruzados a quintal, and some other goods. The pepper would sell in Lisbon for between 30 and 40 cruzados a quintal.

The effects were dramatic. Even in the first decade of the sixteenth

[1] K. S. Mathew, *Portuguese Trade with India in the Sixteenth Century* (New Delhi, 1983), pp. 197–8.
[2] V. M. Godinho, *Os Descobrimentos e a Economia Mundial* 2nd edn. (4 vols., Lisbon, 1981–3), vol. III, pp. 10, 20–2.

century over half of Portugal's state revenue came from West African gold and Asian pepper and other spices. The proportion of the latter soon far outweighed the former. On the obverse, late in the fifteenth century Venice imported about 3,500,000 pounds of spices a year. In 1502–5 her average was 1,000,000 pounds a year, while the Portuguese were importing 2,300,000 pounds a year, 80 percent of this pepper. Even in global terms Portugal was big business. Chaunu has estimated that during the sixteenth century corn traded by sea in the Mediterranean was worth a total of 9000 tons of silver; American gold and silver arriving in Seville was worth 18,000 tons of silver; the sales value of Portugal's Asian commodities was between 7000 and 7500 tons of silver.[3]

This global dimension merits a further discussion. World trade in the sixteenth century and later has been depicted as consisting of a stream of bullion flowing from South America to Iberia and continuing on, with some European goods, to Asia. The return flow was Asian products, pre-eminently spices. The exceptions – Portuguese gold imports from East Africa later in the sixteenth century, and a westward flow of South American bullion to Manila – were comparatively negligible. It may also be noted that Portuguese activities in Asia in fact limited this flow of gold and silver, for they paid much less in Asia for spices than did the Venetians in Alexandria. Despite this, the size of the flow worried the Portuguese – indeed the king had increasing problems in providing capital – and they tried to pay for pepper with local products such as cloths, or other European imports, such as copper.

Unfortunately for the Portuguese, there are several modifications to be made to this rosy picture of huge profits. For most of the sixteenth century this trade was a crown monopoly, carried on in royal ships by crown factors. But before 1506 some private participation had been allowed, from 1570 to 1580 open trade was tried on an experimental basis, and from 1580 to 1597 the crown contracted out the right to this trade. Yet despite this centralization, and the potential for vast profits, Portugal's state finances deteriorated during the century. As early as the reign of João III his treasurer lamented that 'so many motives for despair appear before me when I consider the things Your Highness must

[3] Quoted in Niels Steensgaard, 'Asian trade and world market: orders of magnitude in "The long seventeenth century"', in *L'Histoire à Nice*, Actes du colloque international 1980, vol. III (Nice, 1981), p. 130.

sustain and the state of your treasury' (Livermore, *A New History of Portugal*, p. 151).

In part this was because of the huge cost of trying to maintain the monopoly in Asia: all those forts and fleets cost vast sums of money. Portugal was also affected by the general price rise of the 'long sixteenth century'. The cost of preparing and sending ships to India doubled from 1506 to 1620, and prices of products brought back from India more than doubled between the 1540s and the late 1580s. But more important was simply that this attempt at monarchical capitalism failed in Portugal. It succeeded very largely in blocking the development of an indigenous merchant capitalism which could have competed with the king for more efficient exploitation, but this simply meant the king was dependent on foreign capital, foreign expertise, and foreign sales points. Lisbon was really only a conduit between India and the rest of Europe, with most sales taking place in the Low Countries and elsewhere.

This foreign involvement began in the fifteenth century, and is well seen in some of the earliest expeditions to India. The third expedition, under João da Nova, consisted of four ships, two owned by the king, one by a top noble (a brother of the Duke of Bragança), and one by a Florentine banker. Albuquerque's first expedition in 1503–4 similarly included two ships fitted out by Florentines, and another by a Portuguese businessman. The potential profits in Europe were wasted on a lavish court, the king being the main offender here, or were creamed off by such firms as the Fuggers, the Welsers, and various Genoese. Eric Wolf sums up this matter neatly when he says:

Two Iberian powers, Portugal and Castile, emerged as successful organizations of tribute takers in the course of wars against the Muslim states of the peninsula. In both kingdoms royal control of commerce enhanced the power of the kingship and provided a tribute-taking elite with wealth to purchase goods abroad without altering the tributary structure at home. Yet in both countries that wealth did not suffice to cover the costs of administration and war. Royal bankruptcies and debts transferred control of exchequer and trade to foreign merchant-bankers, turning the two countries into 'the Indies of the Genoese'.[4]

A problem as important as mismanagement in Lisbon was the revival of the Levant trade, for this eroded Portugal's early sixteenth-century quasi-monopoly position. The dimensions of this revival are clear enough. By the 1560s Venice was importing more pepper than she had

[4] Eric R. Wolf, *Europe and the People without History* (Berkeley, 1982), pp. 123–4.

late in the fifteenth century, while Portuguese imports declined, despite a large increase in demand in Europe during the century. The most telling indication of her failure is found in early seventeenth-century figures for pepper production in southwest India, from Honavar to Travancore. The minimum production of this area was put at 258,000 quintals. Of this some 20,000 to 30,000 was bought by the Portuguese and taken to Lisbon. The rest was consumed locally, or exported overland and then distributed outside Portuguese control all over Asia, and via the Red Sea and Persian Gulf to the Mediterranean.

Portuguese success then, in this area where they tried hardest of all, was very small. Their control over other spices – mace, nutmeg, cloves and cinnamon – was even less. Not even one-tenth of the total clove production of the Moluccas found its way in Portuguese ships around the Cape of Good Hope. The Portuguese also traded in this product within Asia; nevertheless, the two together totalled only at most one-third of total production. Even this meagre success was threatened in the 1570s when an anti-Portuguese revolt ended what had always been a rather modest Portuguese political control over the area of the Moluccas. A brief revival in the 1590s was ended by the arrival of the Dutch. Similarly, cinnamon from Sri Lanka was in the late sixteenth and early seventeenth centuries profitable for the Portuguese; again Dutch attacks ended this.

What had gone wrong? Why did the Portuguese, despite formal control over Indian Ocean waters, fail to maintain their monopoly in this vital area? The most general answer is simply that the Portuguese were not operating in a vacuum. Rather they had to cater to local interests, they were faced with often effective opposition from Asian traders and rulers, and there were problems with their system itself. The result was that as one leak was blocked up, another opened. In 1523 the king was told that he must take Diu, for it was the great centre of all 'illegal' trade in pepper. Worse, the goods exchanged for the pepper in Diu, such as copper and cloths, competed with goods the Portuguese were trying to sell in India. Diu was taken in 1535, but the leakage continued. In the 1540s and 1550s Gujarati merchants collected vast amounts of pepper in the Bay of Bengal, and traded in it all over Asia and to the Red Sea. Later in the century the centre of the illegal trade was Acheh, by now a new version of fifteenth-century Malacca, in other words a great entrepot for Asian, including Chinese, and even European products.

We have noted the Portuguese failure to take Aden, and its possession by a hostile Ottoman Turkey after 1538. This left open a vital gap in the Portuguese geostrategic design, as indeed was recognized at the time. There were also problems with the alternative route to the Middle East and the Mediterranean, the Persian Gulf, and in the Malabar production area itself. In Hurmuz the Portuguese were influenced by wider strategic concerns. Their most feared enemy was the Ottoman Turks. Thus during the sixteenth century Safavid Iran, spasmodically at war with Turkey throughout the century, was seen as a vital buffer. To help this *de facto* ally, the Portuguese allowed some spices to pass through their control point at Hurmuz. This policy was intensified after the Ottomans moved closer, taking Iraq and Basra in 1546. The Portuguese also tolerated this trade because the main products used to pay for the spices were horses, plus some rose water and silks; unlike products coming through the Red Sea, these did not compete with Portuguese imports to India. Indeed, as we will see, control of the horse trade was of vital concern to the Portuguese. Thus while the Portuguese tried to control and tax the spice trade via Hurmuz, and also attempted to stop these spices being taken on to the Mediterranean, it is clear that they failed here; later in the sixteenth century Beirut and Damascus were well supplied with spices.

The problem in the production areas of Kanara and Malabar was mostly a matter of Portuguese incompetence. Kanara was located adjacent to Goa, yet the Portuguese achieved surprisingly little control over its pepper production, a production which increased greatly during the century. In Malabar there were a series of problems, which in sum allowed large quantities of pepper to escape either by sea or overland to Coromandel. It is worthwhile to go into this matter in a little detail, for it provides an excellent case study of Indian reactions to the Portuguese attempt to monopolize the spice trade.

In Malabar there was much evasion of the Portuguese system, and in some cases there was open armed opposition to their pretensions. In this opposition the zamorins of Calicut were prominent, for Calicut had been the great Indian centre for the spice trade in the fifteenth century. If Portugal could have enforced its monopoly, Calicut would have been ruined while Cochin, formerly subordinate to Calicut and in the sixteenth century a Portuguese puppet, would have prospered. Thus throughout the sixteenth century warfare between the zamorin and the Portuguese was endemic. In this often brutal war the Portuguese usually did best, thanks to their superiority at sea. Occasional peaces were soon broken by one side or the other and war, either overt or lightly disguised as 'piracy', continued. Nor is this to be wondered at, for the aims of the two sides were fundamentally and diametrically opposed.

Not only the ruler of Calicut, but also her local merchants, resisted the Portuguese claims. The Portuguese wanted to monopolize the trade in Malabar pepper, but this was the main product of the area. The Portuguese forbade trade to Aden and the Red Sea, but this was the main sea route from Calicut. The Portuguese attacked merchants from these two places, but these were the main purchasers of Malabar's products. The Portuguese forced contracts at fixed low prices on the Malabar rulers for the supply of pepper, but other merchants offered much higher prices. The Portuguese later in the sixteenth century treated all ships from Calicut as pirates and sank them on sight, even ships carrying only provisions, and sometimes ships with Portuguese passes. What choice did the merchants of Calicut have but to resist?

Commercially this resistance took the form of continuing to trade in pepper. The trade direct to the Red Sea from Calicut was for a time blocked more or less effectively by the Portuguese and by 1513 the great foreign Muslim merchants of Calicut had moved out to safer parts, such as the Red Sea, or Hurmuz, Gujarat and Vijayanagar. From this time the pepper went to the Red Sea from Kanara, north of Malabar, from the Bay of Bengal, and from Acheh in Sumatra.

It was easy enough for the great foreign merchants to move out and let others bring the pepper to them, and for the Red Sea traders to get pepper from other production areas. The local merchants of Malabar had no such alternatives, but even so they had little difficulty in acquiring pepper in Malabar. They were helped by Portugal's lack of control over the areas where pepper was grown. In Malabar the Portuguese exercised a tenuous control over the coastal area through their puppet rajas, but none at all inland. Given that the Portuguese tried to pay low prices and paid one-quarter of the price in goods (usually copper) for which the growers had little use, it is not difficult to understand how easily the 'illegal' traders found their cargoes. In 1520 a Portuguese official asked an important trader why he had stopped bringing pepper to the coast and selling it to the Portuguese. He replied, 'Because I find that there are many people who beg me to sell it, and pay the price I want in my own house, without troubling me to come to the coast' (*Cartas de Affonso de Albuquerque*, vol. IV, pp. 174–5).

Once they had the pepper, the local traders who chose to ignore Portuguese trade restrictions had two export routes available: overland to Coromandel, and north by sea to Gujarat. The former trade was safe from Portuguese interference, as they had no control over the inland areas of Malabar. Great amounts were transported either by coolie or on bullocks to Coromandel and from there all over eastern India and Bengal. Considerable quantities of this pepper were also taken, especially by Gujaratis, to the Red Sea.

The other route, by sea to Gujarat, was considerably more risky. It was navigated in small, light, oared craft called *paroes*, which could escape up the numerous rivers of the western coast if they were seen by the Portuguese. These Malabari *paroes* sailed in fleets of up to one hundred sail, loaded with pepper. The pepper they carried to Gujarat was usually consumed locally. Some was taken to the Red Sea, but as Portuguese patrolling across the mouth of the Gulf of Cambay improved after they took Diu in 1535 and Daman in 1558, the 'illegal' pepper trade from Gujarat to the Red Sea slackened off. But this did not mean that the Portuguese, having blocked at least partially this escape route, now got more pepper: as we saw, they took less and less to Europe as the century progressed.

The Portuguese were dependent for their supplies on the petty rajas of the producing areas and the merchants who operated between the growers and the exporters. To conciliate the rajas they paid them regular pensions, but these were not always sufficient to ensure their goodwill and co-operation. In 1549 the raja of the main production area, appropriately called the 'king of pepper' by the Portuguese, decided to retaliate against the insults and abuses to which he was subjected by the raja of Cochin. His method was to ally with Portugal's inveterate enemy, the zamorin of Calicut. As a result of this feud between two of their clients the Portuguese were involved in four years of war in the area, during which time it was very difficult for them to get pepper to send to Portugal.

Nor were the rajas of Cochin always totally subservient. The Portuguese thought they should be grateful for all the benefits they had brought them: had not Cochin replaced Calicut as the great spice trade centre in Malabar? Yet they obdurately refused to convert to Christianity, despite many urgings. Indeed, any subject who converted was discriminated against, and treated as if he had lost caste. But the few who converted to Islam were not treated like this. The time for the ritually important moment of the weighing of the first pepper each season was determined by the raja's 'magicians', and not favoured with a Christian blessing.

One of the raja of Cochin's privileges concerned customs duties at his port. In 1530 João III had allowed him to levy duties on goods coming from Southeast Asia and China to western India if they were owned by Portuguese residents of Cochin. They were to pay the raja 6 percent on goods landed in Cochin. Later the raja unilaterally lowered his rates to $3\frac{1}{2}$ percent. As a consequence traders all over western India tried, often successfully, to pass off their goods coming from the east as belonging to a Portuguese resident of Cochin, and thereby entitled to a rate of $3\frac{1}{2}$ percent rather than the usual 6 percent levied at Goa and Cochin. Evasion became so common that the raja in 1584, under pressure from the Portuguese authorities, agreed to a reform. The Portuguese residents of Cochin then revolted, and finally the Goa government was forced to concede the lower rate. Evasion then continued, to the detriment of Portugal's revenues.

The growers of the pepper were mostly Nestorian Christians. They, however, were too afraid of the Portuguese and their Inquisition to bring the pepper to the coast, so they usually sold it to the Muslim traders who traditionally handled this trade. The Muslims sold it to the Portuguese in Cochin and other coastal forts and also to other exporters. Apparently later in the century some of the Christians were persuaded to bring the pepper themselves, but at least for the first part of the century the Portuguese were usually dependent for their pepper supplies on their supposed inveterate enemies, the Muslims. These Muslims often rubbed salt in the wound by supplying pepper that was dirty or wet.

That the Portuguese got poor-quality pepper was, however, due more to their own bad management than to the malice of the Muslim traders. Ideally, the capital to buy pepper should have arrived on the ships from Portugal late in the year. Since the pepper was harvested in December or January, the Portuguese could have used their capital to make purchases at leisure throughout the next year, buying only clean, dry pepper at times when the market was low. About fifteen months after the capital had arrived, the pepper would have been loaded on the next year's ships and sent off to Portugal. In fact the Portuguese were never able to get this far ahead. The capital arrived late in the year, and the Portuguese then had frantically to buy whatever pepper was available, get it loaded, and despatch the ships in time for them to round the Cape of Good Hope before the end of the monsoon.

A succession of letters to the king throughout the century described this unsatisfactory arrangement and urged him to have the capital available for the whole year, but the king could never afford to do this. He had to have his capital, in the form of pepper, back in Lisbon as soon as possible. As a result, his officials were reduced to borrowing money from local Portuguese merchants, the city of Cochin, the raja of Craganore, and even local Muslim traders. This then opened up another gap in the Portuguese system, for in return many local traders were given *cartazes* for trade to the Red Sea. Often pepper was smuggled on these ships, so that from the 1540s there was actually some pepper trade from the centre of Portuguese control, Malabar, straight to the area which was meant to be totally out of bounds, the Red Sea. And even when the capital did arrive in Cochin, a hard-pressed governor would often take part of it for military necessities, despite the king's frequent prohibitions on such behaviour.

One final factor should be mentioned which again decreased the control of the Portuguese crown over the pepper production of Malabar: the tendency of both Portuguese officials and private Portuguese to indulge in the highly profitable 'illegal' trade themselves. In 1519 the governor left for a cruise in the Red Sea. Seizing their chance, the remaining officials in India reportedly sent cargoes of pepper north to Cambay in ships belonging to the 'pirates' of Malabar. A year later an official of the raja of Cochin told the king of Portugal that Portuguese officials bought pepper in Cochin for their own illegal private trade at prices higher than the fixed official price at which it was bought for the king. Now the local merchants wanted to sell all their pepper at this high price. Other reports of Portuguese and local inhabitants of Portuguese areas trading in pepper continue throughout the century and later. In the 1630s even clerics, including one of the inquisitors, were accused of such trade.

A second major Portuguese attempt at monopoly concerned the horse trade. Again local realities limited their success. Before the Portuguese arrival there was an important trade in horses through the Konkan ports of Dabhol, Chaul and Goa. These horses came from the Persian Gulf area, for the Indian subcontinent has never produced good horses. The main local producing area was Kutch, in Gujarat, but horses from there were generally despised. The best came from Arabia and Persia. As Pires said, 'The best are the Arabians, next are the Persians, and third are those from Cambay. These latter are worth little' (Tome Pires, *Suma Oriental*, 2 vols., London, 1944, vol. I, p. 21). A good horse, one suitable for military purposes and also for show, could cost 500 cruzados, and the average price was a high 300 cruzados. The import tax on these valuable animals was a major source of revenue in all three Konkan ports. In Goa each paid total duties of about 40 cruzados. At least 1000 horses came through Goa each year, so that about half the total revenue of the city came from this one source. These horses coming via the Konkan ports were destined for the Deccan sultanates: Vijayanagar received its horses via Cannanore and Bhatkal.

Once Albuquerque had taken Goa, the Portuguese took pains to foster this lucrative trade. Any ship bringing in to Goa at least ten horses from Hurmuz paid no customs duties on its remaining cargo, and merchants who left Goa having bought five horses were given concessions in the customs houses covering Goa's land trade.

The Portuguese also tried to centralize the whole horse trade in Goa compulsorily, so that any ship coming from South Arabia or Hurmuz with horses for the Indian market could come only to Goa. In practice, this was never very strictly enforced, despite some success in the early years. The main chink in the system was that in places outside Goa local rulers and local Portuguese wanted horses for themselves, and both had occasionally to be conciliated by the Goa government for political reasons. There was another difficulty also. The religious authorities in Goa disapproved of Christians selling horses to infidels, as this was forbidden by a Papal Bull. Finally God and Mammon were both served by a decree of 1574. Portuguese were no longer allowed to take horses inland from Goa to sell in Bijapur. Instead the Bijapuri merchants would have to come to Goa to buy them.

From this trade the Portuguese crown derived both financial and political benefits. Horses paid no import duties in Goa, but when they left they paid about 40 cruzados each. As early as 1513–14 this trade was worth 5000 cruzados to the Goa customs. By 1523 this had risen to 18,000 cruzados, and in the 1540s to a very lucrative 65,000 cruzados. But later in the century receipts fell sharply, mostly it seems because the

Portuguese had to allow more horse trade to other ports for political reasons. Around 1580 Goa made 9000 cruzados from the horse trade, but Chaul made 14,000.

The political benefits could also at times be substantial. Vijayanagar and the five Deccan sultanates were frequently at war with one another in the sixteenth century, before Vijayanagar's great defeat near Talikota in 1565. Each was prepared to offer large concessions to the Portuguese in return for a denial of horse sales to their enemies. The Portuguese were thus able to extract various concessions from these supplicants, and play one off against the other to their own benefit.

In their attempts to monopolize the spice trade and the importation of horses we have been able to see Portuguese aims affected by various constraints. Some of these resulted from internal Portuguese factors, but many were responses to opposition from local Indians affected by these policies. A third case study will illustrate even more clearly the responses of different groups and interests in an Indian area to the Portuguese system. The area under review is Gujarat. We have already noted Gujarati traders circumventing Portuguese attempts to monopolize the trade in spices, especially in Diu before 1535, in the Bay of Bengal in the 1540s and 1550s, and in Acheh later in the century. But how did they, and their rulers, respond at home in Gujarat? We can look at nobles and rulers first.

Until his death in 1522 the main adversary of the Portuguese in Gujarat was Malik Ayaz, the governor of Diu. He combated the demands of the Portuguese because acceptance of them would have been disastrous for him. He was successful because he had both military power and influence at court.

Under Malik Ayaz's stewardship Diu at 1500 had risen to be one of the great ports in India. About one half of his income came from the port. This wealth and Diu's strategic location enabled the Malik to acquire a considerable degree of independence from his overlord, the sultan of Gujarat. His initial reaction to the Portuguese seems to have been similar to that of many other independent or quasi-independent rulers of Indian port cities: he was happy for them to come and trade in his port on a basis similar to that of all the other foreign merchants there. As a Portuguese chronicler noted, he was always in these early years pressing them to send to Diu 'two ships loaded with copper and spices so that he could trade with us' (Fernão Lopes de Castanheda,

História do Descobrimento e Conquista da India pelos Portugueses, 9 vols., Coímbra, 1924–33, II, lxxxv). In vain: we have noted Portugal's designs. Malik Ayaz had to choose between resistance or submission. Co-operation in peaceful trade was not offered.

Resistance took two forms, military and diplomatic. In 1508 he helped the Egyptian fleet under Amir Husain defeat and kill the viceroy's son, D. Lourenço d'Almeida, at Chaul. But he feared reprisals, so 'on the one hand he wrote letters of condolence to the viceroy and on the other he fortified the city, as one who expected repayment for the help he had given Amir Husain, which repayment was not long delayed' (João de Barros, *Asia*, 4 vols., Lisbon, 1945–6, II, ii, 9). The viceroy at Diu in 1509 achieved a notable victory over the combined Egyptian–Gujarati fleet.

From then on Malik Ayaz concentrated on guileful defence. In 1513 he was able to out-manoeuvre Albuquerque's attempt to establish a fort in Diu. Seven years later another Portuguese reconnaissance was defeated, as were Portuguese attempts to go above him and get his overlord, the sultan of Gujarat, to allow them a fort. At his death in 1522 he could be well satisfied, for he left a still independent and prosperous Diu to be governed by his son.

Diu's downfall came because it was sucked into closer control by the sultanate of Gujarat. In 1526 a new ruler, Bahadur Shah, came to power. He was able to acquire much closer control over Diu, and change its governors at will. Meanwhile from 1530 he was involved in sporadic warfare with the Portuguese, who had become desperate to conquer Diu and so close it off as a haven for the 'illegal' spice trade. An open Portuguese attack in that year was beaten off thanks to Diu's formidable defences. Five years later Bahadur's situation had changed radically. He had been defeated by the Mughal emperor Humayon, and now desperately needed Portuguese help. In 1535, fatefully, he allowed them to build a fort at Diu. Two attempts by Gujarati forces in 1538 and 1546 to retake the port failed, and by the mid 1550s at least the Portuguese had finally achieved their main objective: all Gujarati ships leaving the great ports of the Gulf of Cambay had now to call at Diu, pay customs duties, and take a *cartaz* which obliged them to call at Diu again on the way back and again pay duties to the Portuguese. This was a very substantial accomplishment indeed. Nor was this Portuguese control threatened when Gujarat was incorporated into the Mughal empire in 1572. Indeed, the great Mughal emperor Akbar tacitly accepted Portuguese control by asking for and receiving a 'free *cartaz*' each year. This allowed him to send one ship each year to the Red Sea without having to pay duties to the Portuguese.

This whole matter shows clearly differing perceptions and interests within the ruling elite of the powerful Indian sultanate of Gujarat. Those members whose interests were threatened by the Portuguese responded vigorously. Thus Malik Ayaz, like the zamorins of Calicut and the Mamluk rulers of Egypt, saw Portuguese demands as intolerable and resisted them, in the Malik's case successfully. Similarly, the two Gujarati sieges of 1538 (helped by the Turks) and 1546 were financed and led not by the sultans but by nobles who were strongly oriented to sea trade, and so found Portuguese control unacceptable. At the other extreme were the land-oriented rulers of Gujarat, and later the Mughal empire, and most of their nobles. Thus Bahadur in 1535 was happy to give the Portuguese a foothold in Diu in the hope that this would help him face the threat on land from the Mughals. Later sultans did little to try and reconquer Diu; for them also it was not a vital resource. The powerful Akbar petitioned for and accepted a free *cartaz* each year. Relations between these sorts of rulers and the Portuguese cannot even really be described as pacific or friendly: contact between the two sides was minimal, the Mughal attitude especially being one of neglect and indifference. One demonstration of this is the very few references (and those casual), to the Portuguese in the very lengthy standard Mughal chronicles.

We need to keep this sort of division in mind whenever we look for responses to the Portuguese presence in India. The vast bulk of the political elite, notably those controlling large land-based inland empires, were unaffected by Portuguese activities on the sea and so ignored them, or accepted their sea-control system when they had to. Only an atypical handful of sea-oriented rulers and governors in littoral western India were vitally disadvantaged by the Portuguese. These people resisted, though usually unsuccessfully.

We described in the previous chapter Gujarat's huge sea trade around 1500. The response of these traders to the Portuguese system shows some similarities and some differences as compared with the responses of the political elite. At first Gujarati merchants were friendly enough, no doubt seeing the Portuguese as simply another new group of traders, and not, on their early showing in Calicut, a particularly effective one. Once Portugal's monopolistic aims became clear Gujarat's merchants tried to resist, for Portuguese claims were both new and arbitrary. This phase ended quickly, for it was soon made very clear that no Gujarati merchantman could resist Portuguese warships. The final, and continuing, response was one of acquiescence in the Portuguese system. Gujarati traders called routinely at Diu and other Portuguese forts to pay their duties and take their *cartazes*.

We noted that members of the Gujarati political elite whose interests were threatened resisted the Portuguese. Merchant interests were apparently at least as gravely affected, yet they soon gave in. There are several explanations for this. In many areas the merchants' interests were in fact not threatened. Thus they continued to trade in spices when they could, and this often was possible in the Bay of Bengal, and later in Acheh. In any case, the spice trade was far from being their only trade. Here the contrast with Malabari merchants is clear. Their main trade was in spices; they had to resist Portuguese attempts at monopoly. But such mainstays of the Gujarati trade as cloths, indigo, saltpetre and a host of other products were not threatened by the Portuguese. Rather they were concerned to foster this trade, for thus Diu's customs revenues expanded. In other words, for most Gujarati trade items and most Gujarati traders, acceptance of Portuguese control really only meant that extra customs duties of about 5 percent had to be paid. This was all Portuguese control meant, and this comparatively trifling sum could be easily recouped by charging slightly higher prices. In any case, the bottom line was that there was no choice. Portuguese fleets patrolling between Diu and Daman made evasion very difficult; here at least their coercion was effective.

There were even advantages in accepting the Portuguese system, at least for some Gujarati merchants. Most Portuguese captains, of Diu and elsewhere, traded extensively, sometimes illegally, on their own accounts, and often used Gujarati agents in this trade. Thus some Gujarati merchants became go-betweens, or intermediaries, forerunners of later Indian groups who did well as commercial agents for British rulers in India. The Portuguese presence also opened up a minor new export trade for Gujarat. Large proportions of the cargoes of the homeward bound ships from Goa were Gujarati products, especially cotton cloths. Indeed, when trade between Goa and Gujarat was blocked by war, there were vociferous complaints from Goan residents whose trade had been ruined by the wars of their elite. On the individual level there was a strong mutuality of interest between Gujarati and Portuguese traders.

One can then accept that in practice Portuguese control was not excessively irksome. It was, nevertheless, control: in Gujarat at least, indigenous sea trade was subjected to and dominated by the Portuguese; this had some effects. There is evidence that the direction of Gujarat's trade changed during the sixteenth century. Around 1500 she stretched out two arms: to the Red Sea and to Malacca. Over the next hundred years the Red Sea became much more important than Southeast Asia. In part this was probably simply a commercial decision, but Portuguese policies also contributed. Their regime in Malacca was sometimes brutal, and usually corrupt. Gujarati traders thus looked for new ports. On the other hand the Portuguese were most strongly opposed to Muslim traders from the Red Sea area and the Middle East in general, and their opposition seems to have helped Gujarati traders, both Hindu and Muslim, to increase their share in trade to this area. A slackening of Portuguese effort also helped here. Later in the sixteenth century, as profits from the spice trade declined, Portugal became more concerned with expanding trade under her control than with worrying overmuch about where this trade went. Increasingly they allowed trade to the formerly forbidden area of the Red Sea. One of the major changes in Indian Ocean trade in the sixteenth century was the increasing dominance of Gujarat's great merchants in the Red Sea area; the Portuguese contributed something to this shift.

In a nutshell, then, most members of the Gujarati elite were unaffected by the Portuguese presence, or ignored them. Those who were affected resisted, but usually were defeated. Among Gujarat's merchant groups, those who traded by sea were directly concerned with the Portuguese, but soon found that resistance was futile, and acquiescence rather painless. Nor is the Gujarati case unique, for in most of India the elite was unaffected, while those who were affected usually were vanquished. Gujarat's merchants, however, are in a sense a special case, for while Portuguese control was tight it was not too irksome. In most of the rest of India this control was much less evident, so that, for example, the powerful *chettyar* merchants of Coromandel were affected hardly at all. And of course this applies completely to the vast majority of India's merchants, those who did not trade by sea. The other area of contrast is with merchants where Portuguese control was both tight and irksome, namely Malabar. Yet even here, as we saw, their control could often be circumvented.

This analysis of the response from Gujarat to the Portuguese system raised two final questions: why did the elite of Gujarat let a wealthy and influential group within the state collaborate with an enemy, the Portuguese; and how can one justify this discrete analysis of the responses of these two groups, given that they were both subjects of one state, and indeed often had close connections based on financial transactions? One answer will suffice for these two questions. In the premodern state of Gujarat, or for that matter Portuguese India, the functions of rulers and political elites were much more limited than is the case in a modern nation state. Thus the merchants were not protected from the Portuguese by their rulers, but on the other hand they were allowed to make what arrangements they wished with them. The land-oriented rulers did not see this as infringing on their sovereignty: as Bahadur said, 'Wars by sea are merchants' affairs, and of no concern to the prestige of kings' (quoted in Conde de Ficalho, *Garcia da Orta e o Seu Tempo*, Lisbon, 1886, p. 118).

This attitude was most clearly seen in a matter where today a state claims complete control, namely trade with the enemy. The sixteenth-century records are rife with accounts of merchants, both Gujarati and Portuguese, ignoring as much as possible the wars of their elites and continuing to trade with each other. The best illustration of this comes not from Gujarat but from Kanara, south of Goa. In 1655 Portugal and the ruler of Kanara were at war; this, however, was a war between two politico-military groupings. Local merchants, both Portuguese and Kanarese, either did not know or did not care. They continued to come to Goa with cargoes of rice. The Portuguese officials (and no doubt their Kanarese counterparts too) protested that such conduct was 'much to be abominated' and 'very damaging to the credit and reputation of the arms of His Majesty, whom God protect' (P. S. S. Pissurlencar, ed., *Assentos do Conselho do Estado*, 5 vols., Bastorá, 1953–7, vol. II, pp. 395–8; diary of Viceroy Sarzedas in 'Noticias dos estados da India', Biblioteca da Academia das Ciências, Lisbon, MSS. Azuis, A58, f. 48). But the rice was sold in Goa anyway.

One rather different case study can be used to complete this analysis of Indian reactions to the Portuguese. It concerns artillery, one of several areas where they did have an advantage and an impact.

Portugal's important victories, such as the conquests of Goa and Malacca, the defeat of Amir Husain in 1509, the defences of Diu in 1538 and 1546, and their general superiority in naval warfare, need some explaining, for the Portuguese were operating with a comparative handful of men. A really big expedition would still include only about 2000 or 3000 Portuguese and *mestiços*. Typically these would be backed up by an at least equal number of local auxiliaries, while the ships on which they travelled would also be primarily crewed by Indians. In the whole empire, from Mozambique to Macao, there may have been a maximum of 10,000 men, Portuguese or Eurasian, available for military service at any one time. There were also complaints that the quality of soldiers sent out from Portugal declined during the century, so that at the end they were mere scum: beggars, jailbirds, and people taken forcibly off the streets of Lisbon. The brittleness of Portugal's land defences was revealed in 1570 when a concerted attack on Portuguese areas (in part provoked by the Portuguese) from the rulers of Calicut, Bijapur, and Ahmadnagar was beaten off with great difficulty; indeed the Portuguese fort near Calicut, at Chalé, was lost.

Portuguese success was based both on the fact that, except in 1570, they were never faced with united opposition from local powers, and on naval superiority. The first is obvious enough. There is no doubt that had the full weight of Deccan armies been turned on their areas in the Konkan and Kanara, in co-ordination with Mughal attacks in Gujarat, then the Portuguese could have been driven out. However most of the time Portuguese activities did not threaten the interests of these land-based states.

The reason why the Portuguese were successful in naval battles, and so could supply besieged forts like Diu from the sea, is also obvious enough. Their ships were better and, crucially, they had artillery on them. At first the Portuguese were confronted by galleys, or large merchant ships which carried soldiers but no cannon. These ships, whether oared or not, were comparatively flimsy because all they needed to be able to do was cruise before the monsoon winds in the Indian Ocean. But the Portuguese ships had to be able to sail from Europe to India, and to withstand much harsher weather.

The key was the cannon on the ships. Artillery had been developed during the fourteenth century in Europe, and was used on ships by the end of this century. In Asia generally crude cannon were occasionally used on land in the fourteenth century, and much more widely later: they played a crucial role in Babur's victories in 1526 which established the Mughal empire. But it does seem that European cannon were better cast, and European gunners more skilful: hence the use of both when available by Indian states. The problem was that the concept of using them on ships at sea was not known when the Portuguese irrupted into the Indian Ocean, partly because Indian Ocean ships, being usually sewn not nailed, were too rickety to survive the recoil of cannon. Here lies the prime reason for their fast early successes. The Portuguese, indeed, were well aware of this advantage. From the very start they were routinely instructed not to board an enemy, but rather to stand off and, using artillery, slaughter the enemy with impunity.

The response of Indian rulers to this situation was a complex one. The advantages of cannon were early demonstrated, as an account of Cabral's voyage in 1500 makes clear. While his fleet was in Calicut the zamorin asked him to capture a coastal ship. Cabral agreed, and the zamorin sent along a Muslim agent to watch how the Portuguese fared. Cabral sent off a caravel armed with a large bombard and sixty or seventy men. After two days they caught up with the local ship,

... and asked them if they wished to surrender. The Moors began to laugh because they were numerous, and their ship was very large, and they began to shoot arrows. And when the captain of the caravel saw this, he ordered the artillery fired, so that they struck the said ship, and it surrendered at once ... The king (zamorin) marvelled greatly that so small a caravel and with so few people could take so large a ship in which were three hundred men at arms. (*The Voyage of Pedro Alvares Cabral to Brazil and India*, London, 1937, p. 78).

This demonstration, and later Portuguese bombardments of his capital from the sea, made the zamorin stop marvelling and start catching up. In 1503 two Milanese cannon makers deserted the Portuguese and joined up with the zamorin. In three years they cast 300 cannon, and taught local people how to make and use artillery. By 1506 the zamorin had a fleet of 200 ships, protected by bales of cotton in the gunwales and carrying cannon on board.

Despite this the zamorin and other Indian rulers proved unable to challenge formal Portuguese naval dominance in the sixteenth century. Geoffrey Parker has provided the best explanation for this. Their ships were not strong enough to withstand an artillery bombardment from the Portuguese, nor to absorb the recoil of large ordinance. There was however no real reason why Portuguese-style ships could not have been built by Asian rulers. It was just that this would not have been cost-effective. It was cheaper to take *cartazes* and so not need to arm one's ships. If the Portuguese failed to honour the protection they had sold, Asian rulers often could retaliate on land. As Parker neatly sums up: 'The ultimate defence of local Asian rulers was, thus, not the gun but the permit and the prison.'[5]

Here then is another area where, when we disentangle a specific case, we find the Portuguese having an impact and an advantage. Their naval dominance, based on artillery on ships, was comparable with other instances we have already noted where they had successes, where they 'made a difference', such as the rise of Cochin and the decline of Calicut; such as their central achievement of establishing a series of fortified areas around the Indian Ocean littoral; such as their contribution to the redirection of Gujarat's massive trade in the sixteenth century.

Yet it needs to be stressed that this sort of impact was rather atypical. Thus their infantry was no better organized than that of most of their opponents. Proper regiments were not formed until the eighteenth century. Before then Portuguese soldiers simply joined up, without proper training, uniform, or even standardized weapons, with a *fidalgo* of their choice for the campaigning season. The companies were disbanded at the end of each season, that is when the rains started in May or June, and the soldiers left for several months to beg for their food in the streets of Goa.

In other technological areas also recent studies seem to make clear that the Portuguese enjoyed few advantages. Habib notes important technological changes in western Europe from 1450 to 1750, which cleared the way for the industrial revolution. In the most general sense, the two main areas of innovation were the development of mechanical devices, clocks, screws, and gear wheels being examples, and the more concentrated application of power and heat. The mass dissemination of many of these innovations in some parts of Europe (Italy, the Low Countries, France and later England, but not Iberia) was of crucial importance in explaining later European dominance in Asia. Indians generally failed to appreciate these new devices; this failure told heavily in the eighteenth century. But two points must be stressed. First, in the sixteenth and seventeenth centuries India was, on most criteria, one of the advanced countries of the world.[6] Second, the Portuguese, at

---

[5] Geoffrey Parker, 'Victory at sea', lecture 3 of the 1985 Lees-Knowles lectures (Cambridge).

[6] Irfan Habib, 'Technology and barriers to technological change in Mughal India', *Indian Historical Review*, vol. v, 1–2 (1978–9), pp. 152–74, and A. Jan Qaisar, *The Indian Response to European Technology and Culture (A.D. 1498–1707)* (Delhi, 1982).

least in the sixteenth century, also knew nothing of these innovations except, ironically, for artillery. Leaving this aside, in the vital area of technology also, the European–Asian balance changed long after the end of Portuguese power.

CHAPTER 3

EVALUATION OF THE OFFICIAL SYSTEM

This discussion of Portuguese policy, and local Indian responses to it, has made clear how variegated was the *official* Portuguese impact: occasionally, in particular places, massive, more often nugatory. We need now to reverse our Indian focus, and investigate a little more closely the strengths and weakness of the Portuguese military–governmental system. This will show that, as well as problems caused by the responses of local people, there were serious weaknesses within the Portuguese structure itself. In chapter 4 we will consider private Portuguese trade, in which all Portuguese regardless of rank or condition traded more or less equally, and under the same conditions as other Asian traders. This private trade will be presented as a paradigm of the *unofficial* Portuguese impact on India, and will lead to a case study of Goa, and a discussion of social interaction, both of them again showing clearly much more reciprocity than domination.

One obvious problem with the Portuguese official or state system was the whole size of their undertaking and the resources available to them. The area they were trying to control was huge. Even the islands and seas of the Malay archipelago cover more area than the continental U.S.A. The round voyage from Lisbon to Goa took one and one-half years, and the distance travelled equalled the earth's diameter. Nor would it be correct to see Portuguese interest as focussed entirely on the Indian Ocean. When D. Manuel successfully besieged Azemmour in Morocco in 1513 he commanded 18,000 men. Albuquerque had only 1000 when he took Malacca in 1511, and 3000 when he failed before Aden in the year of Azemmour. D. João III was often tied up with his dynastic relations with Spain: between 1522 and 1544 he spent 1,790,000 cruzados on this (including 900,000 cruzados as a dowry so he could marry Charles V's sister). In the same period fighting in Morocco cost 450,000 cruzados, and Indian military matters 610,000. Later D. Sebastian was of course even more involved in North African affairs, to the extent of leaving his body there. After 1580 Portugal's Spanish rulers had very far-flung interests to consider. Although the Portuguese empire retained formal autonomy, it was from around this time that

61

Brazilian interests began to compete with, and even outweigh, the metropolitan focus on Asia.

Interest indeed fluctuated, and this was reflected in the availability of supplies of men and money for India. In his first flush of enthusiasm D. Manuel sent off Cabral with 13 ships and at least 1200 men. In the next 5 years a further 81 ships and 7000 men followed. This pace was not sustained: nor could it be, given a home population of 1,000,000. Only in times of crisis would men and supplies be rushed out: the term 'rushed' is used in a purely relative sense, for it took up to a year for news of a crisis to reach Portugal, and for help to reach India.

The total numbers of Europeans and Eurasians available for a major expedition seldom reached 5000. The total number of men capable of military service in the whole empire may have been about 10,000. Figures for departures of ships from Lisbon for India fluctuate decade by decade, but the trend is downwards. The 30-year totals go: 1500–29, 310; 1530–59, 192; 1560–89, 159; 1590–1619, 168, though it must be added that ship sizes rose during the century.

We have noted how international interests dictated that Hurmuz be left open, at least a little, by the Portuguese. Much more important was the failure to take Aden. This was a crucial gap in the Portuguese system, for Aden controlled the entrance to the Red Sea. Without it, a fleet had to be sent each season from Goa to lie off the entrance, usually cruising between Aden and the Bab el-Mandab, and returning to Hurmuz in April. The lack of a closer base created serious logistic difficulties and reduced the fleet's effectiveness. Reports of its operations often come close to farce. The fleet of 1530 consisted of ten ships, and it spread itself across the entrance to the Red Sea 'like a net', with each ship in the fleet nearly in sight of the next. But it took few prizes, as most of those desiring to trade illegally had left early and were already within the Red Sea. In 1562 the armada saw more than fifty ships slip past and into the Red Sea without being able to stop them. We are told that the captain of the 1538 fleet cruised diligently until the middle of April, without stopping anyone, whereupon 'it being time to return, off he went' (Couto, *Da Asia*, V, ii, 7).

A more important and difficult matter is the efficiency of the administrative structure which we sketched earlier. George Winius has noted acutely that viceroys often live better than kings;[1] certainly the

[1] George D. Winius, *The Black Legend of Portuguese India*, Xavier Centre of Historical Research Studies Series 3 (New Delhi, 1985).

Indian viceroy or governor was both an expensive official and a status-conscious one. When Almeida reached Cannanore in 1505 he was meant to build some forts before he made himself viceroy, the idea presumably being that a viceroy with no territory was a nonsense. But he was awaited by an important ambassador from Vijayanagar and status requirements made him proclaim himself viceroy at once. The actual cost of the viceroy and his establishment was considerable, even leaving aside such expensive, but non-recurring, events as D. João de Castro's lavish and self-congratulatory 'Triumph' in Goa after the relief of the second siege of Diu. In 1582 the viceroy's salary was 20,400 cruzados, and a further 6000 cruzados was spent on paying people officially attached to him. These included his guardsmen, a doctor, a surgeon, a trumpeter, and many others.

Within the administration, and especially as regards the allocation of jobs, there was a constant tension between status and suitability. Portuguese noble society was clearly graduated, mostly according to birth. Thus at one dinner Almeida had dining with him nobles down to a certain rank. Those ranked below this had to eat with the *vedor*. One of the clichés of the literature is nevertheless that in the first half of the sixteenth century it was tough old soldiers who did well. It was claimed that da Gama 'would not give captaincies except to those who in war had shown themselves as good soldiers; for he would give the honours of war to those who had won them with their right arms, and however low a man might be he would show him more honour than a gentleman Jew' (quoted in Peter Padfield, *Tide of Empires*, London, 1979, p. 34). But later in the century, we are told, crusty warriors gave way to perfumed popinjays with good connections who spent their time in Goa seducing married women.

The reality seems to be different. It is true that many Portuguese captains in Asia had prior experience in Morocco, hence their automatic visceral anti-Muslim feeling. More generally, past military experience was crucial. It seems that only 2 out of the 33 governors of the sixteenth century had not had prior military experience, and one of these was a very high-ranking noble in that he was a son of the fourth duke of Bragança. He shows that connections and relationships were also important in getting jobs. A Namier-type study of factions, interest groups and interrelationships would reveal an intricate network indeed. As examples, D. Francisco de Almeida (viceroy 1505–9) was the grand-uncle of D. João de Castro (governor 1545–8), while D. Garcia de Noronha (viceroy 1538–40) was a nephew of Albuquerque (governor 1509–15), married to Castro's sister, and a great-great-grandchild of two kings of Castile. This was a very small elite group. In the whole period from 1550 to 1671 one half of the governors were members of only five different noble lineages. One of these was the Noronhas. D. Afonso de Noronha was viceroy from 1550 to 1554. His nephew held the same position from 1564 to 1568. In the next generation another Noronha was appointed viceroy in 1621, but never served. His son however did, being viceroy from 1629 to 1635. And each viceroy or governor looked after his own: witness Almeida's son, several members of da Gama's family, and Castro's sons. It was simply expected that a viceroy would bring with him his sons and other relations, and other clients, and that they would do well while their patron held office. Indeed, the greatest patron was the king himself, who made the final decision on all appointments. Appointment to a position would mean the acquisition of a new client for the king, or it would keep an established noble happy and loyal. The system also served to keep bastards and troublemakers out of sight. One should not, however, think that really important Portuguese nobles served in India, except as governors. In 1538 D. João III wanted to send noble heirs to India to meet the Turkish threat: the noble fathers simply refused.

A powerful noble in India could also recruit followers by providing hospitality. We have a quite precise description of this process from João de Barros: Christavão de Sousa, captain of the fort of Chaul, was

... a fidalgo of high quality, personally energetic and humane, a polished talker, jovial and friendly with everyone; and he was magnificent not only from the continual food which he provided but also from the monetary assistance that he gave to those who had none; as a result more fidalgos spent the rains in Chaul than in any other part of India; and he had so much authority, and so many followers, any side helped by him had a great advantage. (Barros, *Asia*, IV, ii, 2).

Apart from patronage, what were the criteria for selection for office? One, as noted, was past meritorious service. A hero of the first siege of Diu hurried back to Portugal in 1539 with an official document testifying to his services. As a reward he was made captain of Chaul for three years, 'for his defence of the bulwark'. Another hero of this dramatic victory became captain of Cannanore, while his wife, who had also fought well, got a substantial pension. Even a valiant forebear could sometimes ensure a job. The daughter of a deserving *fidalgo* often received from the king for her dowry an office which would go to her successful suitor. Yet getting a letter of appointment was one thing; taking possession of the post was another. Various levels of officials had to be bribed before the post could be taken up. There was often a queue of previous appointees to a post; they all had to serve their three years or die before the last grantee could take over.

Once appointed, an office holder's conception of his responsibilities was still a very personal matter. An appointee's loyalties were not to an impersonal conception of an office in which he (for they were all men) was to discharge certain functions guided by established rules. Rather, Portuguese officials of all grades treated their offices as a service to the king who had appointed them. They owed obedience and loyalty to him personally, or to his deputy; so long as the king or governor was satisfied there were no other criteria to be met.

A Portuguese official's post became in effect his property during his tenure. Any distinction between public and private funds was blurred. The bulk of his salary came not in cash from the capital of Goa but in the form of various privileges and perquisites, such as the right to collect a certain tax or to trade on a particular route. These rights were laid down in the official letter of appointment, but they shaded off into other customary rights (such as the privilege of being allowed to demand a gratuity before issuing a *cartaz*), which were unspecified but hallowed by tradition. These unofficial but tacitly accepted perquisites in turn merged into outright illegal exactions and abuses, notably demanding forced loans from local traders and trading in goods which were meant to be royal monopolies. The perquisites and the unofficial privileges were regarded by king and governor as unexceptional, but they did try to limit the abuses.

This system of payment was reflected in the prices paid for the various offices. The posts were seen as property from which the holder expected to make a profit, and thus they were willing to pay much more for a lucrative post than for one with few opportunities for pickings, even if the status of the latter was higher than that of the former. In a sale of 1618 more than twice as much was paid for the post of judge of the Goa customs house as for the captaincy of the whole city; the high status attached to the captaincy could not compete with the perquisites, legal and otherwise, available to a customs official. The post of captain of Diu was worth five times, and that of Hurmuz fourteen times, that of Goa, for these two forts were notoriously profitable. A critic of 1568 said that such were the perquisites at

Malacca, Sofala and Hurmuz that the captains did not really need any official salary at all.

The prevailing attitude was well expressed by the *fidalgo* who visited a religious house to say good-bye to the inmates before leaving to take up an appointment as captain of a fort. One of the clerics counselled him: 'Be content with what is yours, favour the poor, and do justice.' The *fidalgo* retorted that he fully intended to get all he could, as did all the others, 'because I am not going to my fort for any other reason than to come back rich' (Diogo do Couto, *Diálogo do Soldado Prático*, Lisbon, 1937, p. 14).

One basic problem was that all officials traded on their own behalf, as well as in many cases being responsible for controlling trade in their particular port. We have already seen the way this worked to weaken the official system of Malabar and Gujarat. Some historians have followed the great contemporary chronicler Diogo do Couto and claimed as he did that this increased later in the sixteenth century.

In the old days, when men reached India they asked 'which is the most dangerous outpost?' or 'Where are the fleets in which the most honourable service can be done?' whereas nowadays covetousness has got such a hold, that on their arrival they ask, 'who is preparing for a trading voyage to China or Japan, or Bengal or Pegu or Sunda?' Everybody flocks to those parts, which makes one think that the Muslim proverb will come true, for they say that we gained India like warriors and will lose it like merchants.[2]

But alas: private trade and general peculation had been endemic from the earliest days. A notable early warrior, Tristan da Cunha, was also an investor in several of the early expeditions to India, and saw his own expedition of 1506–7 in strictly commercial terms: the object was to trade or plunder and so make a fortune.

The fuzzy distinction between public and private property can be illustrated by many instances in the sixteenth century. We have already seen examples of abuses in Diu. Complaints about this date from soon after the taking of the fort, but they do seem to increase in frequency late in the century and into the seventeenth century. A captain of the fort of Hurmuz in the 1550s was proud of having made only 33,000 cruzados during his tenure. This was in fact a very substantial sum, but later captains made up to 7 times more than this. The apparent general increase in, but not beginning of, corruption and abuses is no doubt

---

[2] Quoted in C. R. Boxer, *Portuguese India in the Mid-Seventeenth Century* (Delhi, 1980), p. 42.

partly a consequence of better documentation for the later period, but it is to be expected that abuses would increase as Portuguese power declined. Diu's revenues, for example, fell sharply in the seventeenth century thanks to Dutch and English competition. The captains of Diu were more and more driven to abuses to make the profits they felt they should gain from their position.

Dubious practices were legion. In the later years of the century, captains of forts began taking artillery from the forts to use in their own ships. Throughout the century there are records of Portuguese ships seizing and plundering native ships which had Portuguese passes. In 1506 a Portuguese gave a *cartaz* to some Muslim traders which read 'Sir captain, if you find this ship, seize it, and if you don't, let it go' (Marechal Gomes da Costa, *Descobrimentos e Conquistas*, 3 vols., Lisbon, 1927–30, vol. II, pp. 176–7). This was written in Portuguese, which the Muslims could not read. The ship sailed, was seized, and its crew imprisoned for not having a valid *cartaz*. An account of the revenues of Goa for 1545 ended by saying: 'This is what Goa yielded last year, apart from what was stolen by the officials' (*As Gavetas da Torre do Tombo*, 7 vols., Lisbon, 1960–70, vol. III, p. 213). A year later an official complained that he had been trying to get opium for the king's trade, but had been hindered by the fact that the Portuguese officials in charge of trade seemed more interested in sending this product to Gujarat (with which state Portugal was at war at the time) and other places than in obtaining it for the king. Perhaps Diogo do Couto best summed up the state of the administration late in the century when he wrote: 'for the king's property to increase it should pass through few hands, and the fewer hands of officials it has contact with the greater will be its increase' (Couto, *Da Asia*, XII, i, 8).

The most scandalous allegation of all concerns the vital port of Aden. We noted that the failure to take this port left open a crucial gap in the whole Portuguese system of trade control and spice monopoly. Yet in 1513 under Albuquerque, and 1517 under Lopo Soares, the Portuguese missed what seem to have been easy opportunities. It has been suggested that some of their subordinates, and in the latter year even the governor himself, were in favour of the Red Sea remaining open to illegal traders. An open Red Sea left all sorts of opportunities. Many captains liked to cruise off the Bab el-Mandab taking prizes. Many captains and officials in India and the Arabian Sea could make good money by being bribed to allow trade to the Red Sea. On the other hand, the captain of any Portuguese fort in Aden would be holding down a hardship post, one where the climate was impossible and the threat of Muslim attack ever present. The case is not proven, but it seems clear that the interests of many Portuguese were better served by an open Red Sea.

Such instances of what today would be called 'corruption' can usually be explained by the confusion in most officials' minds between public and private property. Such confusion was part of every administration at this time: the distinction has been made explicit, and an attempt made to enforce it, only in the last two centuries. Why then the contemporary criticism just quoted from people like Couto? The explanation is that this criticism was of abuses of the system. The governors and chroniclers were not complaining of corruption in the modern sense (for they were not modern men) but of people who went beyond the bounds of custom in taking perquisites. To take the cannon needed for the defence of an important fort was clearly going too far. So was the plunder of a native ship with a Portuguese pass, or accepting a bribe for exemption from customs payments. Indeed, according to one contemporary the tyranny of the Portuguese captain of Diu caused a frontal attack on the fort from the neighbouring state of Gujarat: 'The captain of the fort caused the siege of Diu because he behaved so badly to the king of Gujarat and the local Muslims that if they had been Christians they would have had good cause to become Muslims' (*As Gavetas da Torre do Tombo*, vol. v, p. 327). Similarly, the revolt of a major opponent of the Portuguese in Malabar was caused by Portuguese abuses. Such abuses were regarded as bad because they could lead to Indian retaliation or increased attempts to evade Portuguese trade control. No one complained because the captaincy of Hurmuz sold for fourteen times that of Goa; the fact of greater perquisites in Hurmuz was part of the system, and appears remarkable only today.

We have then various problems to do with the nature of the Portuguese administration, some gaps in their system, and various, often effective, opposition from interested Indian groups and individuals. The result, some historians claim, was that the Portuguese at least tacitly changed their focus, became less militarist, and concentrated on relatively peaceful trade within Asia. We can accept much of this depiction, but some modifications need to be made. It is clear that from the very start trade was as important, probably more so, as either politics or religion. Even accepting that these three should not be artificially split up, the king's letters on their own make the point that trade and profit was the major concern. Manuel, after all, was nicknamed the Grocer King, not the King of Evangelism or some such. As for the relative dimensions of inter-Asian trade, as compared with the *carreira* to Europe, there is no doubt that the possibilities of the country trade, that is, the inter-Asian trade, were recognized early. In 1510 Albuquerque told the king he could make more money from a system of forcibly centralizing Asian trade on Goa than from taking Asian products to Europe. No doubt Manuel was concerned about how much of the profits from such an Asian-centred system would make their way back to Portugal. Thus he accepted part of this advice. In 1511 he wrote that he wanted to finance the Lisbon-bound cargoes on the *carreira*, and all state expenses in India, from control over country trade. Thus interest in the country trade dates from very early days.

What actually evolved were two rather separate systems. On the one hand was the king's operation, the trade to Europe. He financed the purchase of spices in India, and fitted out the annual fleet to fetch them. The other system involved control over country trade in Asia: the profits from this were meant to pay for all Asian expenses, but did not, despite Manuel's early hopes, cover the spices to send back to Lisbon. Thus the Portuguese empire soon came to be not only self-sustaining, but also self-controlled to a very large extent, with the trade to Europe almost totally discrete from the rest. And even in this arena the king increasingly contracted out his rights, even over pepper from 1580 to 1597. It is possible indeed that this change derived from what has been called a general crisis in Portuguese affairs in the mid sixteenth century, this in turn being part of a general economic crisis in western Europe at the time. Portugal suffered a series of military setbacks in Morocco, declines in revenue, even the death of João III in 1557, which together possibly further reduced royal control over Asian matters. Various data show the distribution of resources in the second half of the sixteenth century. We noted earlier how few cloves went to Europe, but a considerable bulk of them were distributed by the Portuguese in Asia. Similarly, the lucrative horse trade was of course an Asian affair. As to profits made by Portuguese concessionaires on their voyages, the Cape route represented only perhaps 20 percent of the total; 80 percent came from inter-Asian voyages. An estimate of the value of Goa's trade around 1600 finds about one-third taken up on the voyage to Europe, and two-thirds on inter-Asian trade.

Thus it is not surprising that Portuguese captains and governors strove to increase trade, and so customs duties, at their ports, not only because this could increase their own chances for speculation but also because these revenues were vital for the state. If the rigid system laid down in remote Portugal had to be bent a little to do this, then so be it. The clearest case of this was trade to the Red Sea. In the early years the Portuguese tried to ban all such trade, this being a hostile Muslim area. Throughout the century such prohibitions were backed by the clerics, notably in their provincial councils. Their views were more and more often ignored by the governors. There are records of trade licensed by the Portuguese from the Red Sea to Diu from 1537, to Hurmuz from 1539, and to Cannanore from 1546. Most revealing of all was the case of Goa itself. In 1543 Bijapur finally ceded to Portugal the areas of Bardes and Salcette, but in return the Portuguese agreed to allow trade to the Red Sea. They did the same in the case of Cochin from the 1540s. In these two areas, the desire for greater trade, an inability to block illegal trade anyway and the need to conciliate local powers all combined to make the system more flexible. The fact that these licensed ships often took prohibited pepper with them was regrettable, but predictable and unavoidable.

The whole of this and the previous chapter points to the Portuguese being rather unsuccessful in imposing their official system of trade control. We have instead a system where in some areas their naval power enabled them to skim a little off the top. They were really only levying a tribute. Basic structural changes in trade organization were not attempted, nor, to return to our general theme, was their impact the same everywhere all the time. We noted the Chinese beating them off in the 1520s. Further south, their presence in Southeast Asia was usually much more informal and pacific than further west. Malacca never became the great centre for directed trade which Goa and Diu did, mostly because the Portuguese made less effort, and also because Malacca was easier to avoid than was Diu. Around the rest of the Bay of Bengal Portuguese official control was minimal. Malabar certainly was affected, for here local and Portuguese interests were diametrically (and uniquely) opposed. Here there was an impact: Calicut fell and Cochin rose. Portuguese power meant that the overland export route for pepper, to Coromandel, replaced trade by sea from Calicut. Further north, Goa of course flourished as never before or since. Gujarati trade continued to be huge but, partly as a result of Portuguese policies, focussed on the Red Sea now, as compared with Calicut and Malacca in the fifteenth century. Hurmuz, thanks to Portugal's deliberately lax control, continued to flourish, while for a time trade to the Red Sea was hindered. But even as regards the spice trade the Portuguese finally had little success, although it was in this whole matter of trade control that the Portuguese tried hardest. We can conclude this discussion of the 'official' Portuguese system, the one in which they tried to be different and have an impact, by an analysis of three general points to do with the nature of their activities and empire.

One could fill pages with appalling stories of Portuguese brutality, usually directed against Muslims: In 1502 da Gama set alight, and watched burn, a crowded pilgrim ship. Only twenty children were allowed to escape and they were saved in order to be converted. Muslim ships sailing with passports were still likely to be sunk or worse. The Portuguese produced one inveterate opponent in Cannanore after they sewed up his nephew and six others in a sail and threw them overboard to drown. On another occasion, Portuguese pirates seized some *vanias* off a ship with a pass, cut off their hands, and threw them overboard. Malabaris were stoned to death in the streets of Goa. After Albuquerque took Goa for the second time in November 1510 he had killed, over 4 days, 6000 Muslims, men, women and children. Two years later Bijapur attacked Goa again. They were beaten off, and had to surrender 19 Portuguese deserters who had fought for them. Albuquerque had promised not to kill them. He kept this promise, 'but I ordered their noses, ears, right hands and left thumbs to be cut off, for a warning and in memory of the treason and evil that they did' (Henry H. Hart, *Sea Road to the Indies*, New York, 1950, p. 246). On this same occasion Albuquerque had another captured renegade burnt alive.

Not surprisingly, many modern authors have been very critical. One speaks of their 'unbelievably cold-blooded cruelty', another says roundly that 'Whatever balancing factors are allowed, Christ, whose red cross blazed on their sails, was mocked'. On the other hand, some modern Portuguese authors have made very different claims. V. M. Godinho says the brutality was necessary to build up early capital. This seems to be carrying neutral economic history a little too far. An official publication of 1956, a typical product of the Salazar period, claimed that da Gama arrived 'bearing to the Hindustan Peninsula the message of his peaceful intent of commerce and friendship'. Albuquerque's mission was 'primarily the pacification of certain parts of India by the destruction of various sorts of trouble which made for religious division and strife'.[3]

What can be said about this depressing matter? Some late nineteenth-century British authors, notably Danvers and Whiteway, also criticized the Portuguese, but not for brutality so much as on quite racist and anti-Roman Catholic grounds. If one now condemns the Portuguese for anything, is this to share in their invalid stereotypes? It must be said that criticism today is not really a matter of imposing modern morality on the past: some of the fiercest critics were Portuguese authors of the sixteenth and seventeenth centuries. Can one then say that this was a cruel age, and the Portuguese shared in the general disregard for decent behaviour and human life? Certainly one can point to appalling brutalities carried out in other Asian states: sickening massacres, impalings, pyramids of skulls – the nauseating list could go on for ever.

The Portuguese anti-Muslim bias was clear, and openly acknowledged in the sixteenth century. It derived from memories of the struggle to free Portugal from Muslim rule, and from the previous North African service of many of the Portuguese, a service consisting of a hard and brutal struggle with Muslim enemies in which atrocities like mutilation of corpses were common; but be it remembered that here, as in Asia, it was the Portuguese who were the invaders and the aggressors. There is also a distinction to be made between the relatively personal, immediate violence of the Portuguese as compared with later more modern and impersonal barbarity: Coen's actions in the Spice Islands; the Dutch Cultivation System in nineteenth-century Java; the Bengal famine of 1942–3; Kampuchea under Pol Pot; Hiroshima.

There are some signs that the Portuguese behaved worse than other people at the same time. Muslims who fought them, or infringed on their system, or offended in other ways, were likely to be slaughtered: there are few records of such Muslims being enslaved, or held for ransom. But this was done frequently to Portuguese captured by Muslims. The survivors of El-Ksar el-Kebir in 1578 were carefully held and their sale to their relatives went near to bankrupting many Portuguese noble families. The egregious Fernão Mendes Pinto claimed to have been sold sixteen times, and enslaved thirteen. There does seem

[3] Respectively, Henry H. Hart, *Sea Road to the Indies* (New York, 1950), p. 242; Peter Padfield, *Tide of Empires*, vol. I, '1481–1654' (London, 1979), p. 7; V. M. Godinho, *Os Descobrimentos e a Economia Mundial*, 2nd ed. (Lisbon, 1981–3), vol. IV, pp. 220–1; *Portuguese India Today*, 2nd ed. (Lisbon, 1956), pp. 9, 12.

to be a clear difference here, and one not to the advantage of the reputation of the Portuguese.

One cannot push this comparison very far. Nor can one legitimately say that because the Portuguese were European and Christian they should have behaved better than other people in the Indian Ocean area who were neither. Perhaps the only final verdict is that they, like most other people, failed to live up to their own ideals.

The brutality was often not totally random; rather its purpose was to beat off an attack, or enforce compliance with Portugal's imposed trade control system. Here we enter a second area of debate. In a nutshell, would the Portuguese have been better off trading peacefully in Asia?

The Portuguese usually claimed that, faced with united Muslim opposition, they had no option but to use force. We have seen already that the use of force and attacks on Muslim traders were laid down as official policy very early in Lisbon. For example, Cabral in 1500 was told to block the Red Sea. In Diu, Malik Ayaz at least professed a willingness to have the Portuguese come and share in the trade of his port. Certainly he was attacked by the Portuguese, and not vice versa. In Malacca the merchants of Gujarat strongly advised the sultan not to let the Portuguese trade there; a reasonable enough request, for the Portuguese had been seizing their ships for several years.

In Calicut also the Portuguese started the hostilities. Da Gama's whole manner had been overbearing in 1498, and the instructions for the second Portuguese voyage laid down that Muslim ships were to be sunk on sight, and an attempt made to get the zamorin to expel the Muslims (presumably those from the Red Sea only) from Calicut. This second Portuguese fleet found it difficult to obtain a cargo in Calicut, due to the opposition of the Muslim merchants – an opposition using commercial, not military, sanctions. Finally the Portuguese lost their tempers, seized a Muslim ship, and took its cargo. In retaliation a mob burned down the Portuguese factory. The situation from then deteriorated quickly. The Portuguese responded by bombarding the town and then sailing south to Cochin to trade. In 1502 da Gama returned to India, and demanded that the zamorin expel from Calicut all Muslims from Cairo and the Red Sea. The zamorin refused 'to expel more than 4,000 households of them who live in Calicut as natives, not as strangers, and from whom his kingdom had received much profit' (Barros, *Asia*, I, vi, 5).

It is probable that the Portuguese could have traded on a basis of equality in all three of these great ports. Certainly those then in control of the trade would have competed hard, but on past performance it seems that they would not have been the first to use force. As for the rulers, the Portuguese would have been welcomed as merely another group of foreign merchants come to trade and so increase their customs receipts. Further, given the lower costs of the Portuguese route around the Cape of Good Hope as compared with the Red Sea route, they could probably have taken over a large part of the spice trade to Europe. But peaceful competition was never the Portuguese aim.

For the Portuguese peaceful trade alongside Muslims on a basis of equality was impossible, for the crusade element was inherent in their presence in the Indian Ocean. The aim of the fifteenth-century kings was, it will be remembered, not only their profit but also the service of God. God, or at least the God of the Portuguese, could be served by the forcible dispossession of Muslim merchants, especially those based on the centre of the abomination, the city of Mecca. To see these 'Moors' deriving huge profits from their trade was to ignite a short fuse in the easily-combustible Portuguese. If the Muslims could be ousted from the spice trade, not only would God be served, but the true believers would profit on earth, as well as later in heaven, by replacing them.

There was another influence also. The Portuguese empire was of course a state enterprise, directed by the king and serviced by nobles. Such people, while interested enough in their own profits, were also socialized to seek glory, and so renown and promotion to a higher rank in the nobility or membership in an order of chivalry. Hence the compulsion to build a fort somewhere, or anywhere, and have one's name carved for posterity above the entrance. The result was far too many forts: most of them, on a cost-effective basis, could have been abandoned and the system would still have run as well, or badly, as before. Almeida was typical. When he got to Cochin in 1505 the Albuquerque brothers had already built a stockade and a church. This was not nearly grand enough for a viceroy, and anyway they had not been built by Almeida. He desperately wanted to build a stone fort, and of course he got his way. Such people were hardly going to direct a solely mercantile operation in Asia. It is true that some governors wanted lots of forts, and others only a few; nevertheless, they all wanted some forts for a common aim, to dominate the Indian Ocean.

Yet there were plenty of more realistic contemporaries who opposed the militarist policy. An observant early Portuguese noted simply that 'war is contrary to trade' (V. M. Godinho, *Os Descobrimentos e a Economia Mundial*, 4 vols., Lisbon, 1981–3, vol. I, p. 56). A Venetian factor on Cabral's voyage said 'If you wish to trade you do not rob competitors' ships' (Niels Steensgaard, *The Asian Trade Revolution of the Seventeenth Century*, Chicago, 1974, p. 84), while in 1532 the *vedor da fazenda*, himself a noble, said 'To trade and to fight are more opposed than the north and south poles' (Godinho, *Os Descobrimentos*, vol. I, p. 56). Indeed there was even a contemporary model to draw on: they could have obtained concessions for factories like those of foreign traders in Lisbon, or, even more to the point, like the Italians in the Muslim ports of the Mediterranean.

Assuming (and while this is debatable it appears very likely) that peaceful trade would have been possible, several advantages would have followed. The huge expense of the forts and fleets would have been saved, while the Muslims would have been undersold anyway thanks to the cost advantages of the Cape route. The Portuguese could, like other merchants, have simply sat in Calicut and bought what they needed there, instead of being forced, as a result of their own policies, to go all the way to Southeast Asia to get spices. The model of the English and the Dutch in India in the seventeenth century is instructive here, and indeed one Portuguese viceroy in the 1630s envied them, for they had no forts at all. In India the Dutch and English East India Companies traded peacefully, with armed force present only as a rarely used backup in exceptional cases. Portuguese accounts from the sixteenth century show huge expenditures on military and religious matters. Had they followed the Venetians, or the Dutch and English, nearly all of these could have been avoided.

From all that has been said above it is clear why this did not happen. Right from the start the Portuguese effort was based on compulsion and force, not peaceful competition. An incident in 1563–4, described in a manuscript copy of Couto's famous *Decadas*, and only recently discovered, illustrates the whole Portuguese attitude perfectly. They sent an embassy to Constantinople. The sultan suggested that the Turks should get free navigation in the Indian Ocean, and factories in Sind, Cambay, Dabhul, Calicut and other ports, but pay duties to the Portuguese. In return the Portuguese could have factories in Basra, Cairo and Alexandria, and could use any port in the Red Sea. This proposal was turned down flat by the Portuguese, for it aroused several basic fears and anxieties. The three pillars of the empire were the spice trade, the European trade and Indian forts and fleets, and Portuguese private trade. If this proposal were accepted, it was feared that the Turks would out-trade the Portuguese in the Indian Ocean, and thus no Portuguese would go to India. Also the Turks would smuggle spices. Finally, the real aim of the Turks, the Portuguese thought, was to conquer Portuguese India, and this treaty would help them to do so, as it would quickly enable them to find out how defenceless the Portuguese forts were, and how hated the Portuguese were in India.[4] Instead the Portuguese held on to their expensive, rickety, and relatively unsuccessful system.

In terms of general theory, how should we characterize this empire? It was an empire based on the sea, on the attempt to control sea trade, and on the use of the sea for communications, both political and mercantile. Land areas were bases only; revenue was overwhelmingly derived from maritime activities. This however was not deliberate policy. Rather, in most areas of India, the Portuguese were faced by states or societies strong enough to resist any encroachment far inland. Control of the sea meant that the Portuguese could hold on to littoral areas, but penetration further inland was too risky and difficult. The Portuguese made a virtue of this necessity and proclaimed their empire as a new type. Yet even they moved further inland when they had the chance, or when they felt it to be necessary. An example is Sri Lanka, where the Portuguese were drawn into decades of debilitating land warfare in the seventeenth century.

The contrast is clear with other European imperial activities. In South America in the sixteenth century territorial empires were being founded by the Spanish, and by the Portuguese themselves. In Asia, however, they were replaced by the Dutch and British companies. These, being only quasi-state institutions, concentrated on trade, though military force and even conquest of territory was used as a last resort. It was only from the late eighteenth century that European empires in Asia became thoroughly territorial. My predecessor E. D. Ross, reflecting British pride in their Indian empire in the 1920s, made it clear that the Portuguese had really hardly founded any sort of empire at all: there is 'little or no indication of any effort to found an empire; never at any stage did the Portuguese captains assume the offensive on shore, nor did they actually come into contact with any of the great

[4] M. Augusta Lima Cruz, 'The 8th decada of Diogo do Couto's Asia', International Seminar on Indo-Portuguese History (Goa, 1983), typescript, fos. 6–7.

fighting races of India. They depended solely on their control of the high seas.'[5]

A useful notion is to see their non-territorial empire as a network, a series of nodes or focal points connected by maritime routes. As A. B. de Bragança Pereira put it some forty-five years ago:

The Portuguese empire in the East, even at its height, was maritime rather than territorial. It spread along the coasts a network of factories, entrepots protected by forts, from Sofala to Timor and Solor. The armadas provided communications between these foci of the nervous system of the empire, which began at the Cape of Good Hope and ended in the islands of the Pacific.[6]

The net, or network, notion found fuller expression in a study by L. F. Thomaz:

The expression 'Estado da India' in the sixteenth century designates not a well-defined geographic space but an assemblage of territories, establishments, goods, people, and administrative interests, created or protected by the Portuguese crown in the Indian Ocean and the adjacent seas or in the littoral territories from the Cape of Good Hope to Japan. Thus normally empires represent a political structure in a set geographic space, while the Estado da India is essentially a net, that is, a system of communication between various spaces.[7]

Recently Philip Curtin made a somewhat similar point. He sees the Portuguese in the sixteenth century as constituting yet another example of a 'trade diaspora', different from, say, the Armenians only in that theirs was a political system as well, with each 'node' under central control.[8] Certainly we should not say it was a thalassocracy: the lengthy discussions above must at least make clear that this aim was far from achieved.

Even in the areas where some of Portugal's aims were achieved, one must recognize that this did not lead to a substantial change in existing patterns. Rather this was a redistributive empire, where the Portuguese skimmed off a layer of profits for themselves, but were not able to affect radical changes in routes, products or productive techniques at any level. In its simplest terms, the Portuguese system did nothing except

[5] E. D. Ross, 'The Portuguese in India', in *The Cambridge History of India*, vol. V (reprint, 1968), p. 17.

[6] A. B. de Bragança Pereira, *História Administrativa da India Portuguesa* (Bastorá, n.d.), p. 67.

[7] L. F. Thomaz, 'Estrutura politica e administrativa do Estado da India no seculo XVI', International Seminar on Indo-Portuguese History, *Proceedings* (Lisbon, 1985), pp. 515–16.

[8] Philip D. Curtin, *Cross-cultural Trade in World History* (Cambridge, 1984), pp. 136–48.

divert trade in some goods, and force some Asian traders to pay extra customs duties. At most they manipulated, but did not transform. It is significant that they soon loosened such control as their system had, and encouraged all and any trade to everywhere, in order to foster their skimming-off system. A more rational empire would have acted very differently, in other words commercially. Instead of the politico-military attempt to divert the spice trade, the advantages of the Cape route could have been used to win a share, or even control, by commercial means. The Portuguese made no attempt to undercut the Venetians in Europe. This is a most indicative aspect of their activities. Instead of using military control to try and block rival trade and then charging the same prices, a commercially oriented empire would have used the advantages of the Cape route to sell more cheaply in Europe, and so win by non-political means control of, or a large share in, the market. Instead the Portuguese charged as high as possible, and so ensured the continuation of the Levant route, and later the revival of the Red Sea trade.

Within Asia, Portuguese activities, especially the *cartaz* system, have also to be characterized as strictly non-commercial, rather again oriented towards profits based on naval control. What they did is sell 'protection'. A protection cost can be seen as the cost, in an economic activity, of protecting this activity from disruption by violence. The *cartaz* system enshrined this. The Portuguese threatened disruption by violence unless protection – a *cartaz* and the obligation to pay duties – was bought by the local traders. They claimed they provided protection against piracy, but as we have seen much of this was created by their own policies. In effect they created the need for protection, and sold exemption from their own threat of violence. It was, in the modern colloquial sense, precisely a protection racket.

Their saving grace was that they were not very efficient, and so we claim their system never in practice got near achieving their aims. But in what areas did their empire as we have described it represent anything new at all in India? The whole notion of a 'right' to control the activities of others at sea was new, and was based on European practice; in effect the Portuguese introduced politics into Asian maritime affairs. It was in this area of *theory*, of *aspiration*, that they were most innovative and ethnocentric. As part of this attempt to achieve control they conquered several major Asian port cities: Malacca, Diu, Hurmuz and Goa most notably. At certain times in particular places in littoral India their forces created widespread destruction. But generally the theory was much more radical than were the resulting practical changes. It has been claimed that they did concentrate or centralize some parts of Asian trade on their own ports, with a view to collecting customs duties. In the sixteenth century a true world economy began to emerge, we are told, with the whole globe linked at least a little in exchange of preciosities, especially bullion. This claim is difficult to concede. If we return to our much earlier notion of a Eurasian area linked by trade and travel in the fifteenth century, then again we are back to redistribution by the Portuguese, but not a qualitative change. There was some quantitative change also, no doubt, but its precise dimensions are very difficult to elucidate. The commodities of world trade were hardly changed in the sixteenth century. Thus as European demand for spices rose, more came in to meet this demand. Some of these spices came via the Cape. Similarly, South American bullion flowed into Asia, and certainly more bullion was traded in the sixteenth century than in the fifteenth. But the point is that trade within Eurasia continued. The new Cape route allowed the Portuguese to participate in this trade, but on a global view it made little difference to the products traded, the profits to be made, or the communities involved.

Can one then say that the Portuguese at least were harbingers of the future, that their significance lay in the way other Europeans later built on the foundations of their network, improving it and changing its character, and so producing a decisive European impact on Asia? Ironically, the first Europeans to reach Asia did not participate in the emergence of capitalism, the pregnant development beginning in Europe in the sixteenth century; at least in part this was *because* they were the first Europeans in Asia. Easy profits were wasted by lavish court and ecclesiastical groups in Portugal, who thus remained dominant. The Portuguese bourgeoisie never developed, though some Italian and German bankers were helped in their capitalistic development by their share of Portuguese profits. The change in fact occurred in northern Italy, and later Northwest Europe, not in Iberia. Portugal did not share in these changes leading to industrial capitalism, though her activities in Asia provided a little of the fuel for them. Yet it was these changes which made inevitable western European hegemony in India and Asia. In this momentous matter the fact that the Portuguese were there first was of no relevance; hegemony would have been achieved anyway, and the Third World created. To find the beginnings of this process in Asia one needs to look not to Vasco da Gama, but to the Dutch and British East India Companies a century later. If there are straight lines in history, then this is when one began to be traced, one leading to European domination and Asian impoverishment.

CHAPTER 4

INDO-PORTUGUESE SOCIETY

We can now leave this long discussion of the Portuguese 'official' presence and system, and look at areas of social interaction in India. We will present a case study of the Portuguese capital of Goa, and discuss religion separately. The best way to enter this area, however, is to look at Portuguese private trade, for in many ways this exemplified Portugal's unofficial activities in India. In a nutshell, we find interaction, not domination, with the Portuguese contributing something, as also did locals, towards the rich mélange of coastal Asian trade.

It will be remembered that one feature of the official system was the attempt to dominate particular Asian routes. Sometimes these rights were used by agents of the king, but more often they made up part of the package by which the captain of a fort, or holder of some other official position, was paid. In either case, these rights were often sold by the holder. This part of the official system was particularly loose. Trade between the two ports concerned was usually not restricted only to the holder of the official voyage. The advantage of shipping with an official ship was in part greater security, and also some concessions on customs payments. Thus while they made up a very important part of Portuguese official trade – we have noted these Asian concessional voyages produced four times more profits than did the Cape route – in terms of total trade directed by the Portuguese, let alone total Asian trade, they were relatively minor. Indeed they should be seen as similar to the totally private trade.

Trade was important to all the Portuguese living in Asia. There were four occupational groups: officials, including military and naval commanders; soldiers, normally unmarried young men; *casados* or settled, married men; clerics. All four of these engaged in trade on their own account, either directly or through an agent, though naturally the *casados* were most prominent. We quoted Couto earlier complaining that this private trade increased over the sixteenth century, and weakened the Portuguese military presence in Asia. Other writers made similar complaints, and said that this sort of corruption, or at the least lack of attention to official duties, weakened the whole state.

81

But in fact, while there may have been some increase, as the empire became more Asian and more informal over the course of the sixteenth century, there are records from very early days of Portuguese at all levels trading enthusiastically. Albuquerque noted complacently as early as 1513 that 'your people travel securely all over India, by land and sea. In Cambay no one asks them where they are going, and in Aquem and all Malabar they buy and sell, and go about as securely as at home' (*Cartas de Afonso de Albuquerque*, vol. I, pp. 138–9). Ten years later another letter to the king claimed wood for ship building was scarce in Cochin, as it was all being bought by local Portuguese, who intended to settle and die in India, and live by trade. Already they were trading all over Asia: to Malacca, Pegu, Pacem, Bengal, Coromandel, Banda, Timor, Hurmuz, Chaul and Cambay.

We have noted already private involvement on the *carreira* to Portugal at different times, and by different people, not all of them Portuguese. Some idea of the interlocking of private and official strands on this route can be gained from an incident of 1554. The viceroy, D. Afonso de Noronha, was returning to Portugal, and needed another ship to take him and also cargo. He made a contract with Antão Martins, a *casado* in Goa, who 'had in that port a very beautiful *náo* called São Paulo, which he had built in the Ancola River [in Kanara, south of Goa]. Because it was big, new, and very well equipped, the viceroy chose to travel in it' (Couto, *Da Asia*, VII, i, 6), though Martins decided who was to be the captain.

Within Asia the networks in which the Portuguese shared trade with a mass of others were incredibly complex. The great Dutch governor J. P. Coen described it well in 1619:

Piece goods from Gujarat we can barter for pepper and gold on the coast of Sumatra, rials and cottons from the coast [of Coromandel] for pepper in Bantam, sandalwood, pepper and rials we can barter for Chinese goods and Chinese gold; we can extract silver from Japan with Chinese goods, piece goods from the Coromandel coast in exchange for spices, other goods and gold from China, piece goods from Surat for spices, other goods and rials, rials from Arabia for spices and various other trifles – one thing leads to another. And all of it can be done without any money from the Netherlands and with ships alone.[1]

An area favoured by private Portuguese traders for their operations

---

[1] Quoted in Niels Steensgaard, *The Asian Trade Revolution of the Seventeenth Century: The East India Companies and the Decline of the Caravan Trade* (Chicago, 1974), p. 407.

was Gujarat, especially the town of Cambay, trade to which had started by at least 1509. This trade in fact flourished despite opposition to it from both church and political authorities, the former because Portuguese there would have no opportunity to take the sacraments, the latter because they could serve as hostages in the event of war between Gujarat and the Portuguese. When Akbar arrived in Cambay in 1572 he found 50 or 60 Portuguese in residence, although most of those normally resident had fled to avoid the war. In 1594 there were about 100 Portuguese families in Cambay. Many men apparently settled there permanently and married local women, for a Jesuit who baptized 180 people in Bassein in 1573 noted that among them 'were many Eurasian women and boys, children of Portuguese in Cambay' (J. Wicki, ed., *Documenta Indica*, 12 vols., Rome, 1948–, vol. IX, p. 289). These Portuguese were mainly engaged in buying Gujarati goods to be sent to Goa on the *cafilas*, and from there distributed all over Asia, and to Lisbon. Some, no doubt, were agents of big Portuguese merchants in Goa.

Within India, two other areas were also favoured for private Portuguese trade: Malabar and Coromandel. In the former, there was a problem in that the main trade item of the region, pepper, was meant to be a royal monopoly. At times this was ignored, as we have noted, but it does seem that the Portuguese here acted more as redistributors, dealing in goods brought from outside rather than from Malabar itself. Many of these goods came from Coromandel and the Bay of Bengal area; this area was a prime region for private trade.

The official presence in the Bay of Bengal was very limited in comparison with the Arabian Sea, and especially western India. The only major base was Malacca, and even this was hardly effective: we have noted Gujaratis trading in spices in the Bay, and later the rise of Acheh.

There were some attempts to establish other official presences in the area. Viceroy Almeida sent out a preliminary expedition to Coromandel as early as 1507, the purpose being to investigate the general situation, especially relating to trade, and to look for the tomb of St Thomas the Apostle. There were later investigations of the possibility of establishing an official presence, complete with forts and fleets, in Bengal; these came to nothing. By 1517 at least the purported tomb of St Thomas had been found in Meliapur, from 1545 renamed São Thomé and today a suburb of Madras. This port and Negapatam were the two main Portuguese settlements in Coromandel. Both had captains, but while in theory these were appointed by the king, in practice they emerged from the local Portuguese inhabitants and then were recognized by the king. They sometimes were 'appointed' for life, and received no salaries. At times there were no captains at all.

This then was a very different Portuguese presence, one totally dominated by private trade and the church, more comparable with, say, the group of Gujarati merchants in Calicut before da Gama than with the official sixteenth-century Portuguese position in western India. In 1538 the captain of São Thomé was able to collect as many as 400 Portuguese (presumably including *mestiços*) for an expedition. At this time there were 50 *casados* in São Thomé, mostly traders and some who wanted to spend their retirement near the tomb of St Thomas. By 1545 there were over 100 *casados* there.

In Bengal similarly trade and religion was mingled. Private traders had begun to call early in the century, at Chittagong and Satgaon. From around 1580 their main centre was Hughli, which grew into a substantial town with a population of 5000 by 1603. Religious services were provided by members of various orders who chose to live in this area, and from a large Augustinian monastery at Bandel, founded late in the sixteenth century up river from Hughli. There was also a substantial Portuguese presence further east, in Chittagong and Arakan – 2500 including their descendants in 1598.

The absence of an 'official' presence in this area was far from a disadvantage for these private traders: quite the reverse. All of them traded extensively all over the Bay of Bengal area. Around the end of the century they seem to have acquired a quite substantial position in this local country trade, and if this is so then it seems to confirm our earlier argument that the Portuguese generally would have done better from peaceful trade than from their attempts at monopoly. In any case, and regardless of what share they held, these private traders should not be seen as a united or distinctive group. True, their language was new, and was quite widely used in littoral Asia. But economically they made up just one more strand in the rich texture of country trade in the area, in no way different commercially or politically from all the other people there. The lack of differentiation was increased by the fact that their wives, or concubines, were invariably local women. Thus after a few generations there was not even any 'racial' difference.

This description applies to Portuguese in many other Asian littoral areas. They spread all over Southeast Asia. We read of four ships with a total of sixty-three Portuguese on board trading to Siam in the 1520s. In the Hadramaut, at the other end of the Indian Ocean, again we find an active trade in the 1520s: in 1538, 40 Portuguese were present at Dofar.

For the private trader there were two main differences between areas remote from, and areas controlled by, the official system. The first difference is that in the former anything was legitimate, while in the latter one sometimes suffered from official attempts to make one submit to such annoyances as no trade in pepper, or taking a *cartaz*. Like other traders in these areas, such impositions could either be tolerated, or sometimes evaded. A scandalized account of 1623 reflects well the situation. It claimed that each year along the coast from Goa to Daman more than thirty-five oared ships, with a substantial twenty-four oars each, left to trade in the Persian Gulf. Prominent in their cargoes was pepper, which presumably had been obtained from Malabar or Kanara. Worse yet, many of these traders, who were Portuguese and *mestiços*, were soldiers who had taken their muster pay at the start of the campaigning season in September, and then run off through the palm trees and so to Bijapur to get back to a trade financed in part by this stolen money.

The second difference between these two sorts of areas is that in the areas more or less controlled by the Portuguese, one found much more trade by officials. In theory most of this was illegal, nor were they allowed to use Indian agents to trade on their behalf. But this prohibition was almost totally ignored. We noted that many officials abused their positions, indulging in extortion, forced trade, and other peculation. But they, most others, and indeed many clerics, also invested in the country trade. As one example, in Malacca in 1527 a 'society' or partnership was formed between a leading *keling* (Tamil-speaking Hindu) merchant, and two Portuguese, one of them being the captain of Malacca. The venture involved sending ships to Kedah and Perak to buy tin. The only thing distinctive about an official doing this, as compared with a *casado*, was that the official could sometimes use his position to secure an advantage. An example is the gold and ivory trade of the Zambesi valley, which developed after the 1530s and was channelled through the customs house at Mozambique. Both private traders and officials shared enthusiastically in this trade.

Some Portuguese operating outside the official system were not just traders: like some Malabaris, on occasion they became freebooters.

There are various complaints of this in the Arabian Sea area throughout the sixteenth century, and for that matter of renegades serving in Indian Muslim armies, but the main field of operations was the more open Bay of Bengal, where no state claimed to protect traders. Here Portuguese piracy was endemic, and merged in turn into the colourful activities of Portuguese freebooters involved in Burmese and Thai local politics. These men, said a censorious Dutchman, 'live in a manner like wild men, and untamed horses . . . neyther esteeme they any thing of justice, whether there be any or none . . . and are for the most part such as dare not stay in India for some wickednesse by them committed' (J. H. van Linschoten, *The Voyage of J. H. van Linschoten to the East Indies*, 2 vols., London, 1885, vol. 1, p. 95). Sometimes they met their just deserts. In 1632 the Mughal emperor Shah Jahan, fed up with the lawless behaviour and independence of Hughli's inhabitants, launched a massive attack in which the city was taken and pillaged. (This episode is much played up in Portuguese records, but receives only cursory notice in Indian sources. From the Mughal angle, the incident no doubt was simply another routine law and order breakdown which was soon rectified.) In 1607 the king of Arakan killed 600 Portuguese, as he was afraid of their growing power and lawlessness. Yet the participation of freebooters continued: as late as 1786 the Arakan army included 500 'Portuguese' mercenaries (J. J. A. Campos, *History of the Portuguese in Bengal*, Patna, 1979, p. 168). The lives of these freebooters/traders/mercenaries (the distinction is often not clear) are well described in Fernão Mendes Pinto's famous, and at times fanciful, memoirs. We can even sketch what appears to be a typical career: Diogo Soares de Mello, a *fidalgo*, had been involved in several homicides in Galicia, and was banished to India. In 1540 his patron and another *fidalgo* quarrelled over an unmarried woman. Soares's leader killed his rival and was executed by the governor. But Soares was able to flee Goa, and set up as a pirate with twenty men off Melinde, in East Africa. In 1542 he was pardoned by a new governor, but we next hear of him as leader, from 1548 to 1553, of the Portuguese mercenaries fighting for Burma against Siam. Finally he was executed by the Burmese.

Several general points can be made about these private traders. There is first the matter of their effect on the Portuguese state. This was generally deleterious, notably such extreme actions as Portuguese officials trading with enemies of the state and breaking the trade regulations they, as officials, were meant to be upholding. Their activities also produced an unacceptable drain on Portuguese man-power. A critic in the 1590s noted that there were about 1500 men available for service in Goa, but about 2000 others had left Goa for the Bay of Bengal alone.

But can such people be seen as potential agents of Portuguese interest even after they left Portuguese areas, or did they become totally 'submerged'? Some link with the Portuguese language and religion was usually preserved, but apart from these it seems there was little retained: not surprising in a period before nationality was an important categorizing principle. Their position was best described by the VOC (the Dutch East India Company) governor Anthony van Dieman, who in 1642 wrote 'Most of the Portuguese in India look upon this region as their fatherland, and think no more about Portugal. They drive little or no trade thither, but content themselves with the port-to-port trade of Asia, just as if they were natives thereof and had no other country' (quoted in Boxer, *The Portuguese Seaborne Empire*, p. 120).

This raises two final points. First, this lack of differentiation sets off these Portuguese from later Dutch and English private traders, and Indians trading under their protection. Steensgaard[2] points out that such people had a distinct advantage over either the companies themselves or the traditional traders, including the Portuguese private traders, for such privileged traders from the seventeenth century retained the flexibility characteristic of an individual trader, yet also shared in the structural advantages of trading within the company system. The point is well made, and should remind us that we must not over-emphasize the share of traditional trade held by private Portuguese. When compared with official Portuguese trade it was no doubt substantial, though totally unquantifiable. But, in the total Asian context, in most areas it was minor. Even in the Bay of Bengal claims of private Portuguese dominance, even control, seem to be wild exaggerations. More typical was the private Portuguese share in trade on the *cafilas* between Cambay and Goa. This was a major area of Portuguese economic activity. A large part of the cargoes was owned by Portuguese trading on their own account, yet this particular route made up only 5 percent of Gujarat's total trade.

Goa was the main Portuguese town in India from its conquest in 1510,

[2] Niels Steensgaard, 'Asian trade 15th–18th centuries: continuities and discontinuities', *Acts, ICHS* (Bucharest, 1980), 499.

and the official capital from 1530 until 1961. It can be seen as an exemplar of the whole Portuguese presence. A detailed social analysis of the city will let us see the Portuguese empire in operation, and will build on our analysis of private Portuguese trade to demonstrate more clearly the basic theme of this book: a variable Portuguese influence according to time, place and category.

One of the most distinguished of all Goans, D. D. Kosambi, has left us a fine description of his homeland, which will serve to set the scene:

The land itself is one of the most beautiful sights of the world. A heavy rainfall of over 110 inches annual average, compressed mainly into the monsoon months of June to September, covers the earth with dense vegetation whose vivid green contrasts wonderfully well with the red of the laterite soil, and the silvery ribbons of the estuaries. The mountains of the Western Ghats taper off into hills that roll right down to the sea. The inhabitants, however, are much less happy than the idyllic scene would indicate.[3]

We know little enough about this area before the Portuguese. Ironically, it seems that Goa in the decades *before* the Portuguese conquest of 1510 was subject to more stress and change than at any time later in the century. We should first note changes in political control. Goa had been part of the Hindu empire of Vijayanagar until the area's conquest by the Muslim Bahmani sultanate in 1472. In the decade before 1500, as this sultanate fragmented, Goa was included in one of the five successor states, Bijapur. It was conquered by the Portuguese in 1510. Thus in the space of less than forty years Goa was part of four different states. The imposition of a Muslim ruling group in the 1470s must have caused major dislocation, especially as many of these Muslims were foreigners. As a concrete example, after the Bahmani conquest the rate of land-revenue demand by the state was doubled. This was of course a cataclysmic change in an agrarian society. There appear to have been other changes in the all important land-revenue system during the brief period of Muslim rule. According to Baden-Powell,[4] the Hindu system was *ryotwari*, with the state taking a proportion of the actual production of every cultivating family. Under the Muslims, and especially during the decade or so of rule by Bijapur before the Portuguese conquest, a major change occurred. Land revenue became payable in cash, and most import the unit of assessment was

---

[3] D. D. Kosambi, 'The village communities in the Old Conquests of Goa', *Journal of the University of Bombay*, XV (1947), p. 63.
[4] B. H. Baden-Powell, 'The villages of Goa in the early sixteenth century', *Journal of the Royal Asiatic Society* (1900), pp. 261–91.

made not the family but the village as a whole. This increased dramatically the power of the village leaders and land controllers, known as *gaunkars*. It also seems that the method of assessment was changed under Bijapur. Finally, there is evidence that some of the Turkish auxiliaries of the sultan of Bijapur were allowed to seize lands from their Hindu customary holders. It is not an overstatement to say that the imposition of Portuguese rule ushered in an era of stability, a 'Pax Portuguesa', after the shocks and upheavals of the previous forty years.

Why did the Portuguese want to conquer Goa? Generally Goa was well located to control the crucial northwest sector of the Arabian Sea. The port was situated almost midway between the key economic areas of Malabar and Gujarat; fleets from Goa could attempt to control the trade of them both. The area taken by Albuquerque in 1510 (and until 1543 the only area controlled by the Portuguese), consisted of islands, in area 166 square kilometres, called simply Ilhas. The Mandovi River marked the northern, and the Zuari river the southern, coast of the main island of Tissuari, though several smaller islands were also included in the territory of Ilhas. Access to the mainland was available by crossings or fords over the interior creek and the two rivers. This meant that Ilhas alone was strategically vulnerable. For the first half of the passage up the Mandovi from the bar to Old Goa, Portuguese ships were faced with hostile Muslim territory on the northern bank of the river. Similarly with the equally vital Zuari River to the south: its whole southern bank was controlled by Bijapur. Hence, after several foiled attempts, in 1543 the Portuguese acquired two buffer *talukas*, Bardes to the north and Salcette to the south, respectively 264 and 355 square kilometres.

At least by the low standards of the Indian west coast, Goa was a good port. In fact there were two, in the two estuaries of the rivers which surround the island. The harbour in the Zuari estuary was deeper and slightly more sheltered from the southwest monsoon than was the Mandovi; the latter was effectively closed, then and now, between at least June and September by the monsoon.

Goa was protected further inland by the western Ghats, but was not completely cut off. There were a series of breaches in the mountains behind Goa; passes there were under 600 metres, while to the north they were over 900 metres, and to the south over 1800 metres in places. The effective coastal plain stretched inland from 50 to 70 kilometres. Access beyond this became difficult, despite the comparative lowness of the Ghats here.

The existence of these passes contributed to Goa's inland trade in the fifteenth century, but the Portuguese thought they were a disadvantage. They needed the coastal plain for food, but impenetrable mountains behind them would have suited very well. Trade with Bijapur was not essential, but protection from it was.

If Goa were to be a base, it needed adequate supplies of food and water both for its inhabitants and for visiting fleets. Over this matter, as over the importance of Goan trade in the fifteenth century, there is a pronounced difference of opinion between Portuguese writers and foreigners. The Portuguese wax lyrical over the fields and orchards of Goa, its succulent fruit, pure water, and leafy bowers. But Ilhas was sourly described by a Dutchman as being 'most hillie, barren and wild, and full of waste ground' (Linschoten, vol. I, pp. 182–3). Nor did Ilhas have enough good drinking water. In any case, no matter whom one believes, Goa had to import large quantities of food in the sixteenth century.

Goa's function as a port city did change considerably in the sixteenth century. The fifteenth-century accounts tend to expatiate on the great ports of Gujarat, and then pass on quickly to Malabar. The difficulty involved in estimating Goa's importance before the Portuguese conquest lies in the way in which the earliest Portuguese authors make extravagant claims for fifteenth-century Goa. According to them Goa was the main port for both the Bahmani kingdom and for Vijayanagar. It imported spices from Malabar, horses from Arabia, and a host of other products: 'great trains of oxen loaded with merchandise used to come into Goa from very distant kingdoms in the interior' (Pires, *The Suma Oriental*, vol. I, p. 57). These claims are apparently influenced by a desire to puff up the importance of the Portuguese conquest of the city. The true position seems to be that none of the Konkan ports in the fifteenth century were very important. The three biggest were Dabhol, Chaul and Goa; given deficient statistics, it is pointless to try and rank them.

Goa under the Portuguese was always more than itself, more than simply a port city. It was the focus of their entire seaborne empire; its prosperity in the sixteenth century, and its seventeenth-century decline, mark fluctuations in Portuguese fortunes in all Asia rather than any change in Goa and its hinterland.

The clearest indication we have to show which way Goa was focussed in the sixteenth century comes from figures for customs duties collected on inland and sea trade. From these we can work out rough estimates of the ratio of the value of sea trade to land trade. This ratio goes from about 15 : 1 toward the end of the sixteenth century to 12 : 1 early in the seventeenth, and to 6 : 1 in 1616. The relative imbalance is large throughout, and is simply huge in the sixteenth century, the period with which we are most concerned. What the figures also show is a fall in sea trade, and a rise in land trade. This is to be explained by Dutch and English competition from the early seventeenth century.

A further indication of Goa's outward focus is seen in the way the Portuguese were even prepared to watch with equanimity while Goa's production of food, and trade with the interior, declined. Easy pickings from the trade control system made these things seem to be irrelevant. The much praised lushness of the lands of the Old Conquests should have meant that Goa would be able to feed itself, at least after the acquisition of Bardes and Salcette in 1543. Yet increasingly Goa was dependent on food imports.

There were infrequent complaints about this situation, but by and large the Portuguese were prepared to live with it. The seas were relatively secure for Portuguese convoys in the sixteenth century, and profits from other sources meant Goa could afford to import food. In any case, the Portuguese had not come to India to be farmers. In the palmy days of the sixteenth century large areas of what good land there was in Ilhas were apparently used for pleasure gardens and most Portuguese preferred to live by trade, not from agriculture.

A similar outward focus can be seen more generally in the virtual end of trade inland with Bijapur, and instead a strong emphasis on policies designed to direct sea trade to Goa. As we noted, Goa's importance as an entrepot in the fifteenth century is difficult to assess. However, it is clear that it was a true entrepot, channelling exports from the Bahmani kingdom and Vijayanagar, and importing goods for these interior markets.

Under the Portuguese this changed. Immediately after the conquest Albuquerque sent out sea patrols to force ships into Goa, especially those carrying horses. His aim was to use the horses as a bait to tempt the trade caravans to come again from Bijapur and Vijayanagar. This attempt failed, partly because of Bijapuri hostility, but more because the Portuguese soon found that they did not need inland trade, the only exception being the horse trade. Later sixteenth-century accounts describe Goa's 'livings and daylie traffiques' to Bengal, Siam, Malacca, Cambay, China and every way 'both North and South' but not east to Bijapur (Linschoten, vol. I, p. 184). Only food seems to have come from there. Even the local Kanarese and Deccani shopkeepers in Goa sold goods from Gujarat, China, and Bengal, but not from the interior. Early in the seventeenth century, Linschoten put the products of Bijapur in their place when he listed Goa's imports from the mainland as wheat, meat, horse food, and 'much more important than all this, rowers for the oared boats' (Ibid., pp. 256–7). The Portuguese were always scornful of Bijapuri products, preferring to buy cotton cloths, the main trade item, from Gujarat.

What sort of city was this? The 'Golden Goa' image dies hard. A recent author rhapsodizes:

Rich on trade and loot, Goa in the halcyon days of the sixteenth century was a handsome city of great houses and fine churches ... In the eyes of stern moralists the city was another Babylon, but to men of the world it was a paradise where, with beautiful Eurasian girls readily available, life was a ceaseless round of amorous assignments and sexual delights.[5]

Contemporary Portuguese thought the same: 'In terms of size of population and sumptuousness of buildings this city of Goa is one of the greatest and biggest in India' (F. P. Mendes da Luz, ed., 'Livro das cidades, e fortalezas, que a Coroa de Portugal tem nas partes da India', in Studia, no. 6, 1960, f. 6).

We need to try and work out in comparative terms just how big and wealthy it really was, in the context of its sixteenth-century Indian setting. We have no figures for pre-Portuguese Goa's population, not even an estimate, though it does seem that Muslim harshness had made some Hindus flee. Our data for the rest of the sixteenth century are only slightly better. It is clear that the city did grow much larger during the century, a result in part of a claimed 2000 Portuguese leaving home each year for India, mostly for Goa. In 1524 there were 450 Portuguese householders in Goa city, and in 1540 about 1800. The former figure refers to 'pure' Portuguese, while the latter includes descendants of Portuguese and local women, in other words mestiços. There were also 3600 soldiers in the town in 1540. Later in the 1540s, at the time of St Francis Xavier, the city population included 10,000 Indian Christians,

[5] G. V. Scammell, The World Encompassed: The First European Maritime Empires, c. 800–1650 (London, 1981), p. 243.

3–4000 Portuguese, and many non-Christians, while outside the city the rest of Ilhas contained 50,000 inhabitants, 80 percent of them Hindu. Recent estimates put the city population at 60,000 in the 1580s, and about 75,000 at 1600, the latter figure including 1500 Portuguese and *mestiços*, 20,000 Hindus, and the rest local Christians, Africans, and others. In the 1630s the total population of the Old Conquests – Ilhas, Bardes and Salcette – was perhaps a little more than a quarter of a million.

These figures point to two things: that the Hindu population remained large throughout the sixteenth century, a point we will return to in the next chapter, and that Goa was, in Indian (but not European) terms, a medium-sized city. The three largest cities in India around 1600 were Delhi, Agra and Lahore; each had about half a million inhabitants, and several others had several hundred thousand. European cities were much smaller: around 1600 Naples had 200,000 people, Rome 110,000, London 170,000, Madrid only 60,000, and Lisbon, in 1629, had 110,000.

We noted high mortality in sixteenth-century Portugal. It appears that rates were at least as high in Portuguese India. Casualties in the endless skirmishes with Malabaris and others were often substantial. Cholera and malaria also took their toll; one estimate claims that from 1604 to 1634, 25,000 soldiers died in the Royal Hospital in Goa. Of these, according to another and perhaps fanciful account, at least 500 a year died of syphilis, and the 'effects of profligacy'. Be this as it may, mortality was certainly high; a proverb had it 'Of the hundred who go to India not even one returns.' Again an exaggeration no doubt, yet many failed even to reach India. We have a list for the years 1629 to 1634 (signed by that great compiler Pedro Barreto de Rezende) which gives a total of 5228 men leaving Portugal for India in these years. Only 2495 reached Goa. Not that disease was the only reason: some no doubt deserted in Lisbon, and 2 of the 17 ships involved were lost.

We earlier used royal mortality as a rough indicator of death rates in sixteenth-century Portugal. Gubernatorial deaths can play a similar role for Portuguese India, always remembering that these were men who had survived infancy. Of 50 governors, up to 1656, 22 died during their term of office, or while on the way home after it, and another died with D. Sebastian at El-Ksar el-Kebir. Fourteen of the fifty died in India, and one in Malacca. It may be added that, again as in Portugal, social services were rudimentary. The Royal Hospital did the best it could, and was often held up as a model by visitors, despite its appalling mortality rate. Similarly, the Misericordia provided various charitable services.

Was Goa, however, a particularly distinctive or wealthy city? Physically it seems to have been of the same type as any other Indian (or medieval European) city, with bazaars, quarters, a fort and a wall, and (with one exception, the 1500-paces-long Rua Direita) narrow winding streets. Massive buildings devoted to the religion of the rulers dominated all else, just as did *jama masjids* in the Mughal empire and temples in south India. One should recall, however, that most of the colossal edifices that we see in Old Goa today date from the seventeenth century.

In many areas Goa continued to look remarkably like any other Indian city. Thus the Portuguese set aside fixed areas for various categories in the population – Muslims, foreign Hindus, prostitutes – and similarly various occupational groups lived contiguously. Such an arrangement was of course familiar to the Portuguese from European practice, and similarly to Indians, whose cities were also divided into quarters or occupationally-determined localities. In legal matters, the Portuguese were concerned at the propensity to litigation of the local population, and appointed special judges to try minor cases quickly, without recourse to the full panoply of Portuguese law. This however applied only to the Christian minority: Hindus were left with their customary dispute-settling mechanisms. The elite in Goa lived in a very similar style to that of any other elite in India at the time, dressing ostentatiously in public, shielding themselves with umbrellas, accompanied by vast retinues of slaves and servants. Religious processions and festivals were prominent and popular public events, whether for St Catharine's Day, or in other parts of India for Mohurram or Holi. Even in the religious buildings one finds much interaction. Church paintings were often done by Hindus, as were other craft activities and later St Francis Xavier's tomb. The first thirteen of the famous portraits of the viceroys, to be seen today in the Archeological Museum in Old Goa, were drawn by Gaspar Correa but actually painted by a Hindu.

Portuguese male society in Goa was heavily stratified. (In fact the term 'Portuguese' is not quite exact, for there were other Europeans there too, some of whom had come overland. They included Italians, Germans, French, English and Flemings.) This colonial society was divided according to three different, though overlapping, criteria: purity of blood, rank and marital status.

The first criterion was the familiar Iberian gradation, starting with those born in Portugal (*reinoes*) and descending through those born in Asia of Portuguese parents (*castiços* or *Indiaticos*) to those born in Asia of Portuguese and Indian, or Portuguese and African, parentage (respectively *mestiços* and mulattoes). Outside this ranking, and beneath it, were the native Christians, but even the *castiços* and the *mestiços* were regarded with considerable suspicion by the elite. One reads of Nicolao d'Abreu de Mello, 'who, although born here, is the son of Portuguese parents and a well-conducted person' (Arquivo Nacional da Torre do Tombo, 'Documentos remetidos da India', vol. XXIV, f. 34). The received view on *castiços* was that they were 'usually ill-behaved and not to be trusted' (*Ibid.*, vol. XXII, f. 97). *Mestiços* were even more suspect. Late in the 1540s an experienced official told the king that seven new men had recently been hired for clerical positions in a government office: 'Of the seven, four are mesticos, something which absolutely astonished me' (Arquivo Nacional da Torre do Tombo, 'Corpo Chronologico', 1–83–30). In 1634 the viceroy told the king that Portuguese men were needed in Diu, 'because most of the soldiers there are almost niggers' (Arquivo Nacional da Torre do Tombo, 'Documentos remetidos', vol. XXXI, p. 249).

The second criterion is equally familiar – the division of the Portuguese population into the three estates of ecclesiastics, nobility, and people. This division seems to have been most visible on ritual occasions, such as when the oath of allegiance to a new king was being taken. On feast days in Goa anyone who could claim any sort of 'nobility', 300 or even 400 of them, rode to church on horseback.

The third criterion was the simple division between unmarried men from Portugal, who as *soldados* (soldiers) were liable for military service, and those Portuguese or part-Portuguese who had married and settled in Asia, the *casados*. The Portuguese affected by this division were primarily the third estate, the people. It obviously did not apply to the first estate, while the 'nobility', whether married or not, were usually liable and indeed eager to engage in military service until incapacitated by illness or old age.

Below these divisions were local Christians, who shaded 'up' into the *mestiço* group, then unconverted Indians, mostly Hindus, and right at the bottom slaves. We noted earlier the huge slave population of sixteenth-century Portugal: the same applied in Goa, where indeed the numbers seem to have been higher than in Lisbon even. A rich woman could have over 300 slaves, an unmarried artisan about 20. The 100 nuns of the Convent of Santa Monica complained that their 120 slaves were not nearly enough. Various hair-raising accounts make clear how violently they could be treated at times, even favoured black concubines. Their degradation was most apparent at the auctions. Here two products brought the highest prices, horses and slaves. Female slaves were paraded almost naked in the ring, and fetched higher prices if they could sew, sing, dance, or prove to a specialist that they were still virgin. Even so, the dearest woman would sell for up to 30 cruzados; a fine Arabian or Persian horse could fetch over 500.

The divisions in Portuguese society were not completely watertight. In practice a *mestiço* could be a *de facto* noble, and a *casado* could be a soldier, especially in an emergency. A dispute in 1563 showed clearly both tension between different status groups, and also how these were not closed or hereditary. After an incident, a haughty noble struck a *casado*. The governor had the noble arrested. After his release, he was challenged to a duel by the leader of the *casados*, Luis da Francisco Barreto. The latter was killed, but the noble was pardoned as he had offered to apologize. The interesting point is that Barreto was the son of a previous governor, Francisco Barreto (1555–8). One clue to this change, really a drop, in status could be that the father had spent twelve years (1547–59) in Asia. It is possible then that his son was a *mestiço* or perhaps a *castiço*, and even if he was not, this could be seen as a family which had, by reason of long residence, become more oriented to India than to Portugal.

Another family also illustrates this sort of mobility. Manuel de Moraes Supico migrated to Goa at an early age, did well in trade, and as a result before his death in 1630 served on the Câmara, or municipal council, and as president of the Misericordia. Despite his humble origins, wealth became acceptance. His daughter married a governor, and his son a daughter of a *vedor da fazenda* in Goa who later became an ambassador to Sweden. In the next generation a granddaughter married a son of a viceroy.

Within the third estate, two groups with different interests and life-styles need to be distinguished. The settled, married, commercially-minded *casados* were very different from the soldiers, despite the fact that the former were recruited from the ranks of the latter.

The size of the Portuguese soldier population in any fort depended on the season. It was greatest during the period of the southwest monsoon, from June to September, for during this time the strong off-shore winds precluded any patrolling along the western Indian coastline. Up to 500 footloose and idle soldiers could be resident in Goa in this rainy season. During the rest of the year, while the many fleets of small warships were out opposing 'piracy' and checking native ships for 'contraband cargoes', the soldier population of Goa fell to a few hundred. This, however, changed toward the end of the year when the annual fleet from Portugal reached Goa with its supplies of new recruits. These men remained in Goa, independent and subject to no discipline, until they were recruited by a captain, whom they would then follow to his assignment.

During the rainy season of June to September the soldiers usually lived in groups of about ten to a lodging. Their lack of money and occupation soon caused a restlessness which often led to violence. It was 'somewhat dangerous' to walk about Goa after nine at night. We read of sundry knifings, assaults, even murders and pitched battles, in Goa during the rains.

Even when these soldiers had been recruited and were off serving under some captain, strict military discipline was not always in evidence. At times the soldiers were prepared to revolt if they felt that their interests or rights had been violated. A mutiny at sea in 1583 provides an example. After a long battle between twenty small Portuguese warships and a large hostile trader, the enemy capitulated in return for a guarantee of the lives of those on board. But a surrender was not good news for the Portuguese soldiers and sailors; they preferred to board, waving their swords and shouting 'Santiago!' In the resulting confusion all sorts of trifles such as gold and jewels could be picked up, and later disposed of in Goa to a discreet Indian merchant. Thwarted of their sack, the Portuguese mutinied, shouted abuse at their captain, raised the black flag, and took over 14 of the ships. Upon reaching the Portuguese town of Daman, the nearly 300 mutineers terrorized the town officials and the *casados*. Subsequently the 6 loyal ships arrived, and the mutineers attacked them and tried to kill their unsporting captain. A confused battle followed, which even a group of priests, with crucifixes upheld, were unable to stop. The captain fled to the sanctuary of a church. After negotiations, all the rebels were given a share of the prize money, and the mutiny ended (Couto, *Da Asia*, x, iii, 4).

In this instance the soldiers acted independently of, indeed in opposition to, their leaders. Such cases may point to class divisions in

Portuguese colonial society, and indeed divisions of status at least were clearly recognized. Thus a report on the Portuguese defence of their fort at Hurmuz in 1622 listed by name twelve dead – eleven *fidalgos* and a priest – and added 'And many other ordinary people were killed fighting bravely' (Arquivo Nacional da Torre do Tombo, 'Documentos remetidos', vol. XIX, pp. 67–8). Similarly, at an inquiry into a scandal of 1601 a sailor testified that he 'didn't want to know anything about it because big people did it' (*As Gavetas da Torre do Tombo*, vol. VI, p. 395). Nevertheless, a much more frequent pattern was violence by a group of soldiers directed by a *fidalgo*. These crowds were recruited by patronage ties, in a way very similar to what we noted above operating within the nobility.

A lone soldier, newly arrived in Goa or temporarily resident in a west coast port during the rains, had little choice but to live on a *fidalgo's* charity. He usually received no pay at such times, and had no trade or skill. In any case, until he married he could hardly establish himself with a trade or a house, for he was very much of a sojourner. He had no choice but to eat, and even live, with a noble, or to accept charity from the church. In 1548 3 or 5 *fidalgos* gave money to the soldiers in Goa, and the governor fed nearly 800 of them twice a day. In 1609 the French traveller Jean Mocquet was encouraged to emulate all the poor Portuguese soldiers and eat at a noble's table. He speaks of the lords and gentlemen of Goa feeding 20 or 30 each. Indeed, there is even one reference to an important noble having his followers grouped in and around his own house. Behind the Rua Direita 'was another street of the houses of Heitor da Silveira' (Correa, *Lendas da India*, vol. III, p. 162). He presumably lived there, surrounded by men housed and fed by him; in essence, his private army controlled this area.

Such soldiers would be expected to form part of a *fidalgo's* entourage as he rode about the streets and when he went to church on feast days. If he was insulted, or wanted revenge for some other reason, his diners became his private army. More important, and also more legitimate, the main object of this system was its use as a recruitment device for captains newly appointed to command a ship or a fort.

The soldiers were not under the continuing authority of any captain during the rains; every September they were free agents available to whichever captain offered most or had in the past treated them best. The captains received pay for the number of troops sanctioned for their command, 'which done the Captaines bidde their soldiers to a banket, and of their own purses give them something besides their pay, for that every Captaine seeketh to have the best soldiers and buy much victuailes and other thinges at their owne charges, thereby to have their soldiers good willes, and to use them well' (Linschoten, vol. I, p. 190). Clearly the captain who had fed soldiers during all the rains would have little difficulty recruiting them in September.

In 1601 a very revealing incident occurred in Goa. The statue of D. Vasco da Gama, the discoverer of India, was toppled, chopped apart, and distributed around the city: the head and a hand in the town pillory, another hand in the auction mart of the Rua Direita, and so on. The statue had been erected by da Gama's grandson, D. Francisco da Gama, who had been viceroy in 1597–1600. His authoritarian attempts to reform Portuguese India had aroused considerable antipathy, and this apparently was the motive for the desecration. At an inquiry in 1609 most witnesses denied all knowledge of the event, contenting themselves with expressing routine outrage and horror at such a heinous and scandalous crime. This forgetfulness was possibly aided by da Gama's general unpopularity, and certainly total recall was hindered by a public threat to kill any informer. Nevertheless, a few intrepid witnesses did accuse a *fidalgo* 'and his people' or 'and his soldiers' of responsibility. Whatever the motive, it is clear that common soldiers were used by their patrons in the commission of this act.

The *casados* in the various Portuguese settlements had different interests, leaders, and methods of political activity from the soldiers. They had nearly all come out as soldiers to India, and had married and settled down. Given the small number of Portuguese-born women in India, the *casados* born locally must nearly always have been *mestiços* rather than *castiços*. They were apparently outnumbered by the soldiers, but despite this their influence was greater. First, they were permanently resident in Goa and the other settlements, while the soldiers were only sojourners. Second, rates of mortality among the soldiers, from disease rather than violent death, were very high, much higher than among the more settled and stable *casado* population. We will consider the occupations of these *casados* presently.

What can be said of relations between different races in sixteenth-century Goa? W. W. Hunter once noted, with typical Victorian aplomb, that 'the Goanese became a byword as the type of an orientalised community, idle, haughty, and corrupt' (W. W. Hunter, *A History of British India*, vol. I, London, 1899, p. 157). Leaving aside the racist overtones, it is true that a lack of differentiation (to modern eyes most creditable) between Portuguese and Indians can sometimes be seen. Even a viceroy and an archbishop used Hindu doctors. These *pandits* were given special privileges. The governor from 1588 to 1591, and his wife, went even further according to the Inquisition. Not only did they use Hindu doctors, but they consulted Hindu witches (probably astrologers) about when the ships from Europe would arrive. It is hard to see really why one medical system was preferred to the other. In Daman in the 1690s a French visitor was horrified to find a young Portuguese girl with a fever, whose 'Indian physician, instead of letting her blood, had covered her head with pepper' (Priolkar, *The Goa Inquisition*, p. 14). This representative of western science knew what to do: the girl was copiously bled with leaches and, remarkably, recovered from her fever in a few days.

More often European and Asian medicine (or quackery) coexisted. The practice in the famous Royal Hospital in Goa shows this. European patients would be bled frequently to cure their illness, and then, to restore their colour, they were prescribed a glass of cow urine three times a day. 'This remedy has been learnt of the idolators (sc. Hindus) of the country' (J-B. Tavernier, *Travels in India*, 2 vols., New Delhi, 1977, vol. I, pp. 160–1). The astonishing mortality which we noted earlier becomes more explicable by the minute. The prevailing medical theory was best expressed by a French traveller, who noted sagaciously that for local diseases European medicines were useless. 'For this reason the Physitians that go out of Portugal into these parts must at first keep company with the Indian Surgeons to be fit to Practice; otherwise, if they go about to cure these Distempers, so far different from ours after the European manner, they may chance to Kill more than they Cure' (S. N. Sen, ed., *Indian Travels of Thevenot and Careri*, New Delhi, 1949, p. 162).

Two famous visitors, Linschoten and Pyrard de Laval, noted many other aspects of this acculturation. Although bread was available, rice, eaten with the right hand, became the preferred food. In part no doubt this was because European food – the great Mediterranean trilogy of bread, oil and wine, plus some meat – was very expensive. In a clear continuance of caste pollution notions, Goans drank from a pot without letting it touch their mouths, and laughed at newly arrived Portuguese who had not yet mastered this difficult art. Goans chewed *pan*, rubbed themselves with 'sweet sanders', drank *araq*, and washed frequently.

All this, Linschoten pointed out, 'they have learned and received of the Indian Heathens, which have had these costumes of long time' (Linschoten, vol. I, pp. 207–8, 212–13).

This was, however, a 'European' city ruled by Europeans; was the population of Goa very distinctive? Obviously one can say nothing very definite here, but the data quoted earlier point to a comparatively small 'pure European' component in the total of the city, while the country-side was almost completely Indian. Contemporary descriptions give an overwhelming impression of an Indian city, with a small Portuguese population superimposed as rulers. Even this 'Portuguese' population was, in racial terms, often more Indian than European, as again Linschoten noted: 'the posteritie of the Portingales, both men and women being in the third degree, doe seeme to be naturall Indians, both in colour and fashion' (*Ibid.*, p. 184). Nevertheless, the Portuguese stressed fairness of skin as an important part of female beauty. Albuquerque married his soldiers to 'fair' Muslim women. The great Jesuit missionary, St Francis Xavier, while urging the *casados* to marry their local concubines, drew the firmest of colour lines. 'When the concubine was dark in colour and ugly featured, he employed all his eloquence to separate his host from her. He was even ready, if necessary, to find for him a more suitable mate.'[6] Similarly, the most feared enemies of the Portuguese were the Rumes (Turks), the feared 'white men' who fought so bravely and whose hostile presence in Goa was one motive for Albuquerque's decision to attack the town in 1510.

Thus most Portuguese saw 'white' skin as preferable for both love and war. Yet many of them also seem to have had a passion for African women, nearly all of them slaves, while others had to make do with darker-skinned Indians and *mestiças*. We noted earlier sexual double standards in metropolitan Portugal. In Goa the situation concerning sexual morality was quite complex. Many accounts stress not only concubinage on a vast scale, pointing to male sexual 'laxity', but also considerable sexual licence on the part of married women who, we are told, drugged their husbands the better to enjoy their lovers. Yet there is some evidence of a change here, a result perhaps of the influence of the Counter Reformation, and of the greater sexual restrictions among the upper classes which occurred also in metropolitan Portugal. Hence the fatal modesty of the captured noble lady we noted in the first chapter,

---

[6] Georg Schurhammer, *Francis Xavier: His Life, His Times*, vol. II, 'India, 1541–45' (Rome, 1977), p. 228.

and hence also an account by an Englishman of Goan women in the later seventeenth century, who he claimed are 'nurtured up to a lowly Bashfulness, whereby they are render'd unfit for Conversation, applying themselves wholly to Devotion and the care of the House.'

In any case, regardless of the situation for women, Goan men were clearly far from prudish. In the absence of Portuguese women in Goa (up to 1750 only one governor brought his wife with him to India) concupiscence on a grand scale took place, especially as more local women were baptized, for this seems to have lessened clerical hostility to their being used as concubines. The hope, of course, was that marriage would occur sooner or later, though it is hard to see how this could happen in the many cases of Portuguese with whole harems of concubines.

This matter of race relations has been a controversial one for some decades now. During the Salazar period it was bedevilled by the standard government claim, put forward to justify Portugal's retention of her colonies, that race relations were ideal in the Portuguese empire. Any differentiation was based not on colour but on 'degree of civilization'. Hence the injured, sometimes furious, reaction to a book by C. R. Boxer on race relations in the colonial empire.[7] This book mildly pointed out that race relations in this empire were certainly not ideal; they were no better or worse than in other European colonial empires.

The influence of present politics is clear to see. One great apologist of Portugal's empire was the once well-known Brazilian sociologist Gilberto Freyre. His main theme was that sexual interaction and Portuguese tolerance had created a uniquely harmonious racial situation, a Luso-Brazilian or even Luso-tropical (so as to include Portugal's African colonies) civilization. He finds this happy situation deriving from Muslim–Christian interaction and interbreeding in the twelfth and thirteenth centuries, and continued by Prince Henry. Even the slave trade is no problem for Freyre: slaves were well treated, so that slavery was really a form of insurance. Recent (in 1961) signs of racism in Portuguese Africa are a result of British and South African influences. In short, 'after Christ, no one has contributed more towards fraternity among people than the Portuguese'.[8]

Freyre is not alone in being a creature of his own times: all historians

---

[7] C. R. Boxer, *Race Relations in the Portuguese Colonial Empire, 1415–1825* (Oxford, 1963).
[8] Gilberto Freyre, *The Portuguese and the Tropics* (Lisbon, 1961).

are influenced to a greater or lesser extent by the societies in which they live. A clear example, and one related to Portuguese race relations, is a comment in M. Collis's book on the great Portuguese traveller and raconteur, Fernão Mendes Pinto. Collis, in the 1930s a judge in the British colony of Burma, reflected British imperial and racial attitudes. Pinto had been helped by a Muslim from Malacca, and he expressed his gratitude by throwing himself at the captain's feet and embracing his ankles. Collis notes 'Pinto's gratitude was in accordance with the custom of the time, when a European, without demeaning himself, could humbly acknowledge his indebtedness to an Asiatic.'[9] Earlier British writers, like F. C. Danvers and W. W. Hunter, were much blunter: they saw an important cause of Portuguese decline being interbreeding. The well-known traveller and savant Richard Burton was especially racist. On intermarriage: 'experience and stern facts condemn the measure as a most delusive and treacherous political day dream'. As for the results, he noted they are called 'Mestici – in plain English, mongrels'. 'It would be, we believe, difficult to find in Asia an uglier or more degraded looking race than [Goan *mestiços*].'[10]

So much for the minefields which underlie any discussion of race relations. We have already presented information on social interaction and acculturation, and also on economic and even military and political co-operation between Portuguese and Indians of different sorts. Many authors have stressed the survival of the Portuguese language, long after the end of their political power, as showing a similar tendency. Through the seventeenth and eighteenth centuries Portuguese of some sort was a *lingua franca* in several parts of littoral Asia. The chief Indian broker for the East India Company in Surat in 1700 knew Portuguese but not English. Clive, knowing no Indian language, addressed his Indian troops in Portuguese. Even in areas conquered by the Dutch, Portuguese survived. Emerson Tennent in Sri Lanka, then ruled by Britain, noted in 1859 that 'Already the language of the Dutch which they sought to extend by penal enactments has ceased to be spoken even by their direct descendants, whilst a corrupted Portuguese is to the present day the vernacular of the middle class in every town of importance' (quoted in Campos, *History of the Portuguese in Bengal*, p. 173).

[9] Maurice Collis, *The Grand Peregrination: being the Life and Adventures of Fernão Mendes Pinto* (London, 1949), p. 170.
[10] Richard Burton, *Goa and the Blue Mountains* (London, 1851), pp. 88, 97.

Rather than looking to some inherent or organic Portuguese racial tolerance, it seems more profitable to find the reasons for this sort of intermingling in other areas. It is tempting to try and delineate as precisely as possible differences between the cultures and societies of the Portuguese and the local people with whom they interacted. A mammoth task, and one not to be attempted yet, given the present state of research. One place to start, certainly, would be to differentiate levels in societies. Thus the Portuguese political and religious elite had little in common with most Indians, whether elite or not. But perhaps the bulk of the Portuguese who arrived in India, being urban poor or peasants, and thus (as we noted in chapter 1) much less firmly grounded in Portuguese high culture, would be more flexible, tolerant and open when confronted with fellow peasants, who happened to be Indian, and with whom a Portuguese peasant could feel some bonds of commonality on both social and class criteria. This, at least, is the sort of question which needs to be asked.

Freyre and others have found the origins of Portuguese racial tolerance in interbreeding in Portugal itself. This is a very debatable matter. Certainly there was mixing during five centuries of Muslim rule, and indeed after the reconquest. We would expect to find this most in the Algarve, the southern and most Muslim-influenced area of Portugal, and indeed it seems that many Portuguese who went to India were from here and so probably had some Muslim 'blood'. Yet one cannot push this too far, for we have noted already virulent anti-Muslim feeling in many Portuguese.

Two final factors are the related matters of the absence of Portuguese women in India, and the way in which many Portuguese settled permanently in India and Asia. The Portuguese country traders whom we discussed at the start of this chapter, so well described by van Dieman, basically had the choice between celibacy and a relationship with a local woman: they overwhelmingly chose the latter. There is a clear contrast here with the later Dutch and British, who saw themselves as only sojourners in India or Asia.

Yet not all Portuguese stayed. The decision seems to reflect class and status divisions. Those in top jobs in India, and especially governors, always returned to Portugal if they survived. Similarly, the elite seems typically to have had wives back in Portugal, and hence may have kept mistresses, but did not marry, in India. Some Portuguese merchants who prospered in Asia also returned to Portugal, married, and set themselves up as local gentry. But the vast majority, the *casados*, married locally and either through choice or lack of means never returned to Portugal.

Thus one determining factor in race relations was class. Others have claimed that it was not colour which divided people, but religion. Among the criteria of 'civilization' which the Portuguese used in the twentieth century, religion (that is, Roman Catholicism) was an important measuring tool. Thus black Christians were more 'civilized' than paler Muslims or Hindus. But while acknowledging some influence from class, it is difficult to stress religion too much: colour seems to have been overwhelmingly important. We have already noted a general stratification based on 'purity' of blood, and such instances could be endlessly illustrated.

The end result is to confirm Boxer's views, and contradict Freyre's. Predictably, race relations were not perfect. Albuquerque is famous for his encouragement of marriage between his troops and local women in Goa, but we should remember that this did not include marriage to local Malabari women, whom he considered to be 'black', and neither chaste nor comely. He meant marriage to Muslim women, who were 'white and virtuous'. Camoens's great epic *The Lusiads*, which is endlessly quoted as supporting just about every conceivable point of view on almost every topic, certainly does not have many positive things to say about Africans or Indians. Here he reflects the political and military situation in which he was himself embroiled, for friendly natives, like the sultan of Melinde, are praised. Padre Affonso, imprisoned on Ternate for thirty days by the local ruler, was typical. He refused to eat. When food was offered he replied 'What do you think you're giving me? Yams and sago? Am I a nigger? Give me bread and wine!' (Godinho, *Os Descobrimentos*, vol. IV, p. 66).

Albuquerque also was concerned about food. He said that if the Portuguese in Goa ate wheat bread, meat and good fish they would keep a 'manly colour', but not if they ate rice. (Despite this, we have noted that rice became widely eaten in sixteenth-century Goa.) Racial discrimination was certainly noted by an English visitor to Goa: 'The Mass of the People are Canorein, though Portuguezed in Speech and Manners; paying great Observance to a White Man, whom when they meet they must give him the Way with a Cringe and Civil Salute, for fear of a Stochado {rapier thrust}' (John Fryer, *A New Account of East India and Persia*, 3 vols., London, 1909–15, vol. II, p. 27).

It is true that sometimes political factors, and even religion, intruded on race. In 1601 the king wrote to the viceroy that he had previously forbidden Portuguese captains of forts to employ as factors brahmins or Jews. The viceroy had noted that the brahmins were useful, as they often gave the Portuguese important political information concerning the activities of surrounding Indian rulers. In an unusual burst of tolerance (and one soon repealed) the king now said that he was convinced by this: they could use brahmins, but definitely not Jews. Overall, race was central in categorization and discrimination. Donald Lach's comments about how the Portuguese divided up prospects for conversion typifies the whole matter. Black people, Africans and South Indians, were considered, he says, to be hopeless prospects: inferior, incapable of improvement, and stuck in superstition. Whites, Japanese and Chinese, on the other hand, met European standards, may even in some areas have been superior, and were good prospects for conversion.[11]

After this general discussion, we can focus again on Goa. What of the exposure of Goans to a wider European world, and to the Portuguese language? As to the latter, certain Goans by learning Portuguese became in demand as interpreters and go-betweens, and thus acquired, or retained, wealth and influence. The rural language however continued to be Konkani; only in later centuries were attempts made to spread Portuguese widely outside the cities. This language was thus in an analogous position to Persian in Muslim-ruled India at the same time.

As for the first point, it is tempting to see Goan isolation ended by its exposure to the Europe of the Renaissance, Reformation, and Counter Reformation. Here we must first make clear what 'Goa' means. Bardes and Salcette in the sixteenth century were rather remote, with few Portuguese there and the population still Hindu and little affected by Portuguese rule. Urban–rural, or Goa–hinterland, differences were well pointed up in the complaint of an official in Goa in 1566. He had criticized maladministration in Goa, and for his pains was forced to flee the town and seek refuge 'among the Hindus and lax Christians of Bardes'.

Thus one can expect almost no 'European impact' outside of Goa city. But even here one may question the impact of the above three important European intellectual trends. The Reformation was of course hardly

[11] Donald F. Lach, *Asia in the Making of Europe* (Chicago, 1965), vol. I, p. 827.

allowed into Goa at all, while the Counter Reformation (as seen in temple destruction and generally intolerant and muscular Catholicism) in fact had a quite varied impact, as we will see in the next chapter. The impact of the Renaissance was also various. On the one hand one can see beneficial aspects of this broad intellectual trend in Goan church architecture, and in various literary works. The supreme manifestations of this are of course the works of Camoens and d'Orta, and several chroniclers, notably Diogo do Couto, but the inquiring mind of a Renaissance man can also be seen in the navigational–geographic works of D. João de Castro.

But what then of that great disseminator of knowledge, the printing press? The first was introduced to Goa by the Jesuits (as one would expect of this active new order) in 1556. This was the first press in Asia, and indeed, except for Cambridge, Massachusetts, and Mexico, the first outside Europe. It even preceded Moscow by nearly twenty years. It was mostly used to spread a particular part of Renaissance knowledge, the Catholic faith. While it is true that the eighth book printed in Goa was that great monument to Renaissance inquiry, Garcia d'Orta's *Coloquios dos simples e drogas* (1563), more typical was its immediate follower, a virulent anti-Jewish tract published by the archbishop in 1565. Of forty books printed in Goa between 1556 and 1679 only three were not on religious topics. The first books in Bengali, published in Roman characters in Lisbon in 1743, similarly were a Catechism, a Compendium of the Mysteries of the Faith, and a Vocabulary.

In any case, here and elsewhere it is a mistake to see pre-Portuguese Goa as static or isolated. On the contrary, it was a great trade centre and had contacts from this all around the vast and variegated Indian Ocean world. A recent author claims that in the fifteenth century it was also a great embarkation port for the Muslim pilgrimage to Mecca.[12] Nevertheless, the total impact of Portuguese religious, social, economic and political activities on Goa in the sixteenth century was certainly stronger, longer and qualitatively more innovative than any exogenous impacts in previous centuries.

With the conquest of 1510 Goa of course underwent a change of political control. Ostensibly this marks a major change. Goa's rulers changed from Indian Muslims to European Christians. From being a port city subject to an inland state she became the centre of a maritime empire. Nevertheless, a consideration of two general points makes these

[12] J. M. Richards, *Goa* (New Delhi, 1982), p. 18.

changes appear less than dramatic. First, pre-modern states, whether Bijapur, Portugal or any other, usually interfered very little in the everyday lives of most of their subjects. Thus any change at the top political level made very little difference to the bulk of the population: most of the data in this chapter support this position. Second, any upper-level political authority is going to be dependent for political effectiveness on the help, or at least acquiescence, of local power figures. Again continuity, rather than generic change, is ensured despite the displacement of one ruling group (in this case Bijapur) by another (the Portuguese). In the actual conquest and early consolidation of Portuguese rule in Goa a Hindu leader called Timmayya (Timoja) played an important role. Later other Hindus were of crucial help to the Portuguese, so that Scammell's suggestion that 'the art of empire-building was to find the ally within'[13] seems substantially correct.

It is a truism that the Portuguese reserved to themselves the upper-level political positions, excluding as far as possible even Indian-born Portuguese, let alone *mestiços*. On ceremonial occasions, a notable one being the proclamation of Philip II in 1581, only Portuguese took part. On the other hand, village administration was left strictly alone by the Portuguese. The structure of government, with military, civil, legal and financial officials, was little different from common practice in contemporary India. Nor apparently were the standards of conduct of Portuguese officials very different from those prevailing in the rest of the subcontinent. Artisan and craft groups in Goa as elsewhere were governed by guild-like organizations.

Higher-class Portuguese were members of other councils, of which the most important was the Council of State. This was an entirely elite body, for its members, whether ecclesiastical or lay, were all *fidalgos*. The *casados* were thus dependent for their official political voice on the Senado da Câmara, or municipal council. The preferred members of this body were married Portuguese males, though sometimes a *mestiço*, or even a 'New Christian', could force his way in. Members could be, and often were, not humble *casados* but rather *fidalgos*; nevertheless, this elite influence was tempered by the compulsory representation of four men chosen by the 'guilds', and so speaking for lower-class *casados*. The Câmara exercised considerable control over local government matters,

---

[13] G. V. Scammell, 'Indigenous assistance in the establishment of Portuguese power in the Indian Ocean', in John Correia-Afonso (ed), *Indo-Portuguese History: Sources and Problems* (Bombay, 1981), p. 172.

but was of course very much subordinate to the Council of State, which handled the really important matters like war and peace. Nor was the Câmara really very representative: even New Christians and *mestiços* had trouble getting places on it, but Indian Christians were excluded until the late eighteenth century and the vast bulk of Goa's population, those who were not Christian, were never represented at all. There are a few examples of informal consultation with important Hindu leaders, but most of the time Indians, including Christians, were dependent on informal pressure tactics or individual representation.

Not that such methods were necessarily ineffective. The clearest instance, demonstrating Portuguese reliance on Indian co-operation or at least acquiescence, occurred in the 1560s. A new viceroy, D. Francisco Coutinho, described to the king how he found Goa much depopulated when he arrived, with 'the villages ruined, the fields flooded, the river clogged up, and the Hindu inhabitants absent' (Historical Archives of Goa, 'Livro Vermelho', vol. 1, ff. 55–6). The reason was a decree of the last viceroy, D. Constantino de Bragança, a notorious bigot and exemplar of the worst excesses of the Counter Reformation, who had ordered that all Hindus who had left Goa to avoid forcible conversion must return or lose their property. The rate of exodus had increased after this. D. Francisco, after consulting with the Portuguese elite, repealed the offending decrees and promised to restore all confiscated property if the absentees returned within six months. Thus despite racial prejudice and lack of representation, even in political matters the Indian population could on occasion have their say.

The Câmara, on behalf of the *casados*, was most concerned with commercial matters. An example is their constant campaign to restrict competition to their own trade. Thus they got the king to issue a decree meant to stop any converted Jew (that is, a New Christian) or Hindu from acting as agent for Portuguese nobles in their trading activities. Similarly, at their instigation the king tried, albeit unsuccessfully, to restrict the trade of the agents of Lisbon capitalists in India, and to reserve to the *casados* the right to hold government tax-farming contracts.

The Câmara played a role in other commercial matters also. In 1569 it agreed to a rise of 1 percent in Goa's customs duties, though only because the resulting extra revenue would be used to protect the convoys bringing food to Goa. In the early seventeenth century the Portuguese empire's revenues fell sharply due to the competition and hostility of the Dutch and English. Finally a draconian step, a tax on food, was considered. Free trade in food had been one of the city's oldest and most prized privileges. Nevertheless, a general meeting in 1623, attended by the viceroy, *fidalgos*, and members of the Câmara (no Indians were in attendance, though they also presumably ate food) agreed to this new tax, called the *colecta*.

In 1587 the king made a contract with a group of capitalists in Lisbon by which, in return for their paying for five years for the fleets to India, they were given a monopoly on the indigo trade. This threatened to end the *casados'* trade in a very lucrative product. They complained violently, and it took the viceroy, the clergy, and other members of the elite to calm them down and assure them they would still get a fair price for their indigo.

Sometimes *casado* pressure could even affect political and military matters. On two occasions the *casados* of Goa refused to oppose a Bijapuri advance into Portuguese territory. According to them, this sort of martial activity should be done on their behalf by soldiers, not, except in extreme emergency, by them personally. Even in emergencies, they were ready to help with money only on their own terms. In 1586 desperate letters arrived from the captain, bishop and city of Malacca. Acheh was besieging the city, the second most important in Portuguese Asia, and it needed help. The *fidalgos* of Goa rallied immediately, but the viceroy's appeals to the Câmara met a cool response. Finally they agreed to call a meeting of the whole *casado* group, and put the matter to them. After a discussion a loan was agreed to, but only because the viceroy offered to secure it with the revenues of the Salcette area. As a further condition, the *casados* asked that a *fidalgo* acceptable to them be given command of the relief expedition. The viceroy had his own uncle in mind for the job, but was forced to bow to the will of the people.

Finally we have to investigate the economy of Goa. The Golden Goa myth implies that not only was Goa a large town, and a distinctive one, but also that it was remarkably wealthy. It is very difficult indeed to test this claim quantitatively. No doubt in European terms some Goans were fabulously wealthy, but there is an overriding impression that the Portuguese elite in Goa was considerably less rich than, say, their Mughal equivalent. Given the size of the two states, this is of course hardly surprising. Similarly, no Goan public building bears comparison with, for example, the Delhi or Agra fort complexes, or several of the great Mughal or Bijapuri tombs. We do have runs of figures for government revenues in Goa. These are worth at least a brief mention, but it must be stressed that they give little impression of individual wealth. Sixteenth-century governments had rather limited functions, with most areas of the economy outside their control, or even cognizance.

This said, what sorts of revenues were available? Barros claimed that Bijapur got a revenue of 450,000 cruzados from the area of Goa. Under Portugal this revenue seems to have declined. In 1545 revenue was about 350,000 cruzados, in 1586 about 375,00, and around 1600 about 455,000 cruzados. (In all cases I have added in a rather notional 150,000 cruzados to take account of profits from other forts, notably Diu and Hurmuz.) The figures are very rough of course, but they at least seem to show that Goa's government revenue under Portugal was not greatly different from that realized under Bijapur, and indeed was probably smaller.

The Portuguese made very little money from land revenue. We have noted that Bardes and Salcette continued throughout the sixteenth century to be somewhat neglected. They were indeed little needed, except as a mission field, for the Portuguese were able to live from sea trade. Only as this declined under Dutch attack did pressure on Goa's land increase from both *casados* and the religious orders. Just after the conquest Albuquerque issued orders that local landholders and village authorities were not to be disturbed – indeed he remitted one-third of their land revenue. Muslim land, apparently a small amount, was confiscated in 1519, but generally the Portuguese continued a hands-off policy, and this was extended to Bardes and Salcette when these two *talukas* were finally acquired in 1543. This policy was codified in Meixa's famous Charter of 1526, which aimed to preserve what he took to be pre-Portuguese practice. Decisions continued to be made by the *gaunkars* within the villages, or in *taluka*-wide assemblies of village representatives. In Bardes and Salcette in the sixteenth century the Portuguese population was small indeed. It included soldiers in their forts, and perhaps a few *casados* in the several small towns, but the main European representative was the parish priest: in Bardes a Franciscan, and in Salcette a Jesuit. Sometimes these priests had been granted, in return for a quit-rent (*aforamento*), rights over a particular village. The main benefit was the right to collect tribute from the village or villages concerned. This, of course, is not a matter of a transfer of land ownership; village rights and customs were not affected. The situation certainly changed in the seventeenth century, for the reasons noted above: thus in 1628 the king forbade Portuguese to obtain *gaunkar* rights in Goa; one assumes some Portuguese had started to do this as their trade by sea declined. But the Portuguese state made little money from land revenue: in 1586 the whole of the three areas of the Old Conquests paid only about 60,000 cruzados in *foros*, or land revenue.

In the sixteenth century Portugal's main impact on Goan rural society was, first, the beginning of the conversion drive, by no means completely successful at 1600, and second the introduction of new flora, many of which are today firmly established in Goa, and indeed India. The list includes tobacco, pineapples, papaya, maize, sweet potatoes, cashews and red peppers.

Most Portuguese and *mestiços* lived in towns, especially in Goa itself. What did they do there? The occupations of soldiers, nobles and clerics are clear enough, but what role did *casados* play in the Goan economy? The picture that emerges from many scattered sources is that the *casados* normally did not do manual work, but they did engage in larger-scale retail trade. Pyrard claimed the Rua Direita was lined with shops owned by Europeans. These owners would have been a very diverse group, including non-Portuguese, 'pure' Portuguese, agents of metropolitan interests, New Christians, and no doubt some *mestiços*. Indians, whether Christian or not, had their own occupationally-based quarters. But most *casados* seem to have been wholesalers, owners of property including shops, supervisors of groups of non-Portuguese craftsmen, and above all, as we have noted so often, sea traders. The large slave population of Goa helped the Portuguese avoid manual work, as slaves were frequently hired out by the day, or served in their masters' shops. Female slaves were sometimes used as prostitutes by their owners, but whatever the employment a slave's earnings reverted to the owner.

We can close this discussion of the Goan economy by sketching the very large role of Indians. It is clear that the dominant native elite was the Saraswat brahmins. This position apparently continued until the end of Portuguese rule in 1961. In the 1580s the owners of the spice shops and groceries of Goa 'are commonlie the Bramenes, which serve likewise for Priests and Idolatrous Ministers, and have their shops throughout the Cittie. In every place and corner, and under pentises, whereby every man may have to serve him at his need' (Linschoten, vol. I, pp. 229–30). These brahmins were also the controllers of most of the land of the Old Conquests. Further evidence of their wealth comes from a curious proposal of the 1640s. The Câmara wrote to the king suggesting that he pass decrees that 'no brahmin or kshatriya or member of any other caste who is rich or has property' might marry his daughter to anyone except to a Portuguese born in Portugal: such people must also bequeath all their property to their daughters (see M. N. Pearson, *Coastal Western India*, New Delhi, 1981, pp. 96–7 and sources there quoted). The advantages of this forcible cooptation of the wealthy Hindu population would be numerous. The Portuguese would receive an economic shot in the arm from the dowries and legacies their Indian wives would bring with them. Their wives and children would of course be Christian. And this measure would result in the lands of Goa being populated by the earnestly-desired 'white men'. The sons of such marriages would be prepared to bear arms, 'which the brahmins do not do because it is not their custom' (*Ibid.*).

The most convincing evidence we have concerning the role of Indians, especially Saraswat brahmins, in the Goan economy comes from quite detailed statistics concerning the holders of *rendas*, or tax-farming contracts. We have good data for the first seventy years of the seventeenth century. They show that 80 percent of holders were Hindus, and 20 percent Christian. Of the Hindus, Saraswats held nearly 63 percent of the total, and just half of the total of all *rendas*. In terms of the values of these *rendas* (and they made up a considerable sum in total) the distribution changes only a little. Further scattered information from the first half of the sixteenth century and early eighteenth century seems to show that the situation of the seventeenth century was not atypical. Over the whole of this long period it is clear that the Saraswats held a commanding position in this important part of the Goan economy.

Among the local inhabitants of Goa these brahmins were then overwhelmingly dominant, but they appear to have been outranked within the town by a smaller but wealthier group of outsiders, the *vanias* ('banyas') of Gujarat. These were members of a very widespread and economically important group which was found all over the Portuguese area, and indeed seaborne Asia. Many European accounts speak in awe of the vast amounts of capital available to these *vanias*. Goan evidence shows that in an emergency it was more likely that the Portuguese would turn to them for quick funds, rather than to the local brahmins. Similarly, the authorities often measured the prosperity of

Goa, or Diu or other places, by the number of wealthy *vanias* present; these numbers, to the distress of the Portuguese, declined precipitously in the seventeenth century.

The heart of the Gujarati economic position in Portuguese India was their sea trade, based on the products of their homeland. As a viceroy once told the king, the Gujaratis 'have always been the most lucrative group of all in terms of the customs revenues' (Historical Archives of Goa, 'Livros das Moncoes', vol. XXVI B, f. 408). Vast profits from Diu and Hurmuz, based on the trade of Gujaratis, helped to make Goa prosperous in the sixteenth century. The puppet king of Hurmuz was to pay his master, the king of Portugal, 45,000 cruzados a year. However, most of his money came from taxes on Gujarati trade, so it was also provided that if this trade was blocked he was to pay only 18,500 cruzados.

Of equal importance to the Portuguese was the central role of Gujarati products in Portuguese Asian trade, and the sorts of relationships between Portuguese and Gujaratis in the Gulf of Cambay which we noted earlier. As just one example, we have a detailed inventory of the privately-owned part of the cargoes of three Portuguese ships bound for Lisbon in 1630. There were relatively trifling amounts of spices and drugs, and a host of odds and ends, but Gujarati cloths were overwhelmingly dominant. Of these the three ships carried a total of about 4,000,000 metres.

As will be clear from all the above, the Portuguese impact on Goa was variable in the extreme. Sometimes they produced substantial change, yet in many other activities they acculturated and were merged into Indian life, and in yet other areas they deliberately kept aloof. Yet one does not want to go on from this to a Gilberto Freyre sort of paean to cordial race relations and general harmony based on sexual interaction. As C. R. Boxer has so often reminded us, the Portuguese did have very definite aims and prejudices, designed in sum to make a major impact on Indian society. An obvious solution to this apparent contradiction is to say that the Portuguese were not very efficient: their aims may have been large, but their ability to achieve them was limited.

Such an argument has frequently been made, but I think one can go beyond this. In several areas the Portuguese were really not trying to effect generic change. Rather, whether tacitly or not, they were simply altering or redirecting existing patterns. This certainly applies to their trade-control system, as was noted above, and could also well apply in other more social areas, such as those previously mentioned. There was also a negative factor which contributed to the lack of impact. Previously isolated areas like South America and the Pacific Islands were hit hard by European diseases. This of course did not happen in Goa, or indeed Asia generally.

One final and even more general point may be made here to explain these varying and often minor impacts. Western Europe in the sixteenth century was at the beginning of scientific and agricultural revolutions – Marshall Hodgson's 'technicalistic' revolution – which were to transform relations between Europe and Asia. Asian countries either stood still or even declined. This relative shift was plain to see in the second half of the eighteenth century in India. Before this, while in Europe the seeds of change certainly were planted, and later began to sprout, the relative positions were much more equal. Historians have often looked to military conquest to explain western impact, but in a more general sense it seems that it was rather this relative shift which was crucial. While the balance was roughly equal, as applies to the overtly imperialistic Portuguese in the sixteenth century and to the trading Dutch and English in the seventeenth (for although these were the areas where the change occurred, it was at this time still germinating), the impact of Europe was minimal, for Europeans were, like Indians at the same time, essentially 'pre-industrial', in the sense in which this term has been used by Fernand Braudel. Hence their lack of a decisive impact on many areas of society in Goa in what Jan Kieniewicz has called the 'pre-colonial expansion' period (Kieniewicz, 'Contact and Transformation', pp. 45–58). The result was interaction, and the creation out of this process of a unique Goan culture, at least among the Christian population of the Old Conquests. This culture became distinct from the surrounding Hindu areas during the sixteenth century. Later the rest of India was affected to a greater or lesser degree by British rule; Goa, with part of its culture derived from a different European society, remained distinctive.

CHAPTER 5

CATHOLICS AND HINDUS

The preceding chapter focussed on Goa in the sixteenth century. It excluded, except in passing, any discussion of religious interaction in Portuguese India. This forms the subject of the present chapter, which makes both a topical and chronological link with all the previous discussion. Again it shows interaction as well as unidirectional influence, but it also leads to our ensuing study of Portuguese India in its long decline, for this chapter makes no attempt to restrict itself to the sixteenth century.

Leaving aside official statements by Portuguese kings and twentieth-century apologists, who put religious activities in the forefront of their presence in Asia, one can see a general trend in Portugal's attention to conversions. The early years were rather slack and tolerant, but from 1540 the arrival in Goa of the ideology of the Counter Reformation, and its shock troops the Jesuits, increased the tempo and pressure very considerably. But this verve later came to slacken, and be tempered by political realities. Again then we see the need to be very precise when we assess the Portuguese impact on India; it varied widely over both time and space particularly in the category of religion.

The early years are especially interesting, for they were dominated by a very human, and humane, desire to find familiar things in Asia. This explains da Gama's well-known failure, during three months in Malabar, to understand that Hinduism was different from Christianity. True, the images in the temples seemed somewhat grotesque, and some practice clearly unusual or even schismatic: nevertheless the non-Muslim inhabitants of Malabar appeared to be some sort of Christians. This search for the similar continued for some decades. The great compiler Tomé Pires thought Hindus had once been Christian, but had lost their faith thanks to the Muslims. Barbosa, Pires's rival as our best guide to early sixteenth-century littoral Asia, found that Gujarati brahmins attached great importance to a God in three persons; their teachings showed 'many resemblances to the Holy Trinity' (D. F. Lach, *Asia in the Making of Europe*, 2 vols., Chicago, vol. 1, p. 401). Even Castanheda some years later after long experience in India could still' find in Konkani brahmin practice some Christian parallels. Thus, we are told, they venerate the picture of the Virgin, on festival occasions wash themselves as 'a kind of baptismal rite', and 'have hints of the birth of our Lord and his sufferings' (*Ibid.*, p. 387).

This rather tolerant attitude is reflected in the leisurely way in which the official trappings of Roman Catholicism arrived in Goa. It was only in 1534 that a Bull made Goa a diocese. The first bishop arrived in 1538, and in 1539 the cathedral was inaugurated. Goa had to wait until 1560 to get an archbishop. There was some activity even so: as early as 1512, 100 local children were being educated in Cochin. Later other schools were set up in Cannanore and Goa. The state provided both food and books. Around 1540 in Goa there were some 100 priests, though a Jesuit historian tells us they often were ignorant, and most interested in their trade and their concubines. It is tempting to see the new glamorous dynamic Jesuits producing a vitalization of this torpid picture. Yet even allowing for the bias produced by the fact that so many of the best missionaries were Jesuits, and so are later historians, it does seem that the first four decades saw little advance.

All this changed after 1540. Intolerance became the theme. Camoens's *Lusiads* reveals this brilliantly. Published in 1572, it gave a very different account of da Gama's time in a Hindu temple, one which reveals changing Portuguese attitudes. According to him, the Hindu images were 'so many imaginings prompted by the devil. The statues were abominable. . . . Here the barbarous heathen performed his superstitious devotions' (Atkinson, trans., p. 170). The Portuguese in fact now realized Hindus were not unusual Christians who could perhaps be co-opted to help against the Muslims. Rather, at the elite religious level, that of priests, there was a very hard and decisive attempt to convert.

In the watershed year, 1540, in order to encourage conversions all temples in Goa were destroyed. Later this was done in Bardes, in 1573, and in Salcette in 1584-7. Their no doubt distraught brahmin guardians often were able to save the holy images and install them just outside Portuguese territory: hence the several great temples in the Ponda area, acquired by the Portuguese only in the more tolerant eighteenth century. Other discrimination was legion: orphans were kidnapped and converted, rice Christianity flourished, Hindus were discriminated against by the government in a multitude of ways. In 1541 lands which had endowed the temples were turned over to the local priests and the orders. Most Hindu ceremonies were forbidden, including marriage and cremation. These now had to be done in secret, or outside Portuguese territory. In 1623 a Portuguese complained that there were still more than 150,000 Hindus living under Portuguese protection in Goa. They should, he said, be given the choice of converting, paying a poll tax, or leaving Goa.

The aim of all this was of course conversion, and this drive received a new impetus with the arrival of the first Jesuit, Francis Xavier, in 1542. Jesuits soon took over several schools founded by other orders, notably the College of St Paul, and the religious administration of the province of Salcette. As is well known, Xavier travelled very widely, and converted *en masse*. In 1544 over 10,000 villagers in Travancore were converted in a month. In Goa also mass conversions took place. Over a three-day period in 1548, 912 people were baptized in just three of the parishes of the city of Goa. On Divar Island 1538 people were baptized in three months. Important converts were received with great ceremony, *pour encourager les autres*, and rewarded handsomely. The most important Hindu in Goa in the early 1540s was Krishna, who held the top post of *Tanador-Mor*, or overseer, and for three years leased the rights of the newly acquired areas of Bardes and Salcette. In 1548 he was unseated. His rival, Lakshman, decided to convert. The bishop performed the ceremony, the governor stood as his godfather, and eight days of rejoicings followed. Lakshman, now Luquas de Sá, became *Tanador-Mor*, while Krishna and his family, still firmly Hindu, were dispossessed.

The extent of Portugal's commitment was very large indeed. It can be seen in the huge number of convents and monasteries established in Goa. The Convent of Santa Monica in 1606 had over 100 nuns, and many applicants. The largest building in Goa was the Cathedral of Santa Caterina, 250 feet (76 metres) long, begun in 1562 and still being added to in the 1630s. In the town alone there were 7 parish churches, in the countryside 62 more. St Paul's College was the largest Jesuit school in Asia, with 70 religious and in theory 2000 students. Several other monasteries and convents had around 100 inmates each. This commitment cost vast sums of money, as we will see, and also extracted from the population men of military age and women with large dowries: few complained of this.

Another sign of the wide-ranging commitment was the *padroado*, or patronage. By Bulls of the fifteenth and sixteenth centuries the

Portuguese crown was given certain revenues and privileges within Portugal and overseas, and in return had to finance and support the missionary drive in Africa and Asia. Thus the Goa cathedral was the metropolitan church for a vast area from the Cape of Good Hope to China. In all of this area the Portuguese took up, at least to some extent, the obligation to spread their faith. This burden was lessened in 1622 by the establishment in Rome of the Congregation for Propaganda, which could send missionaries to areas neglected by the Portuguese, yet the Portuguese struggled for years against what they saw as usurpation of their rights.

Nor were the Portuguese only concerned with converts. They were much exercised about the purity of a Christian group in India which preceded them, the Thomas Christians. This community numbered anywhere between 80,000 and 200,000 in the sixteenth century. It was believed that their forebears had been converted by St Thomas himself, and by 1517 the saint's tomb had been found in Meliapur, later renamed São Thomé. Thomas Christians may have derived from the hoary past, but the Portuguese of the Counter Reformation considered their practices to be overly tinged with Hindu and Nestorian influences, in a word sloppy, close to heretical. Nevertheless, until 1599 they were under the authority of the Syriac Patriarch of Chaldea, and as he was recognized by the Pope there was little the Portuguese could do. In this year they were able, at the Synod of Dampier, to include them within the authority of the *padroado*, and so directly subject to the wishes of the Pope as interpreted by Portuguese divines in India. Despite this closer control, there were problems with the 'deviations' of the Thomas Christians throughout the seventeenth century.

One disadvantage with being made subject to the *padroado* was that this also meant subjection to the authority of the Inquisition. This institution is generally quoted as the supreme example of the intolerance and bigotry of the Counter Reformation, and of all the discriminatory practices we have just described. Xavier, shocked at the prevalent laxity of Goa, had recommended to the king that it be established, but it was founded only in 1560, eight years after his death. However, even before this, heresy did not go unpunished. In 1543 a New Christian physician was convicted by the ecclesiastical court of relapsing to Judaism. A secular court sentenced him to be burnt, but this sentence was mollified after he confessed and apologized. He was strangled before he was burnt.

The self-styled Holy Office had very wide-ranging powers indeed. It had agents in other Portuguese areas, who had the power to ship off suspected heretics to Goa. The non-Christian population was generally not subject to its authority, though those who hindered someone else from being converted or who caused a relapse were. In any case, given the fast and superficial nature of many conversions, especially in the heady 1540s and 1550s, there were vast numbers of 'Christians' who knew almost nothing of their new faith, and so could easily, in the eyes of the Inquisition, relapse.

The pervasiveness of its authority becomes clear when one considers a sample of the practices it forbade, these all being considered to be signs of continuing Jewish, Muslim or Hindu influence: sending gifts on the day a married woman had her first menstrual period; cooking rice without salt 'as the Hindus are accustomed to do' (A. K. Priolkar, *The Goa Inquisition*, Bombay, 1961, pp. 92–107); wearing a *dhoti* or *choli*; refusing to eat pork. Given these sorts of wide-ranging prohibitions, in many cases of practices which seem to be purely social, it is easy to understand how the Inquisition was able to find 3800 cases to try between 1561 and 1623, and in the whole period of its operation to 1774 no less than 16,172.

The role of the state as an auxiliary of the church, and vice versa, is plain to see. The *padroado* gave the state considerable influence over the clergy. On the other hand, in rural areas the state was often represented solely by the parish priest. Clerics also served on the Council of State as of right and twice in the seventeenth century acted as governors. Royal piety, and the obligations of the *padroado*, made Portugal pour vast sums into religious activities, including the dispensation of charity, such as food for the poor. In Bassein, near Bombay, in 1574 over one-third of total government expenditure was for such activities; by 1588 it was more than one half. Early in the sixteenth century the four orders – Franciscans, Dominicans, Augustinians and Jesuits – cost the state a total of 42,000 cruzados. Nearly one-half of this went to the Jesuits. Nor was the state the only patron, for around 1600 the three-storey Jesuit college at Cochin received three gifts totalling 55,000 cruzados, and another 22,500 to invest in trade.

Some of this money was spent for the rather worldly purpose of putting up a good front. In 1549 the king was informed that the church at Chalé, near Calicut, was small, bare and undecorated, yet surrounded by very sumptuous and lavishly decorated mosques and temples.

Visitors to the church wondered at its poverty. A century later the religious head of Craganore said that his church was also too plain as compared with the surrounding temples. It was agreed to do something, for 'it sets a bad example, and even causes great scandal, to see a Christian church in India less ornate and decent than a Hindu temple' (Arquivo Historico Ultramarino, Lisbon, India, caixa 21, meeting of Conselho Ultramarino, 21 Feb. 1651). The archbishop followed up this happy success by asking for more pay for himself, so that he did not have to go around looking shabby in front of the opulent Hindus.

Apart from finance, the crown also provided much logistic support, such as transport and protection. Indeed, the secular authorities were prepared to bow to clerical pressure quite often. The best illustration of this was a case in 1561. Portuguese forces in Sri Lanka had captured a tooth which Buddhists believed to be from the Buddha himself. It was taken to Goa. The king of Pegu offered at least 300,000 cruzados, perpetual friendship and unlimited rice for Malacca, in return for the tooth. The Portuguese viceroy was D. Constantino de Bragança, a brother of the duke of the same name, and a member of the family which became rulers of Portugal in 1640. Not only was he an eminent noble, he was also a fanatical bigot whose achievements in almost depopulating Goa we described in the last chapter. Nevertheless, there are indications that he found this offer interesting; certainly the secular members of his council did. But the archbishop spoke strongly against the very notion of trafficking in idolatry, and swayed the meeting. The tooth was publicly burnt, or according to another account ground up in a mortar and pestle and the fragments cast into the sea.

What was the result of all this? A new religious community was created in India, but it was a tiny one. By 1600 there were about 175,000 Christians in all India, out of a total population of 140,000,000. Of this total, 100,000 were the low-caste fishers and pearl divers of the Manar coast, where Xavier and later Jesuits had been so successful. In the whole of Goa at the turn of the century there were at least 50,000 Christians, perhaps one-fifth, or even one-quarter of the total population, and this after 60 years of vigorous pressure on the Hindu population. There was more success in the city of Goa, where about two-thirds of the population were Christian.

There are several reasons for this only very partial success. Amongst Muslims the missionaries made almost no converts; they complained about how obdurate these 'Muhammadans' were. Among Hindus also there was strong opposition, or passive resistance. When the temples were destroyed, the brahmins simply took the most holy images and set up again just outside Portuguese territory in more tolerant Muslim-ruled Bijapur.

Another problem was that political and strategic realities often meant that the Portuguese could not be as intolerant as they would have liked. We noted that Bragança's fanaticism drove many Hindus away from Goa; his successor was forced to moderate his policies. In other areas also political and economic realities sometimes softened the conversion drive. In the 1590s the viceroy told the king he quite agreed that all temples must be destroyed in Portuguese India, but this could not be done in Diu. If it were all the *vanias* would leave, and commerce at this most lucrative fort would grind to a halt. In 1609 the king noted that the *vanias* were being forced to pay a special levy in the Diu customs house, the proceeds going to the Jesuit house. Now he decreed that it was to be publicly proclaimed that this levy was voluntary, and no one was to be forced to pay it.

Indeed, even in the sixteenth century there was some toleration, some intermingling, regardless of official bigotry. Not only the political elite, but also the archbishop, members of orders and the College of St Paul in 1548, used Hindu doctors. Linschoten noted generally that while the Hindu ceremonies of cremation and marriage were forbidden in Goa, the Portuguese 'dwell in the towne among all sorts of nations, as Indians, Heathens, Moores, Iewes, Armenians, Gusarates, Benians, Bramenes, and of all Indian nations and people, which doe al dwell and traficke therein, everie man holding his owne religion, without constrayning any man to doe against his conscience' (Linschoten, vol. I, pp. 181–2).

It is sometimes unclear which was the cart and which the horse. Thus the Portuguese could do nothing about the Jains' extreme reverence for animal life. A late sixteenth-century traveller said that 'in Goa I have seen them ransom from the hands of Portuguese boys birds, dogs and cats which the boys, so as to extract money from them, had pretended to want to kill' (Francesco Carletti, *My Voyage Around the World*, London, 1964, pp. 204–5). In Chaul at the same time a rich *vania* died. With what seems to be deliberate malice, he bequeathed 27 cruzados to each of the Christian confraternities of the town, and 3600 to the bird hospital in Cambay. Something of the same sort of attitude, one quite unintimidated by the fulminations of the ecclesiastical authorities, can be seen in the way a traditional Indian caste made a good thing out of Christianity. Hindu painters made nice pictures of Christ, the Virgin and various saints, and sold them door-to-door. The caste head also did altarpieces on demand, and spent the profits on Hindu goods.

Thus, fortunately, even at its height the pressure was not completely intolerable. In the seventeenth century the conversion drive seems to have eased, a slackening which correlates with the decline in Portuguese political and military power, and which may have been caused by it. True, there were still cases of essentially forced conversions. In 1710 a Hindu married an orphan girl who was under ten years old. This made her subject to compulsory conversion, and she was taken away and made Christian despite her husband's opposition. A notorious decree of 1684 seems to fall into this category also, for it made the use of the Portuguese language compulsory. However, this very soon became a dead letter. Indeed, it was claimed that it was passed at the urging of the Franciscans. Priests of this order were too lazy to learn the vernacular, and so tried to cover up by getting this decree issued.

Such intolerance became less frequent in the eighteenth and nineteenth centuries. A sign of the new attitude was Pombal's abolition of the Goa Inquisition in 1774. It was revived three years later and lingered on, a ghost of its former fearsome self, until 1820. Problems in some of the orders contributed to this slackening. A critic said that the Franciscans had done a very poor job in their *taluka* of Bardes. Part of the reason for this was that members of this order were lazy, leaving all the work to Indian secular priests while the European regulars 'live shamelessly without the fear of God, associating with women and having sons from them without any fear of punishment' (quoted in A. K. Priolkar, *The Printing Press in India*, Bombay, 1958, p. 180).

The career of the well-born Italian Jesuit Roberto de Nobili seems to illustrate this change, this decline in cold hard certainty. He is well known for trying to convert brahmins by using their own arguments. To this end he studied Sanskrit texts, and dressed as a brahmin. While this may be admirable, as an example of tolerance and open inquiry, it should be remembered first that de Nobili's aim was still, and always, to make converts, and second that his methods got him into hot water with his superiors.

This sort of calm after the storm of the second half of the sixteenth century continued. Richard Burton sneered that the Portuguese were making few converts (1851) now that compulsion was removed; such as were achieved were really a matter of 'spoiling a good Gentoo by making a bad Christian of him' (Burton, *Goa and the Blue Mountains*, London, 1981, p. 109). By 1956 an official publication could claim, in a caption to a picture of a Goan temple, that 'Portugal respects all religions. The tower of this Hindu temple is not only a remarkable example of religious architecture but also a symbol of toleration and peace.'[1] Thus the bad old days are ignored, though misunderstandings still continue. The tower in the picture is a symbol certainly, but not necessarily of toleration and peace, for it is a gigantic Siva lingam.

We are fortunate that Somerset Maugham left us a fine and evocative pen portrait of Goan Christianity in the 1930s. In what was by then Old Goa,

The churches are large and white, their facades decorated with honey-coloured stone pilasters. Inside they are large, bare, spacious, with pulpits in Portuguese baroque carved with the utmost elaboration and altar-pieces in the same style. In one, at a side altar, a priest, a native, was saying mass with a dark-faced acolyte to serve him. There was no one to worship. In the Franciscan Church you are shown a wooden Christ on a crucifix and the guide tells you that six months before the destruction of the city it wept tears. In the Cathedral they were holding a service, the organ was playing and in the organ loft there was a small choir of natives singing with a harshness in which somehow the Catholic chants acquired a mysteriously heathen, Indian character. It was strangely impressive to see these great empty churches in that deserted place and to know that day by day with not a soul to listen the priests said mass in them.[2]

We have seen interaction and co-operation between Portuguese political and religious leaders in sixteenth-century Goa, and this reminds us that clerics could play roles outside purely religious ones. Needless to say, such activities were, at least in theory, all meant to support and foster religious goals. An example is the three famous Jesuit missions to the Mughal court. The object was of course to convert the emperor, on the 'trickle down from the top' theory, much beloved of Jesuits, of how to win converts. It is symptomatic of the blinkered and closed nature of Counter-Reformation Catholicism (Braudel, noting that European Christians, including priests, were much more likely to convert to Islam than vice versa, concluded 'the Turks were opening doors just as Christendom was shutting them',[3]) that the Jesuits

[1] *Portuguese India Today*, 2nd ed. (Lisbon, 1956), p. 43.
[2] W. Somerset Maugham, *A Writer's Notebook* (London, 1949), p. 282.
[3] Fernand Braudel, *The Mediterranean and the Mediterranean World in the Age of Philip II* (London, 1972–3), vol. II, pp. 799–800.

mistook Akbar's tolerance and inquiring mind for a sign that he was close to becoming Christian. No emperors were converted, but the missions did play a political role of some importance, for the information they gathered was often valuable for the governors of Portuguese India. Intellectually also they played a role: the letters they sent back to Rome were widely circulated as edifying and heuristic; thus Europe saw something of a wider world. Other Jesuits, and members of other orders, played similar political roles in many parts of India. A Jesuit was an important, and quite successful, opponent of the early English in Gujarat. In areas outside formal Portuguese control the only representative of European moral values was the undaunted priest, serving, for example, the lawless local Portuguese population in Bengal and Arakan.

It is doubtful if there was much influence the other way. In Akbar's reign the Jesuits were simply one of many exemplars of particular religions clustered around the emperor and trying to influence him. In the reigns of the later, less tolerant, Mughal rulers the role of the Jesuits was even more obscure. Yet again it is instructive to remember that while Portuguese historical sources contain copious information on Portuguese actions – in this case those of the Jesuits – the vast Mughal chronicles contain only very scattered and rather deflating mentions of the Jesuits or the Portuguese generally. When they do appear, they are not seen as at all unusual or even particularly exotic. Rather the chronicles see them in an Indian context: the Jesuits, for example, as quite interesting holy men, the lawless inhabitants of Hughli as refractory landholders who had to be chastised, and so on.

The role of the church in social integration was of considerable importance. Its members served to link up most areas of littoral Asia: Jesuits in, for example, Peking, Macao, the Philippines, Bassein or Mombasa were all members of the same order, with common standards and a common head, the General in Rome. A good illustration of this role is the Jesuit College of St Paul in Goa. Graduates from here were usually sent back to their native areas to act as secular priests. They all took with them a shared religious faith, a shared ethos, and a shared language of Latin. Thus were integrated a very diverse group of students: in 1556 they included forty-four Portuguese and *mestiços*, thirteen Malabaris, twenty-one Kanarins, and five from the Deccan. The rest were even more diverse: five Chinese, five Bengalis, two from Pegu, three East African Bantus, one Gujarati, one Armenian, six

Abyssinians, and five Muslim converts. Nor was this diversity, now partly subsumed in a common vocation, only to be found in St Paul's College, for the priests coming from Europe were themselves a very heterogeneous group. A list of 1637 finds Jesuits coming not only from Portugal but from Sicily, Naples, Aragon, Germany, Rome, France and Florence. The most famous of all, Xavier, was born in the Basque country.

The integrating role of the church was fostered in two other ways. First, they provided much more continuity than did political leaders. Viceroys served three years: an archbishop could go on for decades. Captains were rotated, or returned to Portugal: clerics usually made a life-time commitment to India. Hence the seventeenth-century Goan jingle: 'Viceroys come and viceroys go; but the Jesuits are always with us.' Second, members of the orders, with the Jesuits again in the forefront, were pioneers in learning Asian languages, the better to convert people. Some, it is true, did better than others at this: we noted above criticism of Franciscans failing here. Several of the early books printed in Goa were in vernaculars, and even in indigenous scripts. Thus, as a side product of the conversion drive, Indian languages began to be standardized.

The Jesuit printing press provides an example of the way in which the orders sometimes acted as agents for change, for the introduction of printing is generally seen as an important social and intellectual innovation. Similar claims have been made, notably by Cipolla, about the importance of accurate clocks. These have been seen as typifying the mechanical advances which laid the groundwork for the industrial revolution.[4] Similarly, it has often been claimed that a regard for precisely-measured time is a characteristic of a 'modern' person. Here again the Jesuits were to the fore. In 1549 the Rector of St Paul's asked the king, João III, for a clock instead of an hourglass. In the 1560s the Jesuits were adjusting their clocks by lunar observations. Soon after watches appeared, and mechanics who could repair, and even manufacture, both clocks and watches. Even in language teaching we find techniques which today appear very familiar. Jesuits learning Konkani were given a six-month intensive course, with two classes a day. They had to practice with native speakers, and were to use only Konkani when talking with fellow students.

[4] Carlo M. Cipolla, *European Culture and Overseas Expansion* (Harmondsworth, 1970), pp. 124–5 and *passim*.

The economic role of the clerics was also considerable. Again the Jesuits were prominent and successful, and indeed were accused of paying far too much attention to Mammon and far too little to Christ. Their response was of course that profits were necessary to save souls. It seems that the religious shared in the general trends of Goan trade. It will be remembered that in the seventeenth century sea trade declined. The result was that in places where Portugal had comparatively large areas of land there was pressure to set up estates and in effect exchange sea trade for landlordism. Apart from Goa, and Sri Lanka, which was turbulent, the largest land areas were in the provinces of the north, in Bassein and Daman. Here the Jesuits had large estates, to a total value of over 180,000 cruzados. It was claimed these should return 10 per cent on their value. Adding in rents from orchards, we find the Jesuits with annual receipts, from the land of about 22,500 cruzados. A traveller in this area in the 1670s claimed that the Jesuits 'govern all [Portuguese] India, in matters both temporal and spiritual, with a superiority and address that render them redoubtable to any who dare to work against this holy Society' (*The Travels of the Abbé Carré in India and the Near East, 1672 to 1674*, 3 vols., London, 1947–8, vol. I, pp. 132–3). The same sort of stereotype is revealed in another seventeenth-century jingle: 'Guard your wife from the Franciscans and your money from the Jesuits.' These comments reflect the prevailing image of the Jesuits, one which contributed to their suppression by Pombal in 1759. Yet they were not the only traders: other clerics also traded enthusiastically, if not as successfully.

We noted that even in the activist days of the sixteenth century official intolerance was sometimes softened in practice. To close this chapter we need to flesh out this impression by investigating a little more closely just what conversion meant, and exactly what the social impact of Christianity was. (Needless to say, we are writing social history, not a work of piety.) We can start at the top, where we would expect to find the greatest impact and 'purity': the seminary of St Paul set up in 1541 to train local clergy. Although at first sight it appears to be an institution pointing to major social change, closer examination shows this to be not completely the case: the trainees became only secular, not regular, priests, and in any case the great majority of them were converted brahmins. These men thus changed from being Hindu priests to being Catholic priests: their status positions remained constant. Similarly, from 1541 much land whose revenue had supported temples was used for financing Christian institutions and the orders. But the sums involved were small, and the point in any case is surely that these lands continued to finance religious activities. For their cultivators the move from Hindu to Christian can have made little difference.

We must consider the nature of the much-publicized conversions to Christianity. It is in no way to impugn the sincerity and fervour of Christianity in Goa either then or now to say that at least in the sixteenth century conversions, whether forced or not, were certainly done hastily and superficially. Church authors admit that many conversions were 'much too hasty . . . Anyone asking for Baptism was at once admitted, and once baptised was left very much to himself. The result was leakage and much ignorance in matters of religion.'[5] It is claimed that this was a problem in the impulsive 1540s, but from 1550 was remedied. Yet in fact mass baptisms, preceded by little or no instruction and succeeded by no follow-up, continued. We have already noted how in twelve days in 1548, 912 people were baptized in only 3 of the parishes of the city of Goa. On 25 August 1559, after some persuasion, 459 people on Chorão Island suddenly decided to convert. They were baptized on the 29th. On Divar Island 1535 people were baptized in three months. Even these feats pale in comparison with Xavier's effort in baptizing over 10,000 villagers in Travancore in one month in 1544.

The results, predictably enough, was less than pure Christian practice. Xavier's own biographer said that 'The wives and male and female slaves of the casados were . . . often so ignorant of the faith that they lived almost like their Mohamedan or pagan relatives and neighbours and shared their superstitions.'[6] Hindu processions continued despite prohibitions and Christians lent jewellery, finery and slaves to the participants, while Portuguese lent guns to fire salutes during the Muslim festival of Ramadan. No doubt Goan Christianity was fervent, and indeed the church at this time stressed emotion and devotion over strict adherence to norms. This was then for most a folk religion like any other, characterized by processions, festivals, fairs, plays, dances and attachment to such symbols as images, bells, pictures and crosses. The lack of differentiation was aided by a similar trend in

---

[5] Carlos Merces de Melo, *The Recruitment and Formation of the Native Clergy in India (16th–19th Century): An Historico-Canonical Study* (Lisbon, 1955), pp. 21–2.

[6] Georg Schurhammer, *Francis Xavier, His Life, His Times*, vol. II, 'India, 1541–1545' (Rome, 1977), p. 213.

Hinduism at this time: the very influential *bhakti* movement also put personal devotion above all else. Hence the agreeable catholicism (in the true sense of the term) of a Christian festival in Diu in 1672, well described for us by a French traveller, the Abbé Carré:

The ninth day of the Feast of the Rosary ended with a solemn service at the church of the Dominican Fathers. There were a sermon and a grand procession of the Blessed Sacrament all round the town, together with music, concerts, and other ceremonies, in which the Portuguese delight. But I was not pleased at the troops of dancing girls and masqueraders, who danced with very indecent postures in front of the procession. This detracted from the devotion and respect due to such a solemn occasion. In the evening, after the blessing, the fete was completed with fireworks, dancing girls, and a comedy acted in the church of the Dominican Fathers. (*The Travels of the Abbé Carré in India and the Near East, 1672 to 1674*, 3 vols., London, 1947–8, vol. I, pp. 135–6)

The continuing influence of Hindu caste notions among Goan Christians is a specific illustration of the way Catholicism adapted, at least a little, to its Indian environment. In part the Portuguese caused this, for as much as possible they encouraged only brahmin converts to enter the seminary. The third provincial council of 1585 said candidates should be 'of respectable and good families and castes, for the reason that the other Christians should look upon them with respect' (quoted in Priolkar, *The Printing Press in India*, p. 165). There does appear to be a difference between Goa and other areas, notably the Fishery Coast and Malabar, where large-scale conversion occurred. In these other areas only lower castes were converted. This homogeneity produced two results: internal stratification within the Christian community was not extreme; and the converts in terms of the surrounding Hindu society simply became another, low, caste grouping. But in Goa converts came from all castes: hence the continuance of caste stratification.

Generations after conversion caste still determined many aspects of social behaviour: marriage, membership of Christian confraternities, where one sat in church. Only in the taking of food was there some relaxation of the strict Hindu custom. A distinguished Christian brahmin claimed that the Portuguese themselves really just became another caste in Goa. A Goan author in 1695, a Christian, proudly described himself on his title page as a Sinai (Saraswat) brahmin from Chorão. In 1827 a British visitor to Goa noted that 'The Native Christians still retain many of the notions and prejudices of the Hindoos; even that of cast is not forgot. A Christian Bramin however poor would not consent to stand in the presence of the Richest Sudra who should be seated.'

Again Somerset Maugham has an interesting comment on the matter, which will serve to conclude this description of the varying impact of Portuguese Christianity on Indian society. In Goa in 1938 he met a Goan priest who, after six years in Rome, was now back home and trying to convert *sudras*. 'He said it was hopeless now to try to do anything with the high-caste Hindus.' He was in favour of a more autonomous native Catholicism in India. Maugham 'had a feeling that even though there were four hundred years of Catholicism behind him, he was still at heart a Vedantist'. He was told that Goan Christians never married out of caste. 'He was not displeased to tell me that there was not in his veins a drop of white blood; his family had always kept resolutely pure. "We're Christians," he said to me, "but first of all we're Hindus." His attitude to Hinduism was tolerant and sympathetic.'[7]

---

[7] Maugham, *Notebook*, pp. 282–3.

CHAPTER 6

DECLINE AND STAGNATION

The decline of the Portuguese empire in India is a much more contentious subject than may at first be apparent. It was something of a favourite for sententious English writers both of the time and through almost to today. Standing in the ruins of Old Goa (which even by the late seventeenth century was being deserted by the elite; the viceroy moved to the present capital of Panjim in the mid eighteenth century and the town became the official capital in 1843), they waxed lyrical, often portentious, as they surveyed the huge churches surrounded by encroaching jungle. The ineffable Dr John Fryer in 1681 said tendentiously that the Portuguese 'generally forgetting their pristine virtue, lust, riot and rapine . . . their courages being so much effeminated that it is a wonder to most how they keep anything, if it were not that they live among mean-spirited neighbours' (quoted in H. G. Rawlinson, *British Beginnings in Western India*, Oxford, 1920, p. 16).

Such comments, which could be multiplied endlessly, provide classic illustrations of historical relativity. English writers in the later seventeenth century, like Dr Fryer, wrote in a context of increasing, and profitable, English trade in India, while Portugal's official and military position was in rapid decline. In Europe, this was the time of the Methuen treaty (1703), which in effect turned Portugal into a British commercial colony. By the late eighteenth century British writers represented a country entering upon a period of world supremacy based on the industrial revolution, and one which had already made much larger conquests in India than the Portuguese had ever achieved. Even more so in the nineteenth century: writers like W. W. Hunter, F. C. Danvers and Richard Burton were exemplars of the calm British assumption, based on world domination, of the inherent superiority of British methods and actions.

From this platform they analysed the fall of their predecessors, and said more about themselves than about the Portuguese decline. Sturdy Protestants almost to a man, they expatiated on the evils of religious influence in government, most especially the Jesuits and the Inquisition. 'Clerical influence' was much discussed, and vigorously condemned, for Victorian Englishmen knew how to keep religion in its place.

It is indicative of the influence of contemporary cultural bonds on commentators that at the time of the decline the very reverse was sometimes put forward: the trouble with the Portuguese was lack of religion. A seventeenth-century French traveller noted, with considerable personal reservations, how contemporaries attributed the decline to

... want of Zeal for Religion ... they say that the Portugueses entring India with the Crucifix in one Hand and the Sword in the other, finding much Gold, they laid aside the Crucifix to fill their Pockets; and not being able to hold them up with one Hand they were grown so heavy, they dropp'd their Sword too. Being found in this posture by those who came after, they were easily overcome. (Sen, ed., *The Indian Travels of Thevenot and Careri*, p. 198).

Some writers got closer to the real nub of the problem when they noted a lack of 'business-like methods'. Portuguese administration was corrupt and personalized, much different from the efficient and honest Indian Civil Service to which so often the critics belonged. R. S. Whiteway (actually quite a good historian) thought that the last good governor was D. João de Castro (1545–8): 'the names of his successors for many generations, some indolent, some corrupt, some both, and all superstitious, are but the mile-stones that mark the progress along the dismal path of degeneration'.[1]

It was not a matter of morality, but of historical time. The sixteenth-century Portuguese administration was pre-modern by definition, just as were those of the British both at home and abroad until the late eighteenth century. As such it had certain characteristics, as did Clive's first period in Bengal, which made it different, and probably less effective, than any nineteenth-century bureaucracy. This comparative dimension was largely ignored by the critics.

Perhaps the greatest explanatory favourite was miscegenation. Even an American author writing in 1955 could see the decline as stemming in part from 'the creation of a half-caste population with the weaknesses of both races and few of their better qualities'.[2] An Italian in the late seventeenth century thought their problems might be 'because they are a mixture of Jews, Mahomedans, and Hindus, either having an admixture of their blood, or having drunk it in their nurses' milk'

---

[1] R. S. Whiteway, *The Rise of Portuguese Power in India, 1497–1550* (London, 1899), p. 324.
[2] Boies Penrose, *Travel and Discovery in the Renaissance, 1420–1620* (Cambridge, Mass., 1955), pp. 73–6.

(Niccolas Manucci, *Storia do Mogor*, 4 vols., Calcutta, 1965–7, vol. III, p. 127). The great orientalist Richard Burton in 1851 categorically saw the decline as a result of 'above all things, the slow but sure workings of the short-sighted policy of the Portuguese in intermarrying and identifying themselves with Hindoos of the lowest castes'.[3]

Not surprisingly, Portuguese historians have rejected most of these claims, and legitimately so, for they are nearly all ethnocentric and often overtly racist. Rather the Portuguese point to *force majeure*, in other words the 'Spanish Captivity' of 1580 to 1640. During this time, they say, Portugal's affairs were subordinate to the wider interests of her Spanish masters, and inevitably suffered. They shared in Spain's lugubrious decline, provided cannon fodder for Spanish Wars, and were attacked because they were part of Spain. Even today anti-Spanish feeling in Portugal runs deep.

Today we can hope to do much better than this. We can reject racist explanations deriving from bastardized Darwinism and Victorian self-esteem. Explanations which are merely anti-Papist diatribes can be dismissed. But international dimensions, such as the influence of Spain, must be evaluated, as must the nature of the Portuguese administration. Three general points will guide our discussion. If the theme of this book, which has stressed a very fluctuating Portuguese impact on India, varying greatly according to time, place and category, is correct, then we need to try and be equally precise concerning where the decline occurred. In areas where there was no peak of influence, can there be a trough? Second, this frequently quite minuscule impact we saw as originating, *au fond*, from the pre-modern character of sixteenth-century Portugal. It will be remembered that we claimed that almost her only decisive advantage lay in her naval superiority, and especially the use of cannon on ships. If this be so, then it logically follows that the arrival of different Europeans, people who were in the process of becoming 'modern', people from countries where scientific and techno-logical developments were beginning to lead to a qualitative change summed up later as the industrial revolution – the arrival of such people was 'inevitably' going to dispossess the Portuguese. In a nutshell, the way in which Portugal in the sixteenth century wasted her Asian profits dictated that the arrival of the Dutch, who had probably done better out of Portugal's Asian trade in the sixteenth century than the Portuguese did themselves, would spell their end. Third, we need to be clear about

[3] Richard Burton, *Goa and the Blue Mountains* (London, 1851), p. 45.

what a 'decline' really is. Is this a crisis or a decline? Who was affected? What was lost? Who survived? These three points will underlie our discussion, but first we must establish firmly the fact of the decline, and try to date when it occurred.

Some almost random examples point to various stresses and reverses. The military aspects are well known. The Dutch, arriving in Southeast Asia in 1596, drove out the Portuguese from this area over the next twenty years. They then reduced Portuguese trade in East Asia. The key fort of Malacca fell in 1641 to the Dutch, the whole of Sri Lanka in 1659, and all their forts in Malabar by 1663. Goa itself was blockaded by the Dutch in 1638–44, and 1656–63. The Persians, helped by the English, took another key possession, Hurmuz, in 1622.

There are other symptoms also. As early as 1606 it was profitable for a French ship to go from Marseilles to Lisbon with a cargo of pepper. By late in the century the population of the city of Goa had declined to 20,000, as compared with about 75,000 in 1600. Now the walls of the city encompassed too large an area. The fate of the famous Royal Hospital is another example. Lavishly praised by early travellers, by mid century it was deteriorating. The French jeweller J.-B. Tavernier allows us to date this fairly precisely. On his first visit, in 1641, it was still splendid, but by 1648 it was in decline and badly managed. State finances declined rapidly. In 1630 the viceroy advised the king to lift the prohibition on Hindu weddings in Portuguese territory in return for a payment. Thus the Portuguese could make up to 3000 cruzados a year. That such a trifling sum could, even as a proposal, dictate such a major policy change is indicative indeed of the Portuguese government's financial straits.

In this same year of 1630 the viceroy complained of the decline in military effectiveness in the state. A habit had grown up of merchants travelling in small boats, so that when a Dutch ship attacked they could more easily beach them and run away inland. In 1662 the ruler of Kanara was deemed to be eminently deserving of punishment for his insolence and hostility. However, given Portugal's lack of military strength, nothing could be done even about so petty an opponent as this. A Scots captain, Alexander Hamilton, toured the remaining Portuguese areas in western India at the end of the seventeenth century. The dominant words are 'poverty', 'calamity', and 'contempt'. His description of Diu says it all. 'It is one of the best built Cities, and best fortified by Nature and Art, that ever I saw in India, and its stately

Buildings of free Stone and Marble are sufficient Witnesses of its ancient Grandeur and Opulence; but at present not above one fourth of the City is inhabited' (Alexander Hamilton, *A New Account of the East Indies*, 2 vols., London, 1930, vol. 1, p. 82).

An attempt to specify when the decline began raises the question of what decline actually means. Some nineteenth-century British writers claimed Castro was the last of the great governors; after his death in 1548 the degeneracy began. A popular Portuguese historian seemed to agree. As early as 1540 she found that 'the vital forces of the race were running out'.[4] The great chronicler Diogo do Couto, writing in the early seventeenth century, claimed that the defeat of the Hindu empire of Vijayanagar in 1565 began the decline, for this ended a very profitable trade through Goa, and also led to a debasement of coinage.

Many modern authors date the decline from the arrival of the Dutch. Up to the end of the sixteenth century Portuguese India was prosperous, its budget balanced, and its possessions secure. The city was at its most opulent in the last decade of the century. It is true that in the second half of the century the trade to Europe, especially the vital spice trade, declined precipitously. This however was more than made up by the inter-Asian trade, which created *casado* and businessman fortunes in Goa, and via the customs duties fed the state coffers. Thus to concentrate on a decline in intercontinental trade is to distort the picture. The almost autonomous Asian empire was flourishing.

Still others, using implicitly an index of decline which relies heavily on loss of possessions, claim all was well until about 1640. To this time the Dutch concentrated on Southeast and East Asia, areas where the Portuguese empire had never been strong anyway. In their core area of the western Indian Ocean only Hurmuz was lost, and this to Persia not the Dutch. Decisive attacks in this area date only from 1636, and the real decline in India is seen only with the disastrous losses of the late 1650s and early 1660s.

The problem with this interpretation of decline is that it is too narrow. Dutch control over Indonesia had ruined Malacca before it was actually conquered in 1641; similarly, Dutch efforts had produced, as we will see, a catastrophic decline in Portuguese country trade in the Arabian Sea long before losses of possessions occurred. If one says that a flourishing Asian trade in the late sixteenth century points to a prosperous empire, then the decline in this same trade in the early

[4] Elaine Sanceau, *Knight of the Renaissance: D. João de Castro* (London, n.d.), p. 61.

seventeenth century must point to problems long before 1640. Territorial losses, in fact, were a symptom, not a cause, of decline. The decline does date from the arrival of the Dutch, with their success in both commercial and military competition. We need now to extend on this, keeping in mind always the precise nature and dimensions of the problem. We can start with international aspects.

Portugal until 1640 was part of Spain. It is, nevertheless, difficult to see this constituting a real problem for her empire. She retained considerable autonomy, even though ruled from Madrid. Her empire was kept strictly separate from Spain's, so that for example there was little contact between Portuguese Macao and Spanish Manila.

Relations with Spain really became a problem only after Portugal regained her independence in 1640. Spain opposed this, and the war in Iberia continued until 1668, though often in a most desultory fashion. Much more important was a general shift in the focus of the empire, and Dutch attacks on what was becoming its most vital part.

One can distinguish four broad phases of Portuguese overseas activities. In the fifteenth century North Africa and gold and slaves dominated, in the sixteenth the Indian Ocean and spices, in the seventeenth and eighteenth Brazil and sugar, and from the nineteenth, after the loss of Brazil in 1822, Africa and slaves until about 1850. The rise of Brazil and sugar is plain to see. The Portuguese population rose from 2000 in the 1540s to 25,000 in 1600, 50,000 in 1650 and up to 100,000 in 1700. The slave population increased even faster, and seems always to have been greater than the Portuguese. (It will be remembered that Goa at 1600 had a Portuguese population of perhaps 1500 to 2000, and this declined over the century; even by the 1630s there were only about 800. In the whole of Asia there were perhaps 16,000 Portuguese and mestiços at 1600.) These Brazilians, both servile and free, were there for the sugar. The number of sugar mills rose from 60 in 1570 to 300 in 1645; sugar production over the same period increased eightfold.

The result of this increasing importance of Brazil to Portugal was that the metropole countered Dutch attacks there much more forcibly than those in the east; after all, the Goa–Lisbon trade had long been in decline. Northern Brazil was occupied by the Dutch in 1635. They were finally driven out in 1654; at least in these years here was the major Portuguese effort. In 1638, 41 ships and 5000 men were assembled in Portugal to relieve Brazil; in 1636–9 only a few ships and 500 men were available for India. Portugal's population around 1650 was at most 2,000,000: her limited resources had to be devoted to the more valuable Brazil. India provided little for the metropole; it got little help against the Dutch.

These international factors also influenced the strength of Dutch attacks in the east. From the late 1630s their attention turned from East Asia to the Indian Ocean. Goa was blockaded from 1638 to 1644. Then Pernambuco in Brazil received their attention, and a truce was declared in the east from 1644 to 1652. It was only after their defeat in North Brazil that they returned to the Indian Ocean. Goa was blockaded again from 1656 until the end of hostilities in 1663.

The statistics of Portuguese losses in India between 1640 and 1663 are, at least by seventeenth-century standards, appalling. During the viceroyalty of Linhares, from 1629 to 1635, they lost 1500 men, 155 ships, and booty of 5,500,000 cruzados. Under the next governor 4000 Portuguese were killed in 3 years. Five hundred were sent from Portugal to replace them. In 1624–5 over 500,000 cruzados was spent on an armada which fought, unsuccessfully, against the Dutch and their English allies. (England made peace with the Portuguese in 1635; the Dutch were always the main opponents.) Huge sums went on other fleets, and on the protracted wars in Sri Lanka with the king of Kandy and his Dutch allies. The list of Portuguese possessions shrank alarmingly: from fifty-odd forts and fortified areas in the sixteenth century, they were reduced by 1666 to just nine: three in Africa, Macao, and in India, now that Malabar was lost, only Goa, Diu, Daman, Bassein and Chaul.

The reasons for these military losses are plain to see. Metropolitan attention and resources went to Brazil. In the east the Dutch were better financed, better armed, and more numerous. The Portuguese were defending a ramshackle and very dispersed empire which could be picked off *seriatim*. As a contemporary noted: 'From the Cape of Good Hope to Japan we were unwilling to leave anything outside our control. We were anxious to lay hands on everything in that huge stretch of over 5000 leagues from Sofala to Japan' (quoted in C. R. Boxer, *Portuguese India in the Mid-Seventeenth Century*, Delhi, 1980, p. 3). The over-extended empire was easy prey.

Not, however, that the Dutch had it all their own way. Several Portuguese forts put up epic defences, notably Malacca, Colombo and Cochin. The latter resisted Dutch attacks for four years. Goa itself was blockaded for a total of fifteen years. Yet the effects of this must not be exaggerated. Portuguese ingenuity enabled trade to continue, and food and supplies to be available. A Dutch commander's complaint about the difficulties of the blockade is ironically almost identical with sixteenth-century Portuguese complaints about how hard it was to block the 'illegal' Malabar pepper trade, or the Red Sea trade:

> Notwithstanding our vigilance merchandise of all kinds are brought into Goa by the rowing vessels and we cannot prevent them as by their swiftness they always elude our pursuit. The merchandises from the North and South coast are landed about five or six miles from Goa and then fetched away by their fregata de remos [oared frigates]. In the same way goods can be sent from Goa, so that our blockade can only prevent their caracks from leaving the harbour. (India Office Records, European Manuscripts, 1/3/22, no. CCCLVIII)

The contemporary who complained of Portugal being over-extended noted that the empire 'could not last for ever, even if we had only the natives to fight against' (Boxer, *Portuguese India in the Mid-Seventeenth Century*, p. 3). In fact various 'natives' humiliated the Portuguese almost as well as did the Dutch. Omani Arab forces had several successes in East Africa in the second half of the seventeenth century. In India their greatest accomplishment was to take and plunder the town of Diu in 1668. The fort was not attacked, but Portuguese forces, both land and sea, performed most ingloriously.

The final blows came from the Marathas, the Hindu fighters who gained control of much of western India in the later seventeenth century. The founder, Sivaji, made what seems to have been a rather half-hearted thrust in 1667. In 1683 his successor, Sambhaji, launched a major attack. He was very close to total success when he was providentially (for the Portuguese) diverted by a Mughal attack on him. This episode is often forgotten. In Indian nationalist terms, what it meant was that India came very close indeed to solving her 'Portuguese problem' some 278 years before in fact this was achieved by the 'liberation' of Goa in 1961. In any case, Maratha pressure continued in the next century. In 1739–41 most of the Old Conquests except the city were occupied by them. It was at this time (May 1739) that the Portuguese lost the extensive lands and quite prosperous town of Bassein to the Marathas. Compensation of sorts was achieved by the later conquest, in the 1760s and 1770s, of seven new *talukas*, the New Conquests, which extended the area of Goa to the north, south and east; the Old Conquests make up about 785 square kilometres, the New

Conquests a little under 3000. They were little valued at the time, but it was here that large deposits of iron ore were later exploited. By the end of the eighteenth century Portuguese India consisted of this enlarged Goa, and a moribund Diu and Daman. The British almost contemptuously garrisoned them during the Napoleonic Wars, and as contemptuously handed them back in 1815.

These political and military defeats are easily explained. Many writers, however, have also looked to administrative weaknesses, in a word corruption, to explain these losses. Here again it is essential to avoid imposing on the sixteenth and seventeenth centuries ideal twentieth-century standards relating to official behaviour. Some perquisites, some peculation, were part of all administrations at this time. It is when these shade over into excesses, abuses, that we can find them contributing to the decline.

Such abuses certainly were present in the seventeenth century. Whether they were greater then than in the preceding century must remain an open question. Much of the evidence points to abuses throughout. If this be so, in other words if detrimental corruption was a constant, then we cannot talk of this causing the decline. The point really is that, regardless of whether abuses were new, or greater than before, their existence clearly did reduce Portuguese military and economic effectiveness when they were faced by the Dutch.

In 1629 Mozambique fort had 300 soldiers on its muster roll, but in fact there were less than 100 there. This was an extreme, but not atypical, case: in all Portuguese forts at least a third of the soldiers on the books were phantoms whose pay was drawn by a very real and very corrupt commander.

Complaints of tyrannical behaviour by captains of forts are legion. Couto claimed around 1560 a captain of a great fort like Hurmuz, Malacca or Sofala would make 30,000 cruzados profit. By the end of the century this had risen to 200,000 or even 300,000. These huge profits came from forced trade and extortion. The effects were serious. Local traders tried to circumvent Portuguese forts, not so much to escape having to pay customs duties as to avoid being shaken down by the captain.

Nor was it only Indians who were disadvantaged. Even Portuguese *casados*, we are told, fled inland to avoid their rapacious fellow countrymen. In the 1630s in Diu, according to Bocarro, one could see the ruins of many fine two- or three-storey houses which had been deserted by their *casado* owners because of the bad treatment they had received from the captains and their relatives and clients. Such an exodus of *casados*, together with huge military desertions, explain the presence of perhaps 5000 Portuguese in just three extra-Portuguese areas, Bengal, Siam and Macassar. St Francis Xavier complained bitterly of the fiscal (and sexual) laxity he found in Goa in the mid 1540s. In a famous indictment he said all official positions led to stealing; 'all go the way of rapio, rapis [I steal, you steal]. And I am astonished at seeing how those who come from there find so many moods, tenses, and participles for this poor word rapio, rapis' (quoted in Georg Schurhammer, *Francis Xavier: His Life, His Times*, vol. II, Rome, 1977, p. 540).

Some Portuguese authors have claimed that the Portuguese became corrupt because the Indian environment was corrupt. We can reject this, and instead agree with an early chronicler who said 'There is no justice in [Portuguese] India because there is none in Portugal' (Correa, *Lendas da India*, vol. II, p. 842). But perhaps the Indian environment contributed in the sense that this was a more open, free-wheeling, frontier society than was metropolitan Portugal. Opportunities for peculation, extortion and plunder were greater, and were usually taken.

Corruption was present throughout the sixteenth and seventeenth centuries. It may have increased in the latter: as Portuguese trade declined captains were driven to more extortion to compensate for a fall in their legitimate profits. But, in what is almost a stereotype of a vicious circle, Portuguese India could not afford this now. As we saw, corruption contributed to military ineffectiveness, and thus to Portugal's sometimes inglorious response to Dutch attacks.

The economic dimensions of Portuguese decline are crucial: if sea trade fell, then the vital customs revenues were diminished, and the state budget went into deficit. Dutch success in commercial competition laid the basis for Portuguese decline and territorial losses. What were the dimensions of this economic decline in India?

We have stressed the rise of country trade in the later sixteenth century as the *carreira* to Portugal declined. By 1630 the ratio in Goa was roughly 15 : 1. The trade to Europe, in difficulties before 1600, declined precipitously thereafter. As early as 1620 the Dutch were importing more into Europe than the Portuguese had done in the last quarter of the sixteenth century. The Portuguese at this time returned 2000 or 3000 tons of shipping a year to Europe; by the middle of the century the Dutch were returning 10,000. These figures become even more significant when we remember that the Portuguese had had a monopoly, while the Dutch did not. Even in the first decade of the century, from 1600 to 1610, the Dutch returned 75 ships to Europe, the Portuguese only 27. Between 1570 and 1595 the Portuguese took about 25–30,000 quintals of spices to Europe a year. By the second decade of the next century this had shrunk to 7500 to 10,000. A belated and feeble attempt to imitate English and Dutch methods, that is by setting up a trading company, lasted only from 1628 to 1635, and failed miserably. The aim was only to ease the strain on royal resources by getting private investment in the Asian enterprise: not surprisingly, this investment failed to be forthcoming.

The decline in the country trade was as great, and much more significant. If the notion of Portugal's empire being a net or network of maritime connections, which we presented in chapter 3, is correct, then clearly such an empire could only survive while these communications could continue. Faced with Dutch and English competition in the country trade, let alone the blockades of Goa later, Portuguese trade deteriorated very quickly. Goa's customs revenues fell by almost one half between 1600 and the 1630s. Estimates of the value of her sea trade, based on these customs figures, show a decline from 2,700,000 cruzados in 1600 to 1,800,000 in 1616–17, 1,400,000 in 1635, and a minuscule 500,000 by 1680. Not surprisingly, the state budget as a result moved into substantial deficit. The balance was made up by cash subsidies from Europe – 512,000 cruzados between 1630 and 1635 alone – and loans from local Goan sources such as the Misericordia and wealthy private capitalists, both Indian and Portuguese. Neither solution could be used indefinitely. Goan capitalists vanished as the economy deteriorated; the metropole, as we saw, increasingly devoted its meagre resources to Brazil.

The Portuguese were soon aware of Dutch commercial competition. As early as 1607 they complained that Dutch and Indian ships traded freely between Surat and Acheh, and Portuguese commerce had already declined as a result. That commercial competition began the rot is clear from a letter from the viceroy to the king in 1629, that is nine years before the Dutch had begun to blockade Goa. The High Court had told the viceroy that although they had no exact figures on present or past state revenues, they did know that ships with cloves from the Moluccas no longer came to Goa, and nor did revenues from Hurmuz or Malacca.

Diu raised less than half, Goa only one-third or one-quarter, compared with twenty years before. Yet at the same time state expenses had risen sharply.

Even natural phenomena seem to have conspired to exacerbate Portuguese problems. Epidemics in Goa, minor in the sixteenth century, increased in number and intensity in the seventeenth. Ship losses increased dramatically. Even leaving aside such one-off disasters as the loss of a convoy of 140 ships in a storm south of Goa in May 1652 (only one ship survived; one of those lost had on board 150,000 cruzados in coin), the long-term trend was unfavourable. In the sixteenth century 768 ships left Lisbon for the east. Up to 1579 only about 10 percent were lost. But between 1580 and 1612 only 63 percent returned safely to Europe. Between 1592 and 1602 alone 38 ships were lost on the *carreira*.

These increased losses had several causes. Climatologists talk of a Little Ice Age between 1550 and 1700 which was at its height late in the sixteenth century. This may explain some of the ship losses, for associated with it were violent storms in the Atlantic. Human factors also contributed. Overloading was endemic, so that sailors and marines had to stumble over and around bales and boxes of merchandise on deck. Mortality from disease and accident was high; in 1614 a ship from Asia arrived off Lisbon with only 16 survivors from a total of 300 who had embarked in her. Even navigational skills may have deteriorated. On one notorious occasion in 1650 a ship bound for India put into Luanda, Angola. The pilot thought he had reached India.

Yet even amidst all this woe, it is important to see the decline as affecting the state, and sea trade, but not necessarily people on the land. The vast bulk of Goa's population, its urban poor and peasants, being largely outside the international economy were little affected by its deterioration. Much more important for them were broad movements in food availability and price. When the food convoys from the south were blocked the urban poor, and even some peasants, were affected. Probably the major event for the bulk of Goa's population in the seventeenth century was not Portuguese decline but the great famine of 1630–2, which devastated large areas of western India and caused huge mortality.

The country trade declined over the century, but of course never completely ended. The result was a move to the land. In the sixteenth century few *casados* in the larger land areas of Goa, Daman and Bassein had left the cities: private sea trade was the preferred economic activity. By the seventeenth century there is evidence of *casados*, and the religious orders, moving to acquire rights over land, and set up landed estates. Travellers' accounts point to such gentry, including the orders, living very well indeed, rich people in a poor state just like their counterparts in Portugal itself. A Frenchman in the 1690s travelled inland from Bassein for 15 miles (24 kms.), and found nothing but 'delightful Gardens' cultivated by a peasant population which while religiously mixed was united in poverty (Sen, ed., *The Indian Travels of Thevenot and Careri*, pp. 168–9). The Scots Captain Hamilton in 1700 described Bassein as 'a place of small Trade because most of its Riches ly dead and buried in their Churches, or in the Hands of indolent lazy Country Gentlemen, who loiter away their Days in Ease, Luxury and Pride, without having the least Sense of the Poverty and Calamity of their Country' (Hamilton, *A New Account of the East Indies*, vol. I, p. 105). Nor did some high officials always display a care for the decline of their state. Peculation continued: office holding was still too often seen as simply an opportunity to make a fortune through speculation and extortion.

CHAPTER 7

TOWARDS REINTEGRATION

Many of the themes of previous chapters will be found writ large in a sketch of the history of Portuguese India from the mid seventeenth century. After the loss of the large and prosperous area of Bassein in 1739, the Portuguese ruled only Goa, Daman and Diu. The latter increased in size in the 1760s and 1770s when the relatively infertile and sparsely populated seven New Conquest *talukas* were added.

If the Portuguese at their height in the sixteenth century had a rather patchy impact on Indian life, how much more did this apply to such a minuscule 'empire'. The official Portuguese presence was, frankly, *opéra bouffe*, strong still on titles and pomp and circumstance, but of no significance in wider Indian affairs. At a lower, or unofficial level, one finds the continuance of powerful religious influence, already touched on in chapter 6, and a continuing role for some Indo-Portuguese traders, usually ethnically Indian. If one can see in the sixteenth and early seventeenth centuries the church and private traders playing important roles under the imperial umbrella, then what happened later was that as the umbrella folded the role of these two groups became more discernible. Their actual functions probably remained rather constant throughout, but this has often been obscured for historians by the dazzle of the imperial canopy, especially in the sixteenth century.

Much of what follows will be tentative indeed. The eighteenth and nineteenth centuries have been neglected by historians. It has been felt that with the decline of empire nothing of interest can be written about the Portuguese in India. All we have are a series of rather tendentious studies of India's 'liberation' of Goa in 1961. Some younger scholars are at last beginning to do new and important work on this dark age, and we can begin to see that beneath the official level there were interesting developments taking place, especially in the economic sphere. The available documentation for the eighteenth and nineteenth centuries is comparatively vast, as any guide to the historical archives of Goa will show. In what follows we will draw on as much new research as is available, and also at times point to some of the more obvious gaps and areas where research is both possible and necessary.

Metropolitan Portugal, enervated by the long war of independence against Spain (1640–68) and perennially suffering from lack of resources and a usually capricious and arbitrary government, staggered through the late seventeenth and early eighteenth centuries. The whole of both centuries was dominated by the Brazilian trade, which provided the major source of both public and private income. Lisbon was able to continue as an entrepot, with sixteenth-century spices now replaced by sugar.

Such public finances as were raised from this trade were ill-used. The Bragança dynasty in the eighteenth century was usually profligate and corrupt, and its members also suffered from an astounding catalogue of illnesses: among them diphtheria, typhoid fever, smallpox, tuberculosis and insanity. Portuguese agriculture remained primitive in the extreme. Private money raised from commercial activities went on ostentation and show: investment in productive activities was minimal, and Portuguese industry remained almost completely underdeveloped.

Not that all this was entirely the fault of the Portuguese. The Methuen Treaty of 1703 with Britain left the country in what today would be called a neo-colonial situation. It gave British merchants and traders outrageous advantages in Portugal. This enabled them to dominate the port wine trade and, more important, syphon off large parts of the profits from slave-grown Brazilian sugar.

Few of these structural problems were solved by the frenetic activity of the Marquis of Pombal, who effectively ruled Portugal from 1755, the time of the great Lisbon earthquake, to 1777. Under his personal, and very brutal, dictatorship many reforms and changes were promulgated. In 1759 the Jesuit order in Portugal was suppressed, and their property confiscated. He vigorously attacked colour prejudice. Slavery was abolished in 1773, and he told the Indian viceroy 'to dispose matters in such a way that the ownership of land, the sacred ministry of parishes, the exercise of public affairs, and even military posts, should be conferred mostly on natives of the soil or on their sons and grandsons not taking into consideration whether they be white or black' (quoted in J. M. Richards, *Goa*, New Delhi, 1982, p. 69). Strong words, yet racial discrimination, and Brazilian slavery, continued, and in any case this all applied only to Christians. Portugal's basic economic problems continued too. The new enterprises set up by Pombal were state run; not surprisingly most of them were unable to compete with British goods, and meanwhile a Portuguese middle class still failed to appear.

The nineteenth century saw little political improvement, but much change. In 1807 the French invaded Portugal, and the court fled to Brazil. A most confused period after the end of the French occupation culminated in Brazil's independence in 1822, and in the same year a liberal constitution for Portugal. The power of the court was greatly restricted. The problem was that Portuguese backwardness made the operation of a relatively liberal constitution almost impossible, so that the liberal period from 1820 to 1851 was characterized by great political instability. This in turn meant even less control over Portugal's diminished colonial empire, something which was exacerbated by the anti-clerical tone of Portuguese governments in the 1830s. The clergy had always operated as a second arm of the state; now this arm also was weakened.

In the second half of the century more conservative elements at least ensured greater government stability. They were however increasingly opposed by liberal and republican supporters. Finally in 1910 the monarchy was overthrown. A very important consequence for the empire was that discrimination based on religion was now outlawed. But Portuguese politics remained chaotic, until the ascetic strongman Dr Antonio de Oliveira Salazar took over in 1928.

A much shrunken Portuguese India could expect little or no help from such a metropole. As a result, politics in Portuguese India were characterized by theoretically autocratic governors presiding over a moribund and impecunious state. Pombal's reforms, by the time they reached India, were more a gentle breeze than the cyclone he intended. There were even problems in finding a capital for Portuguese India. What is now Old Goa had been largely deserted by the end of the seventeenth century. The main reason for the exodus of the elite, excluding clergy, was impure water supplies, which produced endemic cholera and malaria. Many years were spent considering and even planning a move to the more healthy port of Marmagoa. Nothing came of this. Panjim from the mid eighteenth century was the unofficial, and from 1843 the official, capital.

Many examples could show the deterioration of Portuguese India's international position in the nineteenth century. Most obvious was the British occupation of Goa from 1799 to 1815, during the Napoleonic Wars. The aim was to deny France a potential foothold in India. The Portuguese were hardly delighted by the imposed protection, but could do little about it. At first their tiny army was in theory not under

British control, but from 1808 it was. Worse could have followed: the forward-looking Lord Wellesley proposed that Portuguese India, a geopolitical absurdity from his point of view, be permanently ceded to Britain, perhaps in exchange for Malacca.

Nothing came of this, and at the peace Goa was returned in good, or at least no worse, condition. The idea of a British acquisition was revived in 1839. The British were annoyed that some British Indian rebels and outlaws had been using Goa as a sanctuary. The British ambassador in Lisbon offered the insultingly paltry sum of £500,000 for Goa, Daman and Diu. The Portuguese of course turned this down indignantly; yet even much later, in 1873–4, the annual revenue of this state was less than one-quarter of the British offer. Not for the first and certainly not for the last time pride and prestige in Portugal triumphed over cold economic calculation.

By this time Portuguese India was a military and political joke. In 1871 the governor, on a tour to Daman and Diu, had to get transport for his suite in a British steamship. In 1858 a brash eighteen-year-old British midshipman wondered at the decayed glories of Old Goa, and the remaining fortifications, and assured his father that 'now they are so rotten we should soon knock them about their ears' (Edwin Dawes, 'Letters', India Office Records, European Manuscripts, C345, letter to father, 10 Nov. 1858).

Several metropolitan events had their repercussions in Goa. The failure of Pombal's reforms to produce racial equality seems to have sparked a quite large revolt in 1787, which was led by an alliance of clerics, army officers and other Indian Christian elites. Over a century later, in 1890, twenty-three liberals were killed in front of the Margão parish church.

Throughout the nineteenth century, indeed from the 1760s, the Portuguese authorities were faced with a series of revolts by inhabitants of the New Conquests called Ranes, or Rajputs. Twenty are recorded up to 1912; we know too little of their causes or character. The general political instability of the nineteenth century had less sanguinary echoes also. From 1822, as a result of the liberal constitution, Goa had two representatives in the Portuguese parliament, elected, to be sure, on a very restricted franchise. Voters had to know Portuguese, and pay high taxes, so that only 40,000 out of a total population of about 500,000 were eligible: even so, for the early nineteenth century this was a wide franchise. At the time of the political upheaval in Portugal in 1821, white Goan liberals organized a coup against their particularly reactionary governor, who fled to Bombay. Yet liberal influence could not go too far. In 1835 a Goan doctor, Bernado Peres da Silva, was appointed Prefect, the title at this time for the governor of Portuguese India. He was deposed after only seventeen days.

We have already expatiated on the role of the church. There is some evidence that it, and the orders, shared in the general decay. The two most fervent, committed, and intolerant parts of the church were the Jesuits and the Inquisition. The Jesuits, it will be remembered, were suppressed (albeit temporarily) by Pombal in 1759. The Inquisition in Goa similarly was abolished in 1774, later revived in much attenuated form and finally ended in 1820. Yet a slackening of zeal even in the Inquisition seems to be discernible in the seventeenth century, while the Jesuits also by then had lost their earlier élan and enthusiasm, and seem to have concentrated on trade. Symptomatic of this, and of Goa's decline in general, was the closing-down of the Jesuits' famous printing press in 1683. Extraordinarily, Goa then remained without any printing facilities until as late as 1821, when a government press was set up. Only in 1859 was a private press established.

In this period of decay race relations remained uneven. We begin now to have some rather more precise population figures. The total in the Old Conquests in 1750 was 208,000; by around 1800 this had shrunk further to 178,500, in all Goa in 1851 363,750. Of these only 1851 could claim to be European or descended from Europeans. About 63 percent were Christian, a much larger proportion than in the twentieth century. The largest town, Panjim, was a modest 15,000. Pombal's decree laid down, on paper, the equality of all Christians, not all Goans. Only in 1833 were Hindus allowed to practise their rites and ceremonies in Goa, though in fact intolerance had long before then lost its teeth. But discrimination remained a problem. The orders were notoriously reluctant to admit Indians, or even sometimes mestiços or Portuguese born in India. These were forced to make do as only secular, not regular, priests. In this area at least Pombal's reforms had some effect, for when the orders were suppressed in 1834 only 16 out of 300 regular clergy in Goa were Portuguese.

Discrimination was also seen in attempts to make Goans speak Portuguese rather than the local Konkani language. In 1684 an ambitious, unrealistic and racist governor had tried to forbid the use of any vernacular language. This of course failed, yet in 1847 the archbishop decreed to seminaries that 'It is absolutely forbidden both to students and any Ecclesiastic residing in the Seminary to converse with one another in the language of Goa' (Priolkar, *The Printing Press in India*, p. 215). Some years later a scholar wanted a book printed in Konkani. The compositors in Panjim asked for a 25 percent loading, this being applicable to foreign-language books.

Yet with all this, the situation in the eighteenth and nineteenth centuries seems not to have been totally bleak. Official discrimination did not affect the dominant economic position of various Hindu groups in Goa throughout. One of Goa's most famous sons was the Abbé Faria (1755–1819), a distinguished savant, prominent in the French Revolution, and an early practitioner of hypnotism. He was part negro. A better example is the very distinguished Xavier family. They were descended from a convert originally called Narsu Quenim, and apparently had no, or very little, European blood. Despite this they flourished in the eighteenth and nineteenth centuries. Family members held such official positions as interim secretary-general of Portuguese India, secretary to the governor general of Mozambique, president of the municipal council of Mozambique, and commander of the artillery in Lisbon's National Guard. Others were a priest, a doctor, a headmaster, and the famous *littérateur* Filippe Nery Xavier. Even Richard Burton around 1850 noticed this change, this increasing tolerance.

But at Goa all men are equal. Moreover, the heathens may be seen in Christian churches with covered feet, pointing at, putting questions concerning, and criticizing the images with the same quite-at-home nonchalance with which they would wander through the porticos of Dwarka or the pagodas of Aboo. And these men's fathers, in the good old times of Goa, were not allowed even to burn their dead in the land.[1]

This said, it is important to remember that official, legislated, discrimination against non-Christian Goans continued until the revolution of 1910. Only then did all Goans get full equality, only then were Hindus freed from discrimination if not oppression. (And by this time Hindus made up 49 percent of the total population.) After 1910 they flooded to schools, joined actively in public life (until this was terminated for all Portuguese by Dr Salazar) and founded libraries and journals.

Goa on the eve of Dr Salazar was still fragmented, poor and internally stratified. The handful of Europeans (246 in 1900) held most major

---

[1] Richard Burton, *Goa and the Blue Mountains* (London, 1851), pp. 106–7.

posts. About 85 percent of the population lived in villages which, thanks to primitive communications, were still isolated. A semi-official British account of 1920 sneered that Goans were 'hospitable, courteous, and intelligent, though not progressive', that 'Christianity has not improved the industry of the inhabitants', and that those who employ 'Goanese' servants 'are apt to make qualifications in their testimonials to character'.[2]

More to the point is to stress how disaggregated Goa was, really until 1961. Even the almost-universally spoken Konkani language was far from standardized. Hindus and Christians spoke very different versions, as was revealed in the 1950s when the great archivist and historian P. S. S. Pissurlencar tried to address the students of Rachol Seminary in his Hindu Konkani. They could only follow Christian Konkani; finally both sides spoke Portuguese. An even greater Goan scholar, D. D. Kosambi, claimed that at least around 1925 he could place 'any individual to within five miles of locality of origin by his speech'.[3] We must now consider, first, the economy of the Portuguese empire, and then Goa's economy.

Until the loss of Brazil in 1822 Lisbon had always functioned as an entrepot, importing colonial products and in the eighteenth century British manufactures, and exporting these manufactures and some bullion back to her colonies. In the eighteenth century Brazil continued to be all-important. Sugar was still the main product, but to this was joined gold, diamonds and coffee, and the importation of slaves and British goods. Thanks to the Methuen Treaty of 1703 much of this trade was financed by, even controlled by, British capital. Portugal remained impoverished, importing large quantities of basic foodstuffs, even the national dish of *bacalhau* (dried codfish). The disruptions of the Napoleonic Wars benefited Portugal, which for some of this time was neutral, but the improvement was only temporary, for the loss of Brazil ended Lisbon's centuries-old entrepot role. Her remaining colonies, really just Angola and Mozambique, produced little. For the first time Portugal had to survive more or less on her own, paltry, domestic resources.

The exception, and one only now being adequately researched, was the slave trade. Recent research points to Portuguese traders, often in

[2] *Peace Handbooks: Issued by the Historical Section of the Foreign Office*, vol. XIII, section 79, on Portuguese India (London, 1920), pp. 8, 17, 31.
[3] D. D. Kosambi, 'The village communities in the Old Conquests of Goa', *Journal of the University of Bombay*, XV (1947), 66–7.

alliance with, or financed by, British merchants, doing well in the second quarter of the nineteenth century from this trade. The goods used were mostly British.

This trade was of course illegal. From 1817 Britain took to herself the right to stop suspected slave ships, and search them, and from 1839 the British declared that Portuguese slavers would be dealt with as pirates. In 1836 a liberal Lisbon government banned the Portuguese slave trade.

This opposition failed to have any immediate effect for two reasons. British patrols could often be circumvented at sea. Second, we have noted very slight metropolitan control over the activities of colonial African officers. This meant that Portuguese officials in Angola could profit from allowing the trade to continue; indeed they often participated in it themselves. A concrete illustration of the ineffectiveness of decrees issued in Lisbon is that, although they abolished the slave trade in the empire in 1836, until 1844 Angolan officials continued to levy an export tax on slaves.

Being illegal, this trade generated very little state revenue. It did, however, create fortunes for Portuguese traders in the African colonies, and also for Portuguese resident in Brazil. An unquantifiable, but apparently considerable, part of these profits ended up back in Portugal. The result was a writ-large version of something we have seen several times before: rich people in a poor state. It was this wealth which financed a modest economic boom in Portugal in the later nineteenth century. For the first time there was some internal economic development in Portugal.

These profits were curtailed only from 1850, when Brazil began to enforce legislation forbidding the entry of slaves. By 1853 the trade had ended. Slavery nevertheless continued in Portuguese colonies – in 1854 there were about 100,000 slaves in Portuguese Africa. In 1858 Lisbon decreed the end of slavery within twenty years, yet it continued in some parts of the empire until the advent of the republic in 1910, and indeed even after this, now thinly disguised as indentured labour.

Portuguese India played only a small role in this trade. Indeed, her trade with the metropole in the eighteenth and nineteenth centuries was very insignificant. Thus figures from 1886 show that 95 percent of the metropole's trade with her colonies was with Angola, São Thomé and Cabo Verde, in West Africa. Goa and Mozambique were very minor. And in any case Portugal's total colonial trade was insignificant compared with her trade with Britain. In 1876 the ratio between the two was about 1 : 5.

Yet Portuguese India was important for the metropole in other, non-economic, areas, as the part of the empire where Portugal's contact was longest and most extensive and productive. In the 1870s Portuguese India had 39 percent of all primary classes in the whole empire and 54 percent of parishes, and was outranked only by Angola for number of troops and amount of government revenue. But economically India contributed little to the empire. What was important was an Indian Ocean version of the Atlantic pattern we have just described. Just as the slave trade continued in the interstices of British domination of Atlantic trade, so also Portuguese India's traders filled in some gaps, operating within and without the British-dominated Indian Ocean trade of the nineteenth century. From this it was not usually the Portuguese state, nor Portuguese-born people, who profited. It was a few local Portuguese, quite a number of *mestiços*, and especially Indians resident in Portuguese India, and usually citizens of Portugal.

There are several signs of all this, though the subject needs much more investigation. As one example, in the late eighteenth century the newly acquired areas inland from Daman called Dadra and Nagar Aveli produced good teak, which for a while made possible a flourishing ship-building industry in Daman. This was controlled by Gujarati capitalists, among whom Parsis seem to have dominated. In Bengal also the large 'Portuguese' population − one late seventeenth-century estimate puts their number at 20,000 − played some role in the trade of the Bay of Bengal and also worked as artisans, soldiers, and petty traders. From the later eighteenth century Indian groups, mostly Gujarati *vanias*, acquired a considerable economic role in Mozambique and Zanzibar; in the earlier nineteenth century these people dominated Mozambique's rather minor slave trade. As Portuguese citizens they were much less affected by British prohibitions than were other Gujaratis.

In all this we see old patterns still in place. Gujaratis played a large role in Portuguese India's overseas trade when the empire was at its height. This role continued through the nineteenth century. A detailed study of Portuguese India in the 1820s found Goan trade moribund; in Diu the only wealthy inhabitants were *vanias*, and they also dominated Daman's trade. The general point is that while Portuguese India contributed little to the empire and its total trade, some of her inhabitants, especially Gujaratis, participated in a quite flourishing Indian Ocean trade. This has been obscured by the stress in the literature on great power rivalry in the Atlantic, and the importance of the Brazilian trade. In Europe and the Atlantic, Portuguese trade was dominated by Britain; in the Indian Ocean it was controlled by her own Indian citizens.

In the nineteenth century there was for a short time an atypical windfall for the Goan government. This was achieved by operating in defiance of the British government. The East India Company was meant to have a monopoly on the opium trade to China; from 1813 they stopped all opium exports via Bombay. This opened up a new trade for Indian entrepreneurs. They exported Malwa opium to China, avoiding the British monopoly by sailing with Portuguese papers and under the Portuguese flag, leaving from Daman. This was an important trade in the first half of the nineteenth century. The trade itself was done by Parsis and others from Bombay. For the Portuguese the main benefit was a considerable rise in government revenue, derived from the sale of these permits. It has been suggested that the expensive new capital of Panjim, built between 1827 and 1835, was financed largely from government profits from this trade. There are both parallels and differences with Portugal's role in the Atlantic slave trade at the same time. In both cases they flouted a British policy, in the former an attempted monopoly, in the latter an attempted prohibition. But in the former it was the Goa government which profited, in the latter Portuguese traders in Angola and Brazil.

If *vanias* continued to dominate Portuguese India's sea trade, brahmin domination of Goa's internal economy also remained. Portuguese and *mestiços* had been able to set up large estates in Bassein in the seventeenth century. With the loss of this area in 1739 those with some Portuguese blood were apparently reduced to service in the rather rag-tag army. In 1866 there were 2240 *descendentes*, the term now used for *mestiços*, in Goa; 6 years later their position deteriorated further when the standing army was abolished.

In Goa local people, either Hindu or Christians, and usually with no Portuguese blood at all, continued in control of the economy. We have noted already the saga of the very successful Xavier family. In Goan trade and commerce, once the *vanias* had deserted this sinking ship by the mid seventeenth century, local brahmins appear to have dominated. In rural areas this was even more the case. We noted in chapter 4 that the Portuguese preserved the *gaunkar* system which they found in operation at the time of the conquest. This system continued, and villages continued to be dominated by the same families, until 1961.

The *gaunkars* were the male members of the dominant caste, either brahmin or kshatriya, in a village: in theory they were descended from the original settlers of the village. They could be either Hindu or Christian. They ran the village associations which controlled most of the affairs of the village: roads, drainage, irrigation, public security, religion (they supported the local church or temple, depending on whether the village was Christian or Hindu), education and health. More important, they were the primary landowners; the rest of the population were tenants or landless labourers. Tenancy rates were extremely high, in the 1950s ranging from 75 percent to over 95 percent. The system dominated especially the four *talukas* of the Old Conquests; as this is and was Goa's main paddy area, it meant the *gaunkars* largely controlled the production and distribution of Goa's food.

This dominance over at least four centuries by a self-perpetuating group of *gaunkars*, backed by the Portuguese state, no doubt explains the backwardness of Goa's agricultural sector. Methods remained primitive, internal exchange was hindered by almost non-existent communications, and Goa continued to import considerable quantities of food, just as did metropolitan Portugal, and for very much the same reasons.

Nor was the rest of Goa's economy more advanced. The commercial sector remained feeble, there was no industrial development at all. Most symptomatic of all is Portugal's neglect of Goa's iron and manganese deposits. As early as the 1620s a Portuguese report noted that artillery and cannon balls could be made very cheaply in Goa as there were iron mines close to the city. A report during the British occupation, in 1802, reported 'there are mines, in the Province of Ponda, which could afford considerable quantities of very good Iron, if proper Engines were built: there is Water enough in their Neighbourhood to work Mills' (British Library, Additional Manuscripts, 13703, f. 92v). In 1931 the *Times of India Guide* repeated the refrain. Some interest in Goa's manganese had been shown, but overall 'Goa is known to possess rich mineral resources and if these were scientifically explored their exploitation would be a source of wealth to the country and its people. The apathy of the latter and the poverty of the Government, however, combine to render this a possibility almost as remote as it is highly to be desired.' The Portuguese had not even undertaken a geological survey of the territory.[4] Even when D. D. Kosambi wrote about his homeland in 1947 the iron ore was still not being exploited. In this year exports were 14 tons.

It was precisely at this time that Dr Salazar, faced with Indian claims to Goa, at last rushed to develop these mines. Exports rose to 72,000 tons in 1950, and 6,500,000 in 1961, the last year of Portuguese rule. Yet the bulk of Goa's population derived little benefit from this expansion. Conditions for the miners were, and are, primitive in the extreme. The object was to sell unrefined and unprocessed ore to Japan. Licences to mine the ore were given to a handful of the Goan elite, both Christian and Hindu, who made huge profits, and whose concessions were continued after liberation. In 1963 one of these mine owners became Chief Minister. He was succeeded by his daughter who held the office until 1979. The mining has produced no backward linkages to the Goan economy: Japanese importers, a few members of the elite, and the Goan government have been the beneficiaries.

Given a moribund economy presided over by a bankrupt state, the extraordinary role of emigration in the Goan economy and society is easy to understand. Here again the parallels with the metropole are plain to see. Between 1961 and 1974, 1,500,000 Portuguese left for jobs in other countries, leaving a labour force of 3,100,000 at home. From 1974 to 1984 Portugal's population declined by over 200,000.

The situation in Portuguese India was similar. Even in the nineteenth century Goans in British India acquired a reputation as servants, cooks and musicians. In Bombay others entered the professions. Thus there were four Goans among the first eight graduands of Grant Medical College, in 1851. A comparative trickle in the nineteenth century became a flood in the twentieth. The 1900 census showed that 11 percent of the population of Salcette, and 16 percent of Bardes, were migrants. At this time the favoured destination was Bombay. An estimate of the occupations of these migrants found 29 percent were cooks, butlers, and governesses, 21 percent servants and 20 percent clerks.

By 1921, when Goa's population was 469,000, it was estimated that up to 200,000 Goans lived outside – in British India, Burma, East Africa and Mesopotamia – of whom about one-quarter were in the

[4] *Times of India Illustrated Guide to Goa* (Bombay, 1931),p. 28.

Bombay Presidency. In the 1950s the total population of Goa was 547,000, with another 180,000 outside. Of these 100,000 were in India (80,000 in Bombay alone), 30,000 in Pakistan, another 30,000 in Kenya and Uganda, and 20,000 in the Persian Gulf. Of those in Bombay, the main occupations were seamen (37 percent), cooks and waiters (18 percent), clerks, tailors and *ayahs* (each 8 percent) and musicians (2 percent), but another 18 percent were unemployed. The trend since liberation has been away from East Africa, as restrictions and then expulsions were imposed by newly independent governments, and towards the oil-rich Persian Gulf.

This emigration opened a road for mobility for those Goans who found Salazar's politically and economically backward colony stifling. This in turn no doubt minimized discontent in Goa. The adaptability of many Goans is well shown in the area of education. Under Portugal there was only one high school. Though its standards were high, the language of instruction was of course Portuguese. Thus many Goans, especially in the 1950s, attended English-language primary schools in Goa, and then received more English education in India. In Goa in 1958–9 about 19,000 Goans attended all levels of Portuguese-language education; a little under 13,000 were in English medium institutions; over 13,000 attended Marathi primary schools. Ability in English qualified them for jobs in India, and in British areas of east Africa; comparatively few went to the backward Portuguese colony of Mozambique.

There was also an obvious economic dimension. Goa's imports in the twentieth century were at least three times her exports, sometimes four times. The gap was made up by remittances from migrants, and from the money they brought back with them when they returned home to retire. Again the parallels with twentieth-century Portugal are plain to see.

A notable feature of this migration was the way in which village and family ties were maintained. Many migrants, even those who never came back, built houses in their home villages. The famous Goan clubs in Bombay, to which the majority of the community belonged, were village-based. A Goan in Bombay joined people from his home village in a club, and his social life, and many aspects of social welfare, were focussed on these clubs.

Three final points can be made. First, this emigration should not be seen as totally new in the twentieth century. Goa had always, even in pre-Portuguese times, been open to the Arabian Sea and its littoral: the change in the twentieth century was thus quantitative, not qualitative. Second, there was some differentiation between Hindu and Christian Goans. Hindus tended to stay in India, while Christians went further. This phenomenon is easily explained, for Christian Goans had unique advantages in pursuing their essentially service occupations. They knew at least one European language, Portuguese, and often, as we saw, English as well. They knew the Roman script, and via the church had learnt to appreciate and perform western music. Goan food had been influenced by European tastes. Perhaps most important, as Christians they were less caste-bound than Hindu Goans, especially in the crucial matter of food restrictions. Christian Goan cooks could prepare any sort of food. A third general point is that since liberation the flow has continued. Goans now focus on the Persian Gulf area. What has changed is immigration, for as Goans continue to move out to service jobs, they are replaced in the least appealing jobs in Goa by Hindus from India.

We can conclude by surveying Goan politics in the twentieth century, leading up to the liberation of 1961. The political situation in Portugal between the advent of the republic in 1910 and a military coup in 1926 was confused in the extreme. From 1928 *de facto* power in Portugal was exercised by Dr Salazar, who became prime minister in 1932, and remained so until 1968. A recent author encapsulated his policies: 'Among other things, Salazar was a confirmed opponent of consumerism, urbanization, secularism, women's rights, trade unionism and dynamic capitalism. Portugal experienced a long political and social ice age between 1926 and 1974.'[5]

Salazar's colonial policy underwent a major change after the Second World War. Until then Goa slumbered on. In 1900, of a total population of 486,000, 10 percent were literate. The largest town was Panjim, with less than 10,000 people. By 1921 the population had fallen to 470,000, thanks to emigration. Of these less than 12 percent were literate: 17 percent of men and 7 percent of women.

Descriptions of Goa in the 1930s paint a bleak picture. A *Times of India Guide* noted the 'deplorable' condition of the peasants, a result of the degeneration of the soil and of the huge emigration, which had removed many of the most capable men. It expatiated on the 'apathetic

5 Tom Gallagher, *Portugal: A Twentieth Century Interpretation* (Manchester, 1983), p. vii.

indolence of the people', who were, however, 'pious and moral'.[6] D. D. Kosambi found severe economic problems,

... and as the most active elements migrate, the residue sticks far more stubbornly than would be believed to what can only be described as 'the idiocy of village life', accentuated by a certain amount of actual idiocy, apathy (heightened by the poor diet and endemic hookworm) and at the other end energy manifested in quarrels, litigation, violence'.[7]

Nevertheless, before the Second World War the Indian freedom movement had few or no echoes in Portuguese India, partly because likely agitators had all migrated, and partly because it is true that Portugal's appeal, at least for the roughly 45 percent of the population who were Catholic, was considerable. The *Times of India* in 1931 claimed there was little unrest: 'The hold of Portugal upon Goa is as firm as ever, and cemented as it is by a triple bond of politics, religion and language, the years can only strengthen it.'[8]

This hold was challenged by Indian independence in 1947, and increasing pressure on Portugal to follow France's lead and let her enclaves be incorporated back into India. Salazar's response was to stress what he saw as centuries of racial harmony, which meant that Goa was 'an entirely different land' from India. 'There may be', as an apologist wrote in 1959, 'no geographic or economic frontier but there is undubitably a human one: Goa is the transplantation of the West onto Eastern lands, the expression of Portugal in India.'[9] This opinion was supported by diverse people. The Brazilian sociologist Gilberto Freyre found in Goa a prime example of a Luso-tropical civilization based on Catholicism and miscegenation. He was much patronized by the Portuguese authorities. The right-wing English Catholic Evelyn Waugh agreed: 'Goans ... are, in fact, Portuguese. They are not a subject or "protected" people.'[10]

There are problems with these claims. Historically they are weak: it will be remembered that Hindus got equality only in 1910. The Portuguese claim was that all 'civilized' people were Portuguese. Such happy people included everyone in Portuguese India, Macao and Timor, but not in Africa. Here Portuguese racism continued to be overt. An official 1956 publication noted that in the African Provinces

[6] *Times of India Guide*, pp. 30–40.
[7] Kosambi, 'Village', p. 66.
[8] *Times of India Guide*, p. 127.
[9] Frederic P. Marjay, *Portuguese India: a Historic Study* (Lisbon, 1959), p. 7.
[10] Evelyn Waugh, 'Goa: The home of a saint', *Month*, n.s. X (1953), 326.

there were citizens (a tiny proportion) and natives, 'the latter comprised coloured individuals whose development and customs have not risen above the common level of their race'.[11] It is also to be remembered that being a citizen in Dr Salazar's Portugal gave one very few rights indeed. Finally, there is a certain expediency about these claims from the 1950s. They ignore the centuries of racial prejudice we have described earlier. A cynic would smile at the way Portugal tried by a sleight of hand to remove her colonies from the purview of the United Nations. In 1951 the term 'Colonies' was officially replaced by 'Overseas Provinces'; they thus became an internal Portuguese matter and not subject to outside interference.

Portugal in the 1950s also made belated efforts to develop Goa, with a view to making its people clearly better off than those in neighbouring India. In 1952 a Development Plan was decreed. This boosted Goa's fledgling iron ore exports. Revenue from this, and from migrant remittances, meant that per capita income in Goa was some one-third higher than in India. Education was expanded, sanitation was improved. Old Goa was cleaned up for the massive celebrations of the four hundredth anniversary of the death of St Fancis Xavier in 1952. These had a clear political purpose. Among those who attended were the Cardinal Patriarch of Lisbon, Evelyn Waugh and the overseas minister, until the previous year the colonial minister.

These measures were too little and too late. Yet it is doubtful that any measure could have succeeded, for Portugal was swimming against a worldwide tide of decolonization. Goa was not a settlement colony. In 1950 of a total of 637,000 only 517 were Europeans, and 336 Eurasians. Her support came almost entirely from the local Roman Catholic population, who by 1960 made up less than 40 percent of the total. Of the Christians, 83 percent lived in the Old Conquests. In the Hindu New Conquests support for Portugal was minimal. Nor was Christian support total, especially outside Goa. Cardinal Gracias, himself of Goan background, laid down from Bombay that 'as far as the Catholics of Goa are concerned, their culture is not Portuguese but Christian' (quoted in A. K. Priolkar, *Goa Re-Discovered*, Bombay, 1967, p. 40).

Nor had Portuguese policies created much of an economic boom in Goa. We have already noted the very limited impact of iron ore development on the total economy. In 1950 less than 14 percent of

[11] *Portuguese India Today*, 2nd ed. (Lisbon, 1956), pp. 7–8.

Goans lived in urban areas. In terms of occupations, 71 percent were agricultural, with another 8 percent in service industries and the same in manufacturing. The only modern hotel, the Mandovi, was being built around Waugh's ears when he stayed late in 1952. Even literacy was not noticeably higher than in India. In 1960 in Goa it was 30.5 percent, in neighbouring Maharashtra 29.8 percent, to the south in Mysore 25.4 percent, in Gujarat 30.5 percent, and in all India 24 percent.

The population of Goa in the 1950s would be best described as apathetic or neutral rather than supporting either India or Portugal. Soon after Indian independence, in 1950 Nehru approached Portugal, inviting them to discuss a timetable for the transfer of Portuguese India to India. The Portuguese replied that there was nothing to discuss, as Portuguese India was part of Portugal, just like, say, the Algarve. In 1953 India closed its legation in Portugal, and next year took over the isolated enclaves of Dadra and Nagar Aveli, inland from Daman. In 1954 and 1955 Indian nationalists, supported by some exiled Goans, tried several times to launch a Gandhian style *satyagraha* campaign in Goa. These were rather feeble efforts, and received little or no local support. The Portuguese were able to arrest the 'invaders' (in August 1955, twenty-two of them were killed by Portuguese troops), thus incidentally calling into question the effectiveness of these non-violent techniques when confronted by determined opponents.

India's position, nevertheless, was unbeatable. Portuguese rule was increasingly anachronistic. Nehru had support from nearly all Indian political parties, and internationally from the Soviet Union and its allies. In 1961 the revolt in Angola began and, probably not coincidentally, Nehru chose to use force soon afterwards. About 30,000 Indian troops were massed around Goa, Daman and Diu in December. Portugal faced them with 3000 rag-tag troops, no aircraft, a semi-derelict frigate, and 900 Goan police, who promptly deserted. The Indian troops moved on the 17th, and two days later it was all over. Despite Salazar's hopes there was only token Goan opposition. Casualties were 45 Portuguese killed, and 22 Indians.

Neither side emerged with much credit. J. K. Galbraith, the United States ambassador to India at the time, noted in his diary 'The Indians are fabricating great excitement over Goa . . . The Indian case, which has my sympathy, also includes a high component of contrivance.'[12]

[12] J. K. Galbraith, *Ambassador's Journal* (New York, 1970), p. 251.

The chief of staff of the Indian Army told his troops 'You are not going into Goa as conquerors, but as protectors', which was pure cant. On the other side a Portuguese historian, implicitly casting grave doubt on how genuine was Portugal's claimed lack of racism, said that 'The fall of Goa marks a return into the darkness that existed before Vasco da Gama arrived there (*sic*) in 1498.'[13]

In March 1962 Portuguese India was formally integrated into the Indian Union. Portugal refused to accept this. Officially Goa had been temporarily misplaced, not lost for ever. Books with titles like *Our Beloved Goa*, and *Portuguese India: Pledges for her Redemption*, proliferated. The loss was officially accepted only in 1974 when Portugal herself escaped from the shackles of the Salazar–Caetano dictatorship.

Nor indeed were Goans totally ecstatic about being liberated. Especially from the Christian population, there was little support for the Indian army, and since then they have occasionally suffered from heavy-handed 'Indianization' policies. It is symptomatic that in 1967 Goa, Daman and Diu rejected a proposal to integrate them into the surrounding states.

Considerable economic progress has been made, from a very low base in 1961. Between 1961 and 1971 rice production rose 45 percent; from 1961 to 1976 iron ore exports more than doubled. In 1961, 3 villages out of 383 were electrified, in 1980, 330. Communications were improved. Bridges were built over the Mandovi and Zuari rivers, while asphalted road mileage rose 7 times between 1961 and 1980. In the 20 years between 1965 and 1985 the number of secondary schools has risen from 1 to 233, and government primary schools from 176 to 1155.

Liberation has created problems also, for all Goans, both Christian and Hindu. In the most general sense, 1961 was when the new Indian state introduced Goa for the first time to twentieth-century technological society. Tensions are to be expected. Conditions for miners and traditional fishermen are primitive in the extreme. The continuing emigration of talented and educated Goans and immigration of Indian workers (one-third of the population is now non-Goan) has obviously created problems. Similarly with the rapid expansion of the tourist industry, where the number of hotel beds has risen in 20 years from 450 to 5804. The consequent social dislocation and destruction of parts of Goa's heritage are much to be regretted.

[13] Both quoted in R. P. Rao, *Portuguese Rule in Goa, 1510–1961* (Bombay, 1963), pp. 164, 182.

Portugal herself, especially since the 1974 revolution, has also suffered all the problems and disadvantages of mass tourism. Here then we come back full circle to our themes of Goa's essentially Indian character throughout, and of a variable, usually small, Portuguese impact on India. In both Portugal and Portuguese India migration has played a large role. In both, the Salazar–Caetano dictatorship left huge problems to be solved. On many indices Portugal is the poorest, and most unhealthy, country in Europe. All through Portugal's 450 years in India what is striking is the similarities between this European pre-colonial power, one which expanded but did not dominate, and the area in which it operated. In a particular coastal area in 1977, 70 percent of houses had no electric light, 40 percent of the rural population was illiterate, and in 1983 children still had to walk 14 kilometres to get to a primary school.[14] This is not some backward part of Goa; this is in the Alentejo region of southern Portugal.

[14] *Expresso* (Lisbon), 22 October 1983.

BIBLIOGRAPHICAL ESSAY

This bibliographical essay makes no attempt to survey all the literature in the field of Indo-Portuguese history. It is simply a discussion of some of the books and articles I have read over the years and found to be useful. I have deliberately concentrated on work in English, on the assumption that most readers will not be able to use Portuguese-language material. It is true that Portuguese scholarship for much of the twentieth century suffered from the dead hand of censorship under Dr Salazar, as indeed it had earlier, thanks to clerical control. Nevertheless, it is obvious that any serious student of the subject needs to be able to read Portuguese. This is even more the case for anyone thinking of engaging in original research. A very large number of documents and chronicles, especially those relating to the sixteenth century, have been published, but not translated; nor, given their length, are they ever likely to be. Thus the serious student, let alone a potential researcher, has no choice but to learn Portuguese.

There is another reason why this essay makes no attempt to be inclusive. This is because we at last have a comprehensive bibliography available specifically on the Portuguese in India. We all owe a vast debt to Henry Scholberg for his *Bibliography of Goa and the Portuguese in India* (New Delhi, 1982). His book contains nearly 3000 entries in a variety of languages, mostly of course English and Portuguese. Like any other bibliography, it was not complete when it was published, and is rapidly becoming out of date. Nevertheless, it is an indispensable tool. Another very recent bibliography also is fundamental, this time a listing of the complete works, from 1926 to 1983, of one scholar, C. R. Boxer. This is S. George West, *A Complete Bibliography of the Works of C. R. Boxer, 1926–83* (London, 1984). It may seem curious to describe such a book as fundamental, yet in this case it is justified. For nearly sixty years Boxer has been the great authority on the Portuguese colonial empire. No beginner could do better than to read in Boxer as a start. Most of us who began to work in this field over the last forty years at least have started with Boxer, following up his footnotes, and proceeding then to our own original research. Thus West's listing is most valuable, though already no doubt out of date given that Boxer is still a very active author.

We are also fortunate that Boxer has twice reflected on the state of the field which he dominates. He first surveyed this, covering mostly secondary literature, in 'Some considerations on Portuguese colonial historiography', in *Proceedings of the International Conference on Luso-Brazilian Studies* (Washington, 1953), pp. 169–80. More recently he returned to the subject in 'Some second thoughts on Indo-Portuguese historiography', in John Correia-Afonso (ed.), *Indo-Portuguese History: Sources and Problems* (Bombay, 1981), pp. 132–47.

BIBLIOGRAPHICAL ESSAY

I will make no effort in this essay to provide a guide to either archives or published primary materials. This is because the subject is adequately covered in four recent and accessible works. Three of them are Teotonio R. de Souza, *Medieval Goa* (New Delhi, 1979), pp. 294–309; K. S. Mathew, *Portuguese Trade in India in the Sixteenth Century* (New Delhi, 1983), pp. 291–336, and M. N. Pearson, *Merchants and Rulers in Gujarat: the Response to the Portuguese in the Sixteenth Century* (Berkeley and New Delhi, 1976), pp. 161–73. This work includes a discussion of Indian sources as well as Portuguese, and also surveys the literature on Gujarat in some detail. Finally, the extended discussion in Georg Schurhammer's *Francis Xavier: His Life, His Times*, vol. II, 'India, 1541–45' (Rome, 1977), pp. 606–728, must be mentioned. Naturally, given the author's subject, it is strongest for the history of the Jesuits, and especially St Francis Xavier, but he includes copious detail on secular sources for the sixteenth century also. From these four books the reader can gain an entrée into the main archives, in Lisbon and Goa, and to the major published sources, especially the great chronicles for the sixteenth century by Barros, Couto, Castanheda and Correa. A book which appeared late in 1985 gives a good overall impression of the value of Portuguese sources for one important area of India, namely Gujarat. This is K. S. Mathew, *Portuguese and the Sultanate of Gujarat (1500–1573)* (New Delhi, 1985).

Periodical literature is important, for much new research is first presented in this form. Two journals have specialized in our area. The journal *Studia*, from Lisbon, published 45 numbers between 1958 and 1981, and may still continue. It covered the whole Portuguese experience overseas, but usually included much material on their Indian activities. Many important research articles appeared, but the main value of the journal lay in the documents it published. The second journal to be noted, *Mare Luso-Indicum*, concentrated precisely on the Portuguese in the Arabian Sea and west coast of India. Edited by Jean Aubin, it published documents and also meticulously researched articles by Aubin and his colleagues, these always being impeccably researched, copiously footnoted, often a little narrow. This journal produced four numbers between 1971 and 1980, and now unfortunately has been subsumed into *Moyen Orient & Océan Indien, XVIe-XIXe s.* (I, 1984–). Several other journals frequently publish articles of interest to us. Among them are *Indica*, from the Heras Institute of Indian History and Culture in Bombay; the *Arquívos do centro cultural português* in Paris (funded by the most munificent Calouste Gulbenkian Foundation, which has done so much to promote the study of Portugal and its empire); and three Portuguese historical journals: *Anais*, from the Acadêmia Portuguesa da História, *Revista Portuguesa de História*, from Coímbra, and the *Revista de História Economica e Social*. The last-named is edited by the very distinguished historian Vitorino Magalhães Godinho. Beginning in 1978, so far it has published mostly on Portuguese history, as opposed to the history of the Portuguese overseas. It is to be hoped that this will change, and that the influence of the very important French group of *Annales* historians, among whom Godinho must be numbered, will percolate into our area of interest.

BIBLIOGRAPHICAL ESSAY

Keeping up to date in any field of history is difficult. In our case, much new research is first presented at the continuing series of International Seminars on Indo-Portuguese History. The first appropriately met in Goa in 1978, the second in Lisbon in 1980, the third in Goa again in 1983. The fourth was held in Lisbon in November 1985. The proceedings of the second were published from Lisbon in 1985. Selections from the first and third are available under the titles John Correia-Afonso (ed.), *Indo-Portuguese History: Sources and Problems* (throughout this essay I will use short titles if a book has been fully listed earlier), and Teotonio R. de Souza (ed.), *Indo-Portuguese History: Old Issues, New Questions* (New Delhi, 1985). In India these seminars are sponsored by the very active Xavier Centre of Historical Research, which under the vigorous direction of T. R. de Souza also sponsors the publication of other books. Its Newsletter (available from the Centre, Porvorim, Goa 403 521, India) contains news and notes, reviews and reports on research in progress.

SURVEYS

There are numerous surveys of Portuguese colonial history, and even of the Portuguese in India. The obvious place to start is with C. R. Boxer. Pre-eminent in his *The Portuguese Seaborne Empire, 1415–1825* (London, 1969), by far the best introduction to the whole subject, summing up over forty years' of research and reflection, and including a copious bibliography. Recently there have appeared two collections of Boxer's essays and articles, whose subjects are clear from their titles. The first is *From Lisbon to Goa, 1500–1750: Studies in Portuguese Maritime Enterprise* (London, 1984), the second *Portuguese Conquest and Commerce in Southern Asia, 1500–1750* (London, 1985). It is to be hoped that more collections of his shorter pieces, often fundamental yet buried in very obscure journals, will appear soon. Two other books by Boxer may be mentioned here, both of them containing data on the Portuguese in India as well as in other areas. These are *Mary and Misogyny: Women in Iberian Expansion Overseas, 1415–1815, Some Facts, Fancies and Personalities* (London, 1975), and *Race Relations in the Portuguese Colonial Empire 1415–1825* (Oxford, 1963). The latter was controversial when it was published, for it made the (hardly surprising) case that relations between Portuguese colonists and local peoples had not always been totally free from racial prejudice. Under Dr Salazar such a claim could not be tolerated. The official case was that race relations had always been harmonious in the Portuguese empire. The sociologist Gilberto Freyre lent some academic respectability to this in such works as *The Masters and the Slaves* (New York, 1946), and *The Portuguese and the Tropics* (Lisbon, 1961). Today of course Boxer's book is seen as a useful introduction to a complex and important area of investigation.

Three other works also provided good surveys of the Portuguese empire in the east. Bailey W. Diffie and George D. Winius, *Foundations of the Portuguese Empire, 1415–1580* (Minneapolis, 1977), is very detailed, especially for political, military and administrative history. Second are a series of contributions to the *New Cambridge Modern History*, which provide good surveys through to the eighteenth century: H. V. Livermore, 'Portuguese expansion', vol. I (Cambridge, 1957), pp. 420–30; I. A. MacGregor, 'Europe and the east', vol. II (1958), pp. 591–614; J. B. Harrison, 'Asia and Africa', vol. III (1968), pp. 532–58; J. B. Harrison, 'Europe and Asia', vol. IV (1970), pp. 644–71; V. M. Godinho, 'Portugal and her empire', vol. V (1961), pp. 384–97; V. M. Godinho, 'Portugal and her Empire, 1680–1720', vol. VI (1970), pp. 509–40. The third general survey is Malyn Newitt's very recent editing of *The First Portuguese Colonial Empire* (Exeter, 1986). This contains useful articles on the fifteenth-century voyages, on the Portuguese state structure in southeast Asia, on the system of cartazes, and on Goa in the seventeenth century. It also contains useful short bibliographies.

Pride of place for surveys of economic history is held by the distinguished scholar V. M. Godinho. His *Os Descobrimentos e a Economia Mundial* (4 vols, Lisbon, 1981–3) is a truly great achievement, a landmark in our field. This edition, the second in Portuguese, is much to be preferred to the better-known French edition, *L'Economie de l'Empire Portugais aux XVe et XVIe siècles* (Paris, 1969), which is shorter, contains no illustrations, and has no index, while the Portuguese edition, unusually for continental scholarship, does. Godinho has also published two collections of his essays, all of them provocative, stimulating, essential. These are *Ensaios*, vol. I, 'Sobre história universal', and vol. II, 'Sobre história de Portugal' (Lisbon, 1968). Among other wider surveys are a collection of discrete articles by various hands collected in H. V. Livermore (ed.), *Portugal and Brazil: An Introduction* (Oxford, 1953), and the massive on-going work of Donald S. Lach, *Asia in the Making of Europe* (Chicago, 1965–). The latter is a leisurely survey of its subject, collecting information on a vast array of contacts and influences, and especially valuable for its detail on what the Portuguese writers in the sixteenth century saw and wrote in India.

When we narrow our focus down to the history of the Portuguese in India, and to Goa, the quality of the literature declines sadly – hence this book. The best survey of Goa's geography and anthropology is the copiously illustrated Raquel Soeiro de Brito, *Goa e as praças do Norte* (Lisbon, 1966). An older account of the history of Goa is J. N. da Fonseca, *An Historical and Archaeological Sketch of the City of Goa* (Bombay, 1878), which includes some useful data. Afonso Zuquete (ed.), *Tratado de todos os Vice Reis e Governadores da India* (Lisbon, 1962) is useful for dates and political and military detail. It was published just after Goa was 'liberated', and includes essays pledging its redemption and return to the Portuguese fold. Boies Penrose, *Goa: Queen of the East* (Lisbon, 1960) is a discursive, short, bilingual survey, apparently written to order for the Portuguese government, while *Golden Goa* (Bombay, 1980) is a good example of the mythology which surrounds the area, especially as fostered by art historians. Caroline Ifeka in 'The Image of Goa', in T. R. de Souza, ed., *Indo-Portuguese History*, pp. 181–95, makes a start on debunking this sort of nonsense. Finally on Goa, a distinguished English architect, J. M. Richards, recently published *Goa* (New Delhi, 1982). The historical sections are adequate, but the main strength of the book naturally is his informed commentary on Goan architecture, both public and domestic. This would be a good book to read before a first visit to the area.

Turning now to surveys of the Portuguese not just in Goa, but in all India, J. B. Harrison's 'The Portuguese' in A. L. Basham, ed., *A Cultural History of India* (Oxford, 1975), pp. 337–47, is a short, agreeable and occasionally eccentric survey. It is indicative of how little has been done in this area that three older works by English authors are often still used, despite their faults. W. W. Hunter in his *A History of British India*, vol. I (London, 1899) began with a long survey of Portuguese activities. He explicitly saw them as merely the precursors of the more successful, and morally superior, British. Reflecting Victorian certainty (the book is dedicated to the Empress of India), it is today only of historiographical interest. Much better is R. S. Whiteway's survey of the period to 1550, *The Rise of Portuguese Power in India, 1497–1550* (London, 1899 and 1967). Whiteway was a competent historian, though traces of ethnocentrism, directed again more against the Portuguese than against Indians, are to be found in his book also. Much worse is F. C. Danvers, *The Portuguese in India* (2 vols., London, 1894 and 1966). This book is something of a model of how not to write history. It consists of military and political narrative, much of it cribbed almost unaltered from one or two Portuguese chronicles, tendentious and boring in the extreme. It deserves, indeed for decades has deserved, to pass into oblivion. Perhaps the best comment on it came from Danvers's contemporary (and perhaps competitor), R. S. Whiteway, who began his own book by saying 'I have been unable to avail myself of the undoubted erudition of the author [that is, Danvers] as he has not connected his narrative in any way with the general history of India' (p. v).

DISCOVERIES AND SIXTEENTH CENTURY

V. M. Godhinho's *A Economia dos Descobrimentos Henriquinos* (Lisbon, 1962) is basic for economic aspects of the discoveries, while Diffie's section in *Foundations of the Portuguese Empire* is a good survey of the voyages and their causes. Edgar Prestage's older *The Portuguese Pioneers* (London, 1933) is also useful. Carlo M. Cipolla in *European Culture and Overseas Expansion* (Pelican, 1970), a conflation of his earlier two short books *Guns and Sails* and *Clocks and Culture*, is valuable for the European background and prerequisites, such as guns, sails and navigational techniques, for the voyages and conquests. The effects on Portugal are covered in Lach's *Asia in the Making of Europe*, and in detail in R. Hooykaas, *Humanism and the Voyages of Discovery in Sixteenth-century Portuguese Science and Letters* (Amsterdam, 1979). For an overview of the situation in the Indian Ocean at the time of the arrival of the Portuguese, see Geneviève Bouchon, 'Les Mers de l'Inde à la fin du xve siècle. Vue generale', *Moyen Orient & Océan Indien*, I (1984), 101–16. The background to the Portuguese in Goa, that is its history before the fateful year of 1510, is well surveyed in J. M. Pacheco de Figueiredo, 'Goa pré-Portuguesa', *Studia*, no. 12 (1963), 139–259, and nos. 13/14, 1964, pp. 105–225; and in P. S. S. Pissurlencar, *Goa Pré-Portuguesa através dos escritores Lusitános dos séculos*

XVI e XVII (Bastorá, 1962). The latter was director of the Goa archives for many years. He was a fine scholar who published many documents and articles, especially on Portuguese–Maratha relations.

The sixteenth century has of course attracted much attention. In a class by itself is Niels Steensgaard, *The Asian Trade Revolution of the Seventeenth Century: The East India Companies and the Decline of the Caravan Trade* (Chicago, 1974; originally published as *Carracks, Carvans and Companies: the Structural Crisis in the European-Asian Trade in the Early 17th Century* (Copenhagen, 1973). His book has been much discussed, and criticized. It makes a case for seeing a profound disjunction between the activities of the Portuguese and the traditional Asian pedlars on the one hand, and the Dutch and English trading companies on the other. This is an outstanding monograph. As to more usual political surveys, many of the general works listed earlier have detail on this period. There are numerous accounts of political and military history. A recent mostly naval history, often brutally critical of the Portuguese, is Peter Padfield, *Tide of Empires: Decisive Naval Campaigns in the Rise of the West*, vol. 1 '1481–1654' (London, 1979). Also critical, but surprisingly by a Portuguese scholar writing in the Salazar period, is Júlio Gonçalves, *Os Portugueses e o Mar das Indias* (Lisbon, 1947). Much more detailed for military and naval history is Alfredo Botelho de Sousa, *Subsídios para a história militar marítima da India* (4 vols., Lisbon, 1930–56). Less sanguinary aspects of Portuguese activities at sea are described in a fascinating and extended section of F. Schurhammer's great biography, *Francis Xavier*, vol. 1, pp. 3–132, where he describes his hero's voyage from Lisbon to Goa from April 1541 to May 1542. Shorter, and older, political and military surveys are E. Denison Ross, 'The Portuguese in India and Arabia between 1507 and 1517', *Journal of the Royal Asiatic Society* (1921), 545–62, and the same from 1517 to 1538 in *JRAS* (1922), 1–180; by the same author, my predecessor in writing about the Portuguese in India for a Cambridge series, 'The Portuguese in India', *Cambridge History of India*, vol. V (New Delhi reprint, 1968), pp. 1–27; and M. Longworth Dames, 'The Portuguese and Turks in the Indian Ocean in the sixteenth century', *JRAS* (1921), 1–28. One thing to be said in favour of both Ross and Dames, and something which distinguishes them from most of their successors, is that they both used Indian sources in Persian and Arabic as well as the more usual Portuguese sources. Nowadays scholars seem content to learn only Portuguese (or even, amazingly, not even this).

Turning to particular areas, Portuguese activities in Malabar have been described by K. M. Panikkar in *Malabar and the Portuguese* (Bombay, 1929). More recently O. K. Nambiar published *The Kunjalis: Admirals of Calicut* (London, 1963), a book whose theme was better summed up in the title of its first edition, *Portuguese Pirates and Indian Seamen* (Bombay, 1955). A much better book is Geneviève Bouchon, *Mamale de Cananor* (Paris, 1975), a careful study of an early opponent of the Portuguese in Malabar. Like all her work, this is meticulously researched, careful, a little pedestrian. Turning to the other coast of India, L. F. Thomaz's *De Malacca a Pequ. Viagens de un feitor português (1512–15)* (Lisbon, 1966) is a useful case study which, in the introduction, also has some general comments on the limits of Portuguese power. In general, Portuguese activities in the Bay of Bengal have yet to be covered at all adequately. In the meantime, J. J. Campos, *History of the Portuguese in Bengal* (Patna, 1969; 1st ed. 1919) contains some information of value, while G. D. Winius, 'The "Shadow Empire" of Goa in the Bay of Bengal', *Itinerario*, VII, no. 2 (1983), 83–101, is excellent on the subject of private trade and informal empire. For Kanara several of the studies in B. S. Shastry, *Studies in Indo-Portuguese History* (Bangalore, 1981), are useful, as is Sanjay Subrahmanyam's excellent article 'The Portuguese, the port of Basrur, and the rice trade, 1600–50', *Indian Economic and Social History Review*, XXI (1984), 433–62. Turning to Gujarat, the theme of M. N. Pearson, *Merchants and Rulers in Gujarat: the Response to the Portuguese in the Sixteenth Century* is summed up in its title, while Jean Aubin wrote a detailed study of early Portuguese contacts in 'Albuquerque et les négociations de Cambay', *Mare Luso-Indicum*, I (1971), 3–63. K. S. Mathew's *Portuguese and the Sultanate of Gujarat* contains both case studies and some original sources.

The administration of the empire in the sixteenth century is covered in George D. Winius's sections of Diffie and Winius, *Foundations of the Portuguese Empire*. The same author has published a study of corruption in the empire in *The Black Legend of Portuguese India*, Xavier Centre of Historical Research Studies Series 3 (New Delhi, 1985). Steensgaard's *Asian Trade Revolution* is also basic for corruption, as is M. N. Pearson, *Coastal Western India: Studies from the Portuguese Records* (Xavier Centre of Historical Research Studies Series no. 2, New Delhi, 1981), pp. 18–40. For the administration in general two important books are F. P. Mendes da Luz, *O Conselho da India* (Lisbon, 1952), and V. M. Godinho, *Les Finances de l'État Portugais des Indes Orientales (1517–1635) Matériaux pour une étude structurale et conjuncturelle* (Paris, 1982), which includes both discussion and documents. C. R. Boxer in *Portuguese Society in the Tropics: The Municipal Councils of Goa, Macao, Bahia and Luanda* (Madison, 1965), included a very useful account of the work of this important council in Goa.

Particular studies for this period are of course legion. Among them is G. Bouchon, 'Le Premier Voyage de Lopo Soares en Inde (1504–1505)', *Mare Luso-Indicum* III (1976), 57–84. Good biographies are surprisingly few and far between. One of the better is Elaine Sanceau, *Knight of the Renaissance: D. João de Castro* (London, n.d.), not that this complex figure was really much of a knight or a renaissance man. Thumbnail accounts of all the governors and viceroys can be found in Afonso Zuquete (ed.), *Tratado de todos os Vice Reis e Governadores da India* (*sc.* for Portuguese India), while Anthony R. Disney has under preparation a study of the great seventeenth-century viceroy the count of Linhares (1629–35). G. V. Scammell wrote a typically graceful account of early Indo–Portuguese relations in 'Indigenous assistance in the establishment of Portuguese power in the Indian Ocean', in J. Correia-Afonso (ed.), *Indo-Portuguese History*, pp. 163–73. For Goa see M. N. Pearson, 'Goa during the first century of Portuguese rule', *Itinerario*, VIII, no. 1 (1984), 36–57. Many years ago the great student of Indian land systems, B. H. Baden-Powell, turned his attention to Goa, and published 'The villages of Goa in the early sixteenth century', *JRAS* (1900), 261–91. There is a vast survey of Portuguese colonialism in A.G.C. Germano da Silva Correira, *História da colonização portuguesa na India*, 6 vols (Lisbon, 1948–56), which contains masses of only partially digested data. Finally two collections of articles can be noted. B. S. Shastry in *Studies in Indo–Portuguese History* wrote on the early collaborator, Timmayya, and on Portuguese relations with various South Indian states, while topics covered in M. N. Pearson, *Coastal Western India*, include corruption, piracy, the role of Indians in the Portuguese Indian economy, and popular political activity.

SEVENTEENTH TO TWENTIETH CENTURIES

Much of this period is still *terra incognita*. The number of worthwhile studies are few indeed, though we can look forward to some forthcoming work of quality. These include Disney's already-mentioned study of Linhares, and economic studies for the eighteenth and nineteenth centuries by Rudolph Bauss and Gervaise Clarence-Smith. There are a few reliable books for the seventeenth century. C. R. Boxer recently published his *Portuguese India in the Mid-Seventeenth Century* (Delhi, 1980), in which he investigated conquest, navigation and commerce. His article 'Portuguese and Dutch colonial rivalry, 1641–1661', *Studia*, no. 2 (1958), 7–42, is basic for its subject. Recently Leonard Blusse and George D. Winius presented a new, and short, reinterpretation of this subject: 'The origin and rhythm of Dutch aggression against the *Estado da India*, 1601–1661', in T. R. de Souza (ed.), *Indo-Portuguese History*, pp. 73–83. Next to be mentioned is A. R. Disney's fine monograph *Twilight of the Pepper Empire: Portuguese Trade in Southwest India in the Early Seventeenth Century* (Cambridge, Mass., 1978), an excellent book which, apart from the coverage described in its title, also has good data for the sixteenth century, and on Portuguese business society in the metropole. Finally, Teotonio R. de Souza has published a splendid study of Goa in the seventeenth century, *Medieval Goa* (New Delhi, 1979), a fine monograph and, it is hoped, a harbinger of many more studies by young Goans.

Steensgaard's *Asian Trade Revolution* is of course important for the earlier seventeenth century. A. J. R. Russell-Wood's 'Seamen ashore and afloat: the social environment of the carreira da India, 1550–1750', *Mariners' Mirror*, LXIX, no. 1 (1983), 35–52, is a sophisticated study with an interesting theoretical angle. A. K. Priolkar's *The Printing Press in India* (Bombay, 1958) contains good detail on the early Jesuit presses, though his lists should be supplemented by reference to C. R. Boxer's authoritative 'A tentative checklist of Indo-Portuguese imprints', *Arquívos do Centro Cultural Português*, IX (1975), 567–99.

Goa's expansion into the New Conquests in the eighteenth century is described in José de Oliveira Boléo, 'A incorporação das "Novas Conquistas" no Estado da India', *Studia*, no. 8 (1961), 335–90. The condition of Goa early in the nineteenth century is well set out in Gonçalo de Magalhães Teixeira

BIBLIOGRAPHICAL ESSAY

Pinto, *Memórias Sobre as Possessões Portuguezas na Asia Escriptas no Anno de 1823 . . . com Breves Notas e Additamentos de J. H. da Cunha Rivara* (Nova Goa, 1859). This book deserves to be better known than it is; the extra material from Cunha Rivara is as usual sensible and valuable. Cunha Rivara was a high civil servant in Goa in the mid nineteenth century, and a formidable amateur historian. Indeed for a time he was able to turn the official government gazette into a vehicle for publishing long runs of sixteenth-century documents. For later in the nineteenth century A. Lopes Mendes, *A India Portugueza* (Lisboa, 1886), accumulates much data.

Among descriptions of Goa in the twentieth century we may note a survey done by the British just after the First World War, *Peace Handbooks*, vol. XIII, section 79 on Portuguese India (London, 1920) and another from the *Times of India* in 1931, *The Times of India Illustrated Guide to Goa* (Bombay, 1931). As Portuguese rule was challenged by India the government had written *Portuguese India Today*, 2nd ed. (Lisbon, 1956), an apologia for Portuguese rule and valuable in that it constitutes a clear statement of Portugal's rationale for retaining its empire in the 1950s and 1960s. But by far the best account of Goa in the twentieth century is that written by one of its greatest sons, the savant D. D. Kosambi, 'The village communities in the Old Conquests of Goa', *Journal of the University of Bombay*, XV, no. 4 (1947), 63–78. The liberation struggle has yet to find its author. R. P. Rao at least gives us a basic chronology in *Portuguese Rule in Goa, 1510–1961* (Bombay, 1963), while T. R. de Souza's 'Capital input in Goa's freedom struggle: the Bombay connection', in de Souza (ed.), *Indo-Portuguese History*, pp. 102–13, is an example of the sort of work which needs to be done. Descriptions of modern Goa can be found in R. S. de Brito, *Goa*, and J. M. Richards, *Goa*, cited above, while B. G. d'Souza *Goan Society in Transition: A Study in Social Change* (Bombay, 1975) is a useful account of Goa's society and its historical evolution. By far the best short account of the impact of 'liberation' on Goa is R. S. Newman's 'Goa: the transformation of an Indian region', *Pacific Affairs*, LV, no. 3 (Fall 1984), 429–49.

SPECIAL STUDIES

Economic history, and especially the history of the spice trade, has been well covered in several works. V. M. Godinho's *Os Descobrimentos* is vital for both. Among particular economic studies may be mentioned a stimulating overview by Jan Kieniewicz, 'Le Commerce en Asie et l'expansion portugaise vers l'océan indien au XVI siècle', *Acta Poloniae Historica*, XVIII (1968), 180–93, and Geneviève Bouchon's fine socio-economic study of 'Les Musulmans du Kerala à l'époque de la découverte portugaise', *Mare Luso-Indicum*, II (1973), 3–59. For the early pepper trade by far the best source is K. S. Mathew's excellent recent monograph, *Portuguese Trade in India in the Sixteenth Century*. Jan Kieniewicz, 'The Portuguese factory and trade in pepper in Malabar during the sixteenth century', *Indian Economic and Social History Review*, VI (1969), 61–84, is also important, while C. R. Boxer wrote a useful study of 'A note on Portuguese reactions to the revival of the Red Sea spice trade and the rise of Atjeh, 1540–1600', in the *Journal of Southeast Asian History*, x (1969), 415–28. For the late sixteenth and early seventeenth centuries Disney's splendid *Twilight of the Pepper Empire* is basic. F. C. Lane was the first to point to a revival of the Red Sea spice trade around the middle of the sixteenth century; his important studies were conveniently collected in F. C. Lane, *Venice and History: Collected Papers of F. C. Lane* (Baltimore, 1966). Two other particular studies of the spice trade are E. Ashtor, 'Spice prices in the Near East in the fifteenth century', *JRAS* (1976), 26–41, and C. H. H. Wake, 'The changing patterns of Europe's pepper and spice imports, ca 1400–1700', *Journal of European Economic History*, VIII, no. 2 (1979), 361–403.

Much heat, and occasionally some light, has been shed on the controversial matter of religious interactions and conversions. For the great missionary St Francis Xavier, Schurhammer's *Francis Xavier* is of course essential. C. R. Boxer's *The Church Militant and Iberian Expansion, 1440–1770* (Baltimore, 1978) is a fine survey of the role of the church in several areas, while A. K. Priolkar has written a (deservedly) critical account of the Inquisition: *The Goa Inquisition* (Bombay, 1961). Two good, and much neglected, studies of Christianity in Goa are Carlos de Merces de Mello, *The Recruitment and Formation of the Native Clergy in India (16th–18th centuries)* (Lisbon, 1955), and Anthony D'Costa, *The Christianisation of the Goa Islands* (Bombay, 1965). Vincent Cronin's *A Pearl to India: the Life of Robert de Nobili* (London, 1959) is a readable account of this unusual Jesuit.

TRAVELLERS' ACCOUNTS

Goa has been visited by many travellers over the last five centuries; their accounts of their experiences often provide interesting data which, because of its familiarity, are not included in accounts written by locals. Thus travellers can be 'participant observers' for the modern historian. The two best known for the late sixteenth and early seventeenth centuries respectively are by the Dutchman J. H. van Linschoten, *The Voyage of John Huyghen van Linschoten to the East Indies* (2 vols., London, 1885), and Francois Pyrard de Laval, *The Voyage of Francois Pyrard of Laval* (2 vols., London, 1887–90). Early in the seventeenth century J. A. de Mandelslo spent a little time on the west coast: his account was edited by M. S. Commissariat as *Mandelslo's Travels in Western India, AD 1638–9* (London, 1931). S. N. Sen edited the accounts of two travellers, both of whom visited Goa, in *Indian Travels of Thevenot and Careri* (New Delhi, 1949). Dr John Fryer later in the seventeenth century had some truculent things to say about the Portuguese in his *A New Account of East India and Persia* (3 vols., London, 1909–15), and Alexander Hamilton added his comments in *A New Account of the East Indies* (2 vols., London, 1930). The Abbé Carré was more sympathetic: *The Travels of the Abbé Carré in India and the Near East, 1672 to 1674* (3 vols., London, 1947–48).

Apart from some unpublished descriptions dating from the period of British occupation, the only nineteenth-century account of much note is Richard

Burton's extraordinary *Goa and the Blue Mountains* (London, 1851). Leaving aside its flights of fancy, this early work by the great adventurer is notable for vigorously expressed prejudice, directed at both Indians and Portuguese. In the twentieth century two famous English writers left us accounts of late-colonial Goa. Somerset Maugham's evocative and sympathetic account is included in his *A Writer's Notebook* (London, 1949). Evelyn Waugh visited for an exposition of the body of St Francis Xavier, and had some typically snobbish and racist observations to make. These can be found in his own article, 'Goa: the home of a saint', *Month*, n.s. x (Dec. 1953), 325–35, and in an edition of his letters by Mark Amory, *The Letters of Evelyn Waugh* (London, 1980). Finally, at the time of 'liberation' the American ambassador to India happened to be the ineffable J. K. Galbraith. In his *Ambassador's Journal* (New York, 1970) he had some acerbic comments to make about the behaviour of both sides in the crisis.

PORTUGAL

Metropolitan Portugal has a vast literature of its own. I will simply list here a few works which provide an entrée to this. Godinho's two volumes of *Ensaios* are a good and challenging place to start. Two basic references are Joaquim Veríssimo Serrão, *História de Portugal* (6 vols. to date; Lisbon, 1977–82), a vast political chronology from a conservative view point; vol. VI takes us up to 1807. More useful is Joel Serrão (ed.), *Dicionário da história de Portugal* (4 vols., Lisbon, 1963–71), which includes articles by many fine scholars. The best survey in English is that by A. H. de Oliveira Marques, a liberal Portuguese scholar: *History of Portugal*, 2nd ed. (2 vols., New York, 1976). His *Daily Life in Portugal in the Late Middle Ages* (Madison, 1971) is social history in the G. M. Trevelyan mould, and contains copious information for the period of the twelfth to late fifteenth centuries. H. V. Livermore in *A New History of Portugal* (Cambridge, 1966) provides a sound chronology of Portugal's history. Two particular studies are Rodney Gallop, *Portugal: A Book of Folkways* (Cambridge, 1936), useful for its depiction of Portuguese peasant life, and Dan Stanislawski, *The Individuality of Portugal: A Study in Historical-Political Geography* (Austin, 1959), a work described in its title. The Revolution of 1974 atracted much attention. Two recent books which describe its origins and course are Tom Gallagher, *Portugal: A Twentieth Century Interpretation* (Manchester, 1983), and Richard Robinson, *Contemporary Portugal* (London, 1979).

COMPARATIVE AND THEORETICAL

Several surveys of European colonialism provide data to enable the activities of the Portuguese to be put in context. K. M. Panikkar's popular survey *Asia and Western Dominance* (London, 1953) was very widely read, even though he insisted on discerning a 'Vasco da Gama Epoch of Asian History' stretching from 1498 to 1945. As it progresses, D. F. Lach's *Asia in the Making of Europe* will be more and more important for purposes of comparison. J. H. Parry's *The Age of Reconnaissance* (New York, 1964) is a good survey of the early European explorations, while J. H. Elliott, in a book complementary to Lach's, but much more succinct, discusses the impact of the discovery of America on Europe: *The Old World and the New, 1492–1650* (Cambridge, 1970). Ralph Davis's excellent *The Rise of the Atlantic Economies*, 2nd ed. (London, 1975), has useful comparative data. G. V. Scammell's *The World Encompassed: The First European Maritime Empires, c. 800–1650* (London, 1981) is quite splendid, a wide-ranging and humanistic survey which teems with comparisons and usefully looks at continuities in European expansion over the whole period covered. A new book by Philip D. Curtin, *Cross-Cultural Trade in World History* (Cambridge, 1984) is very useful in enabling the reader to place the Portuguese in a broader context, that is as another example of a 'trading diaspora', unusual only in that theirs was a political entity with each 'node' under central control. A recent book by K. N. Chaudhuri provides something of a model for all who aspire to write on the Indian Ocean, or on maritime history: *Trade and Civilisation in the Indian Ocean: An Economic History from the Rise of Islam to 1750* (Cambridge, 1985). Finally, the Leiden journal *Itinerario* is consciously devoted to the field of colonial history, and has already published many valuable reports and articles. Indeed, colonial history *per se* seems to be reviving again. For a while those who wrote it were sometimes accused (in some cases with justice) of being old-fashioned or neo-colonialist; now that formal colonialism at least is virtually ended a more objective reassessment is being made. In this effort a recent article by Frank Perlin is much to be recommended for stimulation and provocation: 'Proto-industrialization and pre-colonial South Asia', *Past and Present*, no. 98 (1983), 30–95.

Any selection of work which can be loosely described as 'theoretical' must be arbitrary in the extreme, for my attitudes, and ideas about human conduct, obviously derive from all sorts of literary and other influences. Three very important books about perspectives, and about how Europeans should look at other cultures, are J. C. van Leur's early and very innovative *Indonesian Trade and Society* (The Hague, 1955); Marshall G. S. Hodgson's large and very provocative *The Venture of Islam: Conscience and History in a World Civilization* (3 vols., Chicago, 1974), a work which tries to return Islamic history to its correct perspective, and Edward Said's even more inflammatory *Orientalism* (New York, 1978), a magnificent excursion into the history of ideas. Denys Lombard has also contributed in this area, in an iconoclastic piece called 'Questions on the contact between European companies and Asian societies', in Leonard Blusse and Femme Gaastra (eds.), *Companies and Trade* (Leiden, 1981), 179–87.

Fernand Braudel's work is of course much discussed at present. It has influenced me too, though not so much for what he says about Asian societies and economies in his *magnum opus Civilization and Capitalism, 15th–18th Century* (3 vols., New York and London, 1979–84) as for his account there, and in his earlier *The Mediterranean and the Mediterranean World in the Age of Philip II* (2 vols., New York and London, 1973) of early modern European societies. There are so many suggestive ideas, parallels, to be drawn with Asia at the same time. Many of Braudel's concerns can be found discussed in a Portuguese context in Godinho's *Os Descobrimentos*. F. C. Lane's important concept of 'protection costs' was set out in papers now included in his *Venice and History*: the notion was used explicitly by Steensgaard in his *Asian Trade Revolution*, and in the same author's 'Violence and the rise of capitalism: Frederic C. Lane's theory of protection and trade', *Review*, V, 2 (1981), 247–73.

Studies of early imperialism can be seen as contributing to our understanding of the creation of underdevelopment in the third world. In this context one book stands out, Eric R. Wolf's brilliant *Europe and the People without History* (Berkeley, 1982). Immanuel Wallerstein's theories about world economies and world systems are presented in *The Modern World-System: Capitalist Agriculture and the Origins of the European World-Economy in the Sixteenth Century* (New York, 1974), in vol. II of this on-going study, *The Modern World-System II: Mercantalism and the Consolidation of the European World-Economy, 1600–1750* (New York, 1980), and more synoptically in 'The rise and future demise of the world capitalist system: concepts for comparative analysis', *The Capitalist World-Economy* (Cambridge, 1979), pp. 1–36. Jan Kieniewicz's two stimulating articles, 'L'Asie et l'Europe pendant les XVIème-XIXème siècles. Formation de l'État arrière et confrontation des systèmes des valeurs', in *L'Histoire à Nice*, Actes du colloque international (Nice, 1981), vol. III, pp. 217–29; and his 'Contact and transformation: the European pre-colonial expansion in the Indian Ocean world-system in the 16th–17th centuries', *Itinerario*, VIII, 2 (1984), 45–58 make important contributions to this debate. Braudel in vol. III of *Civilization and Capitalism*, pp. 21–88, provides a friendly critique of the world-system and world-economy notions. The senior Indian economic historian K. N. Chaudhuri has also evaluated Wallerstein's ideas in his 'The world-system east of longitude 20. The European role in Asia, 1500–1750', *Review*, V, 2 (1981), 219–45. In the whole field of Indo-Portuguese history, the most innovative and stimulating work being produced today is coming from Niels Steensgaard, who is providing exciting synoptic views of Asian trade and European impacts on it, in studies well grounded in theory yet drawing on control of the sources also. His current concerns can be followed up in 'Asian trade and world economy from the 15th to 18th centuries', in T. R. de Souza (ed.), *Indo-Portuguese History*, pp. 225–35; 'The companies as a specific institution in the history of European expansion', in Blusse and Gaastra (eds.), *Companies and Trade*, pp. 245–64; 'Asian trade 15th–18th Centuries: continuities and discontinuities', *Acts, ICHS* (Bucharest, 1980), 488–500; and 'Asian trade and world market: orders of magnitude in "The long seventeenth century"', in *L'Histoire à Nice*, Actes du colloque international 1980 (Nice, 1981), vol. III, pp. 129–47.

This essay must end with a plea for historians to use theory, as is done in the works listed above, more consciously. Far too many of the works listed in the body of this essay, let alone the vast literature not mentioned here, are antiquarian in the extreme. Comparison and a self-conscious use of wider theoretical statements are of the essence, the way forward for our field of study. At the least, those scholars who prefer to tell us only 'what the documents say' should accept that their work, valuable and time-consuming though it is, is only a beginning. The wave of the future must be for historians to use the data generated by such historians, along with their own original research, to revitalize the field. It is a golden opportunity, for the history of the Portuguese in India is the history of the early European impact on a major area of the third world. The precise nature of this impact, and Indian reactions to it, should make up a vital and exciting area of research, of interest to historians and other social scientists working in many different areas. The torch is waiting to be picked up.

INDEX

Acheh, 44
Aden, 25, 26, 29, 31, 45, 62, 67–8
Akbar, Mughal emperor, 27, 52, 53
Albuquerque, Afonso de, 30–1, 32, 63, 82, 91, 105, 111
Almeida, Francisco d', 30, 63, 64, 74
artillery, 56–9
Azores, 5, 6

Bahadur Shah, 52
Bengal, 84, 86
Brazil, 136, 150
Burton, Richard, 103, 123–4, 133, 149

Cabral, Pedro Alvares, 5, 10, 13, 30, 58
Cafila, 39
Calicut, see Zamorin
Camoens, Luis de, 6, 105, 107, 117
Carreira da India, 69, 140–1, 142
Cartaz, 38–9, 78
Castro, D. João de, 18, 107, 132
Cheng Ho, 12
Christianity, in Portugal, 16–18; in India, 116–30; numbers, 121; nature of conversions, 127–30
Cochin, 30, 45, 47–8
conversions, see Christianity in India
Coromandel, 83–4
Counter Reformation, 15, 18, 21, 101, 107, 116, 117–19, 124
Country trade, 69, 81–7, 134–5, 140–2
Covilham, Pero de, 11

Diu, 29, 31, 33, 34, 44, 51–3, 122, 134–5
Dutch, attack Portuguese, 134–8

Franciscans, 123
Freyre, Gilberto, 102, 158

Gama, Vasco da, 3, 5, 10, 11, 13, 19, 30, 32, 63, 73, 116
Gaunkars, 89, 111, 154

Goa, 31, 32, 35, 50: description of, 88–90; pre-Portuguese, 90; trade of, 90–2; characteristics, 92–4; society, 94–9; race relations, 99–106; government, 107–10; economy of, 110–14; revenue, 111–12; religion in, 116–30; blockaded by Dutch, 134, 137–8; in decline, 146–50, 151–7; liberation, 157–61; since 1961, 161; see also Portuguese
Gujarat, 53–6, 83; natives of in Goa, 113–14; see also Diu

Hajj, 27, 107
Henry, king of Portugal, 17
Henry, Prince, the Navigator, 7–8
Horse trade, 49–51
Hurmuz, 31, 45

India, rulers' attitudes to sea, 26–9, 53
Indian Ocean, situation at 1500, 23–9; trade routes, 25–6
Indians, help Portuguese conquests, 32; opposition to Portuguese, 45–49; response to Portuguese system, 51–60; role in Goan economy, 112–14; see also Goa; Portuguese
Inquisition, in Portugal, 15; in Goa, 119–20, 123, 148
Iron ore, 154–5, 159, 161

Jesuits, 107, 117, 118, 120, 125–7, 131–2, 145, 148; missions to Mughals, 124–5
Jews, 15, 19, 32, 109, 119
João III, king of Portugal, 16, 17, 42–3, 61

Kosambi, D. D., 88, 150, 158

Lusiads, The, see Camoens

Macao, 33

INDEX

Madeira, 5, 6
Malacca, 25, 26, 29, 31, 55, 134, 135
Malik Ayaz, *see* Diu
Mamluk Egypt, 33
Manuel, king of Portugal, 5, 15, 16, 19, 30, 61, 62, 69
Maugham, Somerset, 124, 130
Methuen Treaty, 145, 150
Mughals, 27, 52, 124–5
Municipal Council, 108–10
Muslims, Portuguese hostility to, 17–18, 72–4; role in Indian Ocean trade, 23–4

Navigation, Portuguese, 9
Nehru, Jawaharlal, 160
New Christians, *see* Jews

Ottoman Turks, 32, 33–4, 45

Padroado, 118–20
Pedlars, 24–5
Piracy, 29
Pombal, Marquis of, 123, 145, 146, 147, 148
Population: Portugal, 14–16; India, 23; Goa, 92–3, 148; migration from, 155–7; empire, 136
Portugal: in fifteenth century, 7; in sixteenth century, 14–22; under Braganças, 145–6; in nineteenth century, 146, 150–1; in twentieth century, 157
Portuguese: early voyages, 5–10; significance of, 10–14; aims of sixteenth century, 29–30; conquests, 30–2; administration in India, 34–6, 62–8, 132, 139–40; economic policies, 36–9,

73–6; and spice trade, 40–9; and horse trade, 49–51; and Gujarat, 51–6; evaluation of official system, 61–71; brutality, 71–3; nature of empire, 76–80, 115–16, 136; private trade, 81–7; decline of empire, 131–43; after 1650, 144–57; in twentieth century, 157–61; *see also* Goa
Printing press, 107, 126, 148

Race relations, 99–106, 148–9
Rendas, 113
Saint Paul, College of, 118, 122, 125–6, 127–8
Saint Thomas, 83, 84; St. Thomas Christians, 119
Salazar, Dr. António de Oliveira, 146, 155, 157, 158, 159, 160, 161
Saraswat Brahmins 112–13, 153
Sebastian, king of Portugal, 17, 22, 61
Senado da Câmara, *see* Municipal Council
Ships, Portuguese, 9
Slaves, 6, 14–15, 136, 145, 150–1; in Goa, 95–6, 112
Society of Jesus, *see* Jesuits
Spices, 6–7, 25–6, 36–7; Portuguese attempt to monopolise, 40–9
Sri Lanka, 25, 26, 31, 76

Van Leur, J. C., 24–5

Waugh, Evelyn, 158, 159, 160

Xavier, St Francis, 101, 118, 126, 128, 140

Zamorin, ruler of Calicut, 13, 28, 45–8, 58, 73

THE NEW CAMBRIDGE HISTORY OF INDIA

I The Mughals and their Contemporaries

JOHN F. RICHARDS, *Mughal State and Society*
M. N. PEARSON, *The Portuguese in India*
CATHERINE B. ASHER, *Mughal Architecture*
MILO C. BEACH, *Mughal Painting*
PETER HARDY, *The Ideas and Beliefs of the Moghuls*
BRUCE B. LAWRENCE, *Indian Sufism and the Islamic World*
BURTON STEIN, *Vijayanagar*
RICHARD M. EATON, *Social History of the Deccan*

II Indian States and the Transition to Colonialism

C. A. BAYLY, *Indian Society and the Making of the British Empire*
P. J. MARSHALL, *Bengal: The British Bridgehead*
STEWART GORDON, *The Maratha Empire*
OM PRAKASH, *The Northern European Trading Companies and India*
RICHARD B. BARNETT, *Muslim Successor States*
J. S. GREWAL, *The Sikhs in the Punjab*
DAVID WASHBROOK, *South India*

III The Indian Empire and the Beginnings of Modern Society

GORDON JOHNSON, *Government and Politics in India*
F. CONLON, *Modern Maharashtra*
SUGATA BOSE, *The Agrarian Development of Modern Bengal*
DAVID LUDDEN, *Agriculture in Indian History*
SUSAN BAYLY, *Caste in South Asia*
B. R. TOMLINSON, *Economic Growth, Change and Stagnation*
THOMAS R. METCALF, *Ideologies of the Raj*
K. W. JONES, *Social and Religious Reform Movements in British India*
B. N. RAMUSACK, *The Indian Princes and their States*
GORDON JOHNSON, *Government and Politics in India*

IV The Evolution of Contemporary South Asia

PAUL BRASS, *The Politics of India since Independence*
ANIL SEAL, *The Transfer of Power and the Partition of India*
RAJ CHANDAVARKAR, *The Urban Working Classes*
GERALDINE FORBES, *Indian Women in the Twentieth Century*
FRANCIS ROBINSON, *Islam in South Asia*
GYAN PANDEY, *Peasants and Politics*
SHAHID AMIN, *Economy, Society and Culture*